Development Centre Seminars

Electronic Commerce for Development

Edited by
Andrea Goldstein and David O'Connor

OECD

DEVELOPMENT CENTRE OF THE ORGANISATION
FOR ECONOMIC CO-OPERATION AND DEVELOPMENT

ORGANISATION FOR ECONOMIC CO-OPERATION AND DEVELOPMENT

Pursuant to Article 1 of the Convention signed in Paris on 14th December 1960, and which came into force on 30th September 1961, the Organisation for Economic Co-operation and Development (OaECD) shall promote policies designed:

- to achieve the highest sustainable economic growth and employment and a rising standard of living in Member countries, while maintaining financial stability, and thus to contribute to the development of the world economy;
- to contribute to sound economic expansion in Member as well as non-member countries in the process of economic development; and
- to contribute to the expansion of world trade on a multilateral, non-discriminatory basis in accordance with international obligations.

The original Member countries of the OECD are Austria, Belgium, Canada, Denmark, France, Germany, Greece, Iceland, Ireland, Italy, Luxembourg, the Netherlands, Norway, Portugal, Spain, Sweden, Switzerland, Turkey, the United Kingdom and the United States. The following countries became Members subsequently through accession at the dates indicated hereafter: Japan (28th April 1964), Finland (28th January 1969), Australia (7th June 1971), New Zealand (29th May 1973), Mexico (18th May 1994), the Czech Republic (21st December 1995), Hungary (7th May 1996), Poland (22nd November 1996), Korea (12th December 1996) and the Slovak Republic (14th December 2000). The Commission of the European Communities takes part in the work of the OECD (Article 13 of the OECD Convention).

The Development Centre of the Organisation for Economic Co-operation and Development was established by decision of the OECD Council on 23rd October 1962 and comprises twenty-two Member countries of the OECD: Austria, Belgium, Canada, the Czech Republic, Denmark, Finland, France, Germany, Greece, Iceland, Ireland, Italy, Korea, Luxembourg, Mexico, the Netherlands, Norway, Portugal, Slovak Republic, Spain, Sweden, Switzerland, as well as Argentina and Brazil from March 1994, Chile since November 1998 and India since February 2001. The Commission of the European Communities also takes part in the Centre's Advisory Board.

The purpose of the Centre is to bring together the knowledge and experience available in Member countries of both economic development and the formulation and execution of general economic policies; to adapt such knowledge and experience to the actual needs of countries or regions in the process of development and to put the results at the disposal of the countries by appropriate means.

 THE OPINIONS EXPRESSED AND ARGUMENTS EMPLOYED IN THIS PUBLICATION ARE THE SOLE RESPONSIBILITY OF THE AUTHORS AND DO NOT NECESSARILY REFLECT THOSE OF THE OECD, THE DEVELOPMENT CENTRE OR THE GOVERNMENTS OF THEIR MEMBER COUNTRIES.

*
* *

Publié en français sous le titre :
Commerce électronique et développement

Foreword

This publication falls within the 2001-2002 Development Centre work programme under the title "Globalising Technologies and Domestic Entrepreneurship in Developing Countries". The project has produced a number of outputs as well as this book whose chapters are derived from papers delivered to a May 2001 conference organised in co-operation with the School of Development and Institutional Change of the University of Bologna, under the patronage of Italy's Ministry for Foreign Affairs.

Acknowledgements

The Development Centre and the School for Development and Institutional Change (SDIC) acknowledge the support of Telecom Italia Lab, Fondazione Cassa di Risparmio in Bologna, Endaveours and Sun in organising the conference held in Bologna on 4-5 May 2001 under the patronage of the Italian Ministry for Foreign Affairs. The interest and support received from the Government of Italy in the context of this project is gratefully acknowledged.

Table of Contents

PART THREE

COUNTRY EXPERIENCES AND LOCAL EXPERIMENTS

Preface

In the last part of the past century, the application of information and communication technologies (ICT), including the internet, has become widespread in global business. This has been made possible by technical progress as well as policy changes such as market opening to trade and foreign investment and service market liberalisation, notably in telecommunications. Although new technologies appear to be improving economic performance and welfare among user populations, in the OECD countries the link between ICTs and economy-wide productivity advance has been notoriously elusive. Early studies for developing countries also fail to detect a significant association between economic growth and use of ICTs. A possible hypothesis is that investing in these technologies bear fruit only once certain networks and organisational changes are implemented. Individual firms investing in ICT, particularly internet-based management systems, at this early stage in the development of e-business might find the return on investment quite low. Over time, as more suppliers and customers use the internet in their front-office and back-office systems and to connect with their trading partners, the benefits of internet-enabled collaboration will likely become more pronounced.

What does then the widespread diffusion of the internet and web-based e-commerce imply for developing countries? Can their small producers use these technologies to break into high-value segments and increase profitability and competitiveness? Or, on the contrary, do they increase "commoditisation" and strengthen the bargaining power of global buyers, mostly based in the OECD countries? These questions are of increasing relevance to policy makers everywhere. Poorer countries must devise appropriate strategies to turn new technologies into building blocks towards their insertion into the global economy, but their OECD partners must make sure that erecting barriers in the virtual marketplace does not offset the support provided through development assistance.

The linkages between the internet and global market structures are far from clear. The OECD's pioneering role in developing e-commerce policy led the Development Centre in 2000 to start research on the development implications of the application of internet in business practices. This project, included in the 2001-02 programme of work under the title "Globalising Technologies and Domestic Entrepreneurship in Developing Countries" has so far produced a number of outputs.

Two Technical Papers have been presented by Development Centre staff in Brazil, Chile, Italy, Japan, Lebanon, Malaysia, Mexico and Poland. A joint op-ed piece on the *Financial Times* and other still unpublished papers have also been produced. In May 2001 a conference was organised in co-operation with the School of Development and Institutional Change at, as I remarked at the time, the world's oldest university in Bologna under the patronage of Italy's Ministry for Foreign Affairs. On this occasion, scholars, practitioners and policy makers from both OECD Member and non-Member countries analysed different questions associated to e-commerce, trying to go beyond the veil of the digital divide to better understand what can be expected from the new medium in terms of development.

As multinational corporations integrate the internet into their cross-border business operations, firms from developing countries run the risk of exclusion from global value chains if they cannot establish electronic ties with their major business partners. In this context, it would be useful to focus on the ways in which ICTs affect the growth prospects of firms in specific sectors. Further research should concentrate on how net-based applications change organisation routines, modify the pool of corporate resources and interact with strategy in firms of different size, nationality, ownership and industries. Where does the quality of ICT assets, including internet access, make the greatest difference to firm and industry competitiveness?

Policy makers need such detailed analyses for the design of policy and investment measures to upgrade ICT infrastructure and promote ICT diffusion. This volume is a major contribution to an area of economic research which is still in its infancy, despite the current preoccupation with ICT.

Jorge Braga de Macedo
President
OECD Development Centre
2 October 2002

An Introduction to the Debate on Electronic Commerce and Development

Andrea Goldstein and David O'Connor*

The "digital divide" literature focuses on low rates of internet penetration and high costs of access in much of the developing world. Most developing countries do still have weak information and communications technology (ICT) infrastructures as well as limited systems know-how. Still, consistent with Moore's law, ICT products and services have experienced significant cost reductions over time, which is permitting developing countries, including some of the poorest, to improve their access to and use of modern ICT at an impressive rate. While low incomes do continue to pose a constraint to broader internet diffusion, perhaps more crucial is the establishment of a conducive competitive and regulatory environment in the telecommunications and internet service provider (ISP) sectors.

Assuming that ICTs continue to become more affordable, what does this imply for entrepreneurs in developing countries? How can they use these technologies to their advantage? What does the widespread diffusion of the internet and web-based e-commerce mean for their profitability and competitiveness? The linkages between the internet and global market structures are far from clear. Do they make it easier for small producers to break into high-value segments and compete on a global scale, or, on the contrary, do they increase "commoditisation" and strengthen the bargaining power of global buyers, mostly based in the OECD countries?

The novelty of the internet means that there is little historical evidence on which to venture projections of future trends, even in the OECD countries. E-commerce is evolving rapidly, with the corporate landscape continuously transformed by start-ups,

---

* Our thinking on these matters owes a lot to the comments received on presentations of our paper "E-Commerce for Development: Prospects and Policy Issues" in Beirut (UN Economic Commission for Western Asia), Brasília (Presidencia da República), Cagliari (Italian Economic Association), Santiago (Chilean Academy of Diplomacy), Singapore (Asian Development Bank Institute), Tokyo (Japanese Bank for International Co-operation), Tijuana (Colegio de la Frontera Norte) and Warsaw (Leon Kozminski Academy of Entrepreneurship and Management).

acquisitions and failures, and with new technologies coming to market almost daily. Digital trade in goods and services already makes it easier for artisans, musicians and other artists in developing countries to access world business-to-consumer (B2C) markets, cutting out layers of middlemen and improving the creators' bargaining power. For some developing countries, B2C e-commerce may offer important export as well as local market development opportunities. Globally, however, the biggest potential appears to be in the business-to-business (B2B) market. It includes a broad range of inter-company transactions such as wholesale trade, corporate purchases of technology, parts, components and capital equipment, and trade in services, including financial services such as insurance, commercial credit, bonds, securities and other assets (Lucking-Reiley and Spulber, 2001). How can developing country entrepreneurs position themselves to participate in B2B markets? The papers presented at the Bologna Conference and published in this volume deal with both sorts of e-commerce, as well as with the broader question of how the internet may be reconfiguring global value chains and inter-firm relationships along them.

Internet and the Organisation of Global Markets

In theory at least, market exchange is impersonal, episodic and carried out at arm's length. All that matters is how much the seller is asking and how much the buyer is offering. Incomplete information in the international market, however, creates difficulty in matching buyers and sellers and interferes with the ability of prices to allocate scarce resources. Information technologies have the potential to reduce such market imperfections. Information-sharing networks among internationally dispersed agents can improve the allocation of resources, although their effectiveness depends on whether they include all potentially important market participants. If certain large low-cost producers of a particular good do not have network access, potential benefits may not reach consumers. While the internet is more inclusive than early-generation proprietary electronic networks such as EDI (Electronic Data Interchange), it is still far from universal. Moreover, the existence of a network technology infrastructure is not itself a sufficient condition for the emergence of a durable social or business network. That depends on repeated interactions through which parties build reputations for trustworthiness and gain confidence in one another. This still poses a challenge for prospective new entrants into established networks. Does physical disintermediation — i.e. the shift from face-to-face to virtual transactions — render it easier or harder for developing-country newcomers to enter global markets? This question lies at the core of the debate on e-commerce and development, since to different answers correspond contrasting predictions of the chances for poor countries to break through the glass ceiling to prosperity.

In his contribution to this volume, Gary Gereffi compares the three main drivers of economic globalisation in the latter half of the 20th century: investment by transnational corporations, international trade and the internet. Producer-driven and buyer-driven value chains characterise the phases of investment-based and trade-based globalisation. The emergence of the internet holds the potential to undermine traditional models of commodity-chain organisation, substituting one in which new "info-mediaries" (e.g. owners of B2C or B2B portals) provide the main impetus to the organisation of transactions. By making markets they erode the market power of traditionally dominant commodity-chain participants (buyers or sellers). Gereffi also presents two alternative scenarios. In one the internet becomes the ultimate instrument of consumer sovereignty, putting enough information at consumers' disposal to permit arbitrage to squeeze sellers' profits. In the other, the lead firms in existing value chains, whether producer-driven or buyer-driven, largely capture the e-commerce benefits. He suggests that, at present, this last scenario appears the most probable.

The experience of Italian small and medium scale enterprises (SMEs) was invoked as potentially relevant to SMEs in developing countries. Annaflavia Bianchi, discussant of Professor Gereffi's paper, argued that such enterprises are unlikely to be excluded entirely from the benefits of internet use. The technologies are broadly affordable and becoming more so, and e-commerce application tools are available on a pay-for-use basis, avoiding the obstacle of large fixed investment costs. The internet also makes possible greater specialisation of functions and more division of labour in administrative tasks (witness the outsourcing of back-office functions), which could perhaps benefit small enterprises that lack expertise in, say, accounting, finance and marketing.

The literature on Italian industrial districts, a form of business network that has attracted much interest in development circles, also offers possible lessons. The competitive success of these districts is thought to lie in how firms become embedded in supportive local socio-economic environments that allow them to overcome their size limits in terms of managerial know-how, financial capital and technology. The emergence of the internet raises the question whether such rich networks of supporting institutions can be replicated in virtual space, or are too heavily dependent on relationships of trust and the intensive personal interactions permitted by physical (and cultural) proximity.

Patrizia Fariselli observes that the pervasive use of ICT infrastructures, services and goods is changing the relationships between firms and the configuration of business networks themselves. Established networks become unstable as interactivity increases, global multipurpose technological platforms develop and business activities can be de-composed and re-composed at low cost. Networking effects can give rise to increasing returns, so that the standard models used to analyse productivity performance in the "old economy" find their heuristic power diminished and the problems of measurement become more difficult. Yet one recent attempt at measuring ICT-related network economies (or productivity spillovers) for the US economy finds scant evidence of their existence (Stiroh, 2001)[1].

The internet's most significant impact to date has been in B2B markets. E-commerce is reshaping the competitive dynamics in traditional producer-driven and buyer-driven value chains such as automobiles and coffee.

Automobiles

The automotive industry has traditionally pioneered in new management and organisational techniques, from mass production Taylorism in the 1920s to lean manufacturing and just-in-time (JIT) in the 1980s. More recently automotive manufacturers have reached a high level of sophistication in outsourcing the design, manufacture and assembly of increasingly complex systems (e.g. Anti-blocking Brake Systems, ABS) and modules (e.g. the vehicle cockpit), in the process narrowing the immediate supply base to trusted Tier I suppliers. Car assemblers are also among the largest multinational companies in terms of assets located outside their home markets, and producers of motor vehicles are consistently ranked among the largest investors in developing countries.

Two papers in this volume analyse the impact of internet technology in the car industry in developing countries. Sagren Moodley examines the prospects and challenges for the Kwa-Zulu Natal automotive components sector in South Africa. He notes that reaching the ideal type of lean supply chain managed over the internet will be expensive and requires a sort of industry-wide co-operation not generally prevailing in the South African automotive components industry. The critical mass needed to reap positive network externalities is not yet present in the sector. An important insight from this study concerns the role of leadership by original equipment manufacturers (OEMs) and the large Tier I suppliers in defining e-business standards for all value-chain participants and in creating incentives that attract more companies to join digital supply chains. Early adopters can also play a catalytic role in promoting the diffusion of e-business in the components sector.

Research by Andrea Goldstein explores the use of e-business in the Indian car industry, taking Fiat India as a case study and looking in particular at the effects on domestic companies in the supply chain. Although net-based solutions are expected to streamline the automotive supply chain, they have less importance than progress in implementing lean manufacturing, which the internet can facilitate. Fiat produces a homogeneous product for emerging markets in eight countries, including India, and has been very successful in optimising supply-chain management in Brazil, where it operates one of the largest non-OECD car factories. The auto business in India, and supplier-OEM relationships in particular, are not immune from global pressures, including oversupply, industry consolidation, modular assembly and the increasing use of the internet. The last appears as a core element in the internal organisation of major auto manufacturers such as Fiat and as taking a progressively more important role in inter-firm relationships as well. Thus far, however, tangible effects on the supply chain in India appear more in e-information management (knowledge management, research and development and marketing) than in procurement.

Still, the auto industry has no unanimity on how the internet will shape the organisation of supply chains and relations between OEMs and suppliers or between different tiers of suppliers. To caricature, the industry has two contrasting supply-chain models, one epitomised by Toyota and the other by General Motors (GM). The Toyota model stresses durable supplier-customer relationships, in which OEM and

Tier 1 suppliers share major responsibilities for model design and development. The GM model involves sourcing from the lowest-cost supplier, even if that means frequent switching and repeated short-term contracts. These contrasting models are perhaps more accurately used to describe, on the one hand, the relationship between OEMs and Tier I suppliers (Toyota) and, on the other, the relationship between the first two and lower tier suppliers (GM), where the latter make more standardised components and parts. The internet may have the greatest impact in the second type of relationship by fostering greater price competition among suppliers (e.g. through on-line bidding) and pooling the demands of OEMs or other buyers to reap ever greater scale economies. What remains unclear is whether the criteria for participation in on-line exchanges such as Covisint — the exchange established by major auto OEMs and parts manufacturers — will act as major barriers to entry to prospective new suppliers.

The discussant, John Humphrey, suggested that the threat posed by internet-based procurement to longstanding customer relationships might be more perceived than real, citing the example of the horticultural industry. There, UK consumers have become more demanding of assurances that the fresh produce on their supermarket shelves is produced according to certain standards (e.g. regarding use of pesticides, GMOs, etc.). As a result, the wholesalers and retail chains are more inclined to stick with trusted suppliers than to search for new, lower cost suppliers via the internet.

Coffee and other Commodities

Morten Scholer describes the first on-line coffee auction, highlighting the potential that e-commerce holds for certain commodity producers in developing countries. The first auction, for premium Brazilian coffees, was organised in 1999 with considerable outside technical support, notably from the International Trade Centre (an UNCTAD/WTO joint venture). The Brazilian industry saw value in repeating it in 2000 on a purely commercial basis. The precise designs of auction mechanisms will vary by commodity. The success of the Brazilian auction depended in part on sending samples for tasting to pre-qualified bidders. Evaluation of physical samples may or may not be critical for other commodities. Where grading is used to gauge the quality of an auctionable commodity, the prospective bidders' degree of trust in the graders is crucial. The Brazilian coffees commanded above-average prices largely by virtue of their pre-selection for quality. Conventional markets tend to undervalue such premium products. For standardised commodities, the distribution of surplus may favour consumers rather than producers, although that is not a foregone conclusion. An interesting question raised by David Hallam, paper discussant, was what long-run effect the internet can be expected to have on commodity price variability.

Country Experiences and Local Experiments

Several papers present experiences of ICT use in developing countries or their administrative divisions, rather than in specific sectors of the economy. They demonstrate the catalytic effect that governments and NGOs can have on ICT and internet use. According to Kyle Eischen, the state government in Andhra Pradesh, India, has pursued a pro-active ICT strategy, partly to build the infrastructure and human capital base for attracting investments in the software and services industries that, in earlier days, had gone mostly to Bangalore in Karnataka. Numerous government services, including land titling and taxation, can now be transacted on-line, with significantly reduced processing times. The move to e-government has generated a local demand for network software developers.

The Grameen Phone experiment in Bangladesh is particularly well studied. Its intent is to make village pay phones (VPP), based on cellular radio technology, available in rural areas of Bangladesh. Salahuddin Aminuzzaman highlights as one interesting feature of this experiment the reliance on the credit-evaluation capabilities and the infrastructure of the Grameen Bank to facilitate selection of VPP operators and bill collection. As with Grameen microcredit borrowers, the phone operators are overwhelmingly women, while the users are still predominantly men. The VPPs appear to have provided significant benefits, including reduced isolation and fragmentation of village economies, extension of the boundaries of the local market, timely price information and improved terms of trade for farmers and recipients of overseas remittances, and faster communication between family members and enhanced kinship bonding. The income generated by the phone business has improved the status of women within the household, while their command of a wealth of valuable information has increased their status outside the home. This "infomediary" function of the village phone operator will likely take on added importance if the internet is to have much value to the illiterate. A still under-explored aspect of the Grameen Bank/Grameen Phone experience is the degree to which access to mobile telephony by poor rural women can leverage investments made with micro-credits and/or open new investment opportunities.

Carey-Ann Jackson and Johan Eksteen describe two government-supported pilot projects in South Africa, emphasising that, in the particular context, creation of local content should also be seen as part of a "nation-building" effort. One of the projects supports the creation of micro-enterprises to add value to agricultural and other primary commodities. One component (cited as an example of a "livelihoods approach" to e-commerce) consists of developing an architecture for a virtual trade house for these value-added products. Typical generic functions are designed into the virtual trade house such as distribution, payments, optimisation, centralisation, auditing and customer account management. The issue of branding must still be resolved, with implications for the distribution of income from, for example, royalty payments to participating communities. The project is still too new to enable impact evaluation. A second project deals with cultural preservation, in part through the promotion of local content creation for virtual cultural tourism. Jackson's paper notes the tension between the need to retain a degree of authenticity and making the web site as appealing as possible to the virtual tourist. The latter becomes all the more important if the site is seen as an important medium for promoting actual tourism.

The Road Ahead

The most powerful message from the Bologna conference says that as multinational corporations integrate the internet into their cross-border business operations, firms from developing countries run the risk of exclusion from global value chains if they cannot establish electronic ties with their major business partners. Beyond this general proposition, however, an evident need persists for detailed sectoral analyses of how ICTs transform the way business is done and the place of developing country firms in this "brave new world".

Although new technologies appear to be improving economic performance and welfare among user populations, in the OECD countries the link between ICTs and economy-wide productivity advance has been notoriously elusive. Temple (2000), for instance, observes that productivity gains have occurred mostly in sectors intensive in ICT — e.g. the introduction of ATMs in the financial services sector — and have consisted largely of gains in labour productivity rather than total factor productivity (a point confirmed by Stiroh, 2001). An early study for developing countries also fails to detect a significant association between economic growth and use of ICTs (Rodríguez and Wilson, 2000). More recent work by Pohjola (2001) corroborates it. A possible hypothesis is that the networks and organisational changes necessary to take advantage of these technologies take time to implement (cf. Askenazy and Gianella, 2000). Individual firms investing in ICT, particularly internet-based management systems, at this early stage in the development of e-business might find the return on investment quite low. Over time, as more suppliers and customers use the internet in their front-office and back-office systems and to connect with their trading partners, the benefits of internet-enabled collaboration will likely become more pronounced.

At this stage in the development of ICT in developing countries, a more fruitful avenue of research than seeking to detect broad growth impacts would be to focus on the ways in which ICTs affect the growth prospects of firms in specific sectors, given a detailed knowledge of industry organisation and dynamics. Research should focus on how net-based applications change organisation routines, modify the pool of corporate resources and interact with strategy in firms of different size, nationality, ownership and industries. Where does the quality of ICT assets, including internet access, make the greatest difference to firm and industry competitiveness? Policy makers need such detailed analyses when designing policy and investment measures to upgrade ICT infrastructure and promote ICT diffusion.

Note

1. Stiroh finds that ICT capital investment is significantly related to labour productivity but has no significant effect on total factor productivity. He argues that it if ICT capital is different from other types of capital investment in terms of its productivity effects, this should show up in TFP.

Bibliography

ASKENAZY, P. and C. GIANELLA (2000), "Le paradoxe de productivité: les changements organisationnels, facteur complémentaire à l'informatisation", *Économie et Statistique*, No. 339-340.

LUCKING-REILEY, D. and D. SPULBER (2001), "Business-to-Business Electronic Commerce", *Journal of Economic Perspectives*, Vol. 15, No. 1.

POHJOLA, M. (ed.) (2001), *Information Technology, Productivity, and Economic Growth: International Evidence and Implications for Economic Development*, Oxford University Press, Oxford.

RODRÍGUEZ F and E.J. WILSON, III (2000), "Are Poor Countries Losing the Information Revolution?", INFODEV Working Paper, May, processed.

STIROH, K.J. (2002), "Are ICT Spillovers Driving the New Economy?", *The Review of Income and Wealth*, No. 1(48).

TEMPLE, J. (2000), "Summary of an Informal Workshop on the Causes of Economic Growth", OECD Economics Department, Working Papers No. 260.

PART ONE

INTERNET AND THE ORGANISATION OF GLOBAL MARKETS

Chapter 1

The Evolution of Global Value Chains
in the Internet Era

Gary Gereffi*

Shifting Forms of Value-Chain Governance

There have been three main drivers of economic globalisation in the latter half of the 20th century: investment by transnational corporations, international trade and the internet. Each has expanded the scope of global integration by altering how people, resources and places are connected in economic transactions. This can be seen in three broad and to some degree overlapping phases of globalisation:

1)   *Investment-based globalisation (1950-70)* — International production networks were the primary vehicles for this form of globalisation. In the 1950s and 1960s, the spread of transnational corporations accelerated in a growing number of manufacturing and raw material industries, and the ability of global companies to try to manage the world as an integrated unit was seen by some as a threat to national sovereignty (Vernon, 1971; Barnet and Müller, 1974).

2)   *Trade-based globalisation (1970-95)* — In the 1970s, there was a marked shift to export-oriented industrialisation as a preferred development strategy in many parts of the developing world, beginning with East Asia, but spreading in the 1980s to Latin America, Africa, and elsewhere (Gereffi and Wyman, 1990). This shift in national development strategies towards exports was premised on the rapid and diversified industrialisation of a wide range of developing nations.

3)   *Digital globalisation (1995 onward)* — In the mid-1990s, the information revolution and a growing acceptance of the internet began to create an explosion in connectivity owing to the open and almost cost-free exchange of a widening

*   This chapter originally appeared as an article in the *IDS Bulletin*, Vol. 32, No. 3, 2001. Permission to reprint is gratefully acknowledged.

universe of rich information (Evans and Wurster, 2000). Asymmetrical access to the Internet has given rise to concerns about a "digital divide" between those countries and firms that were connected to modern information technology, and those that were not.

Globalisation has been defined as "not merely the geographical extension of economic activity across national boundaries but also — and more importantly — the *functional integration* of such internationally dispersed activities" (Dicken, 1998: 5, italics in original). But what underlies this functional integration of globalisation processes? At the most fundamental level, information and the mechanisms for delivering it are the unifying force that holds together the structure of business. In the investment-driven phase of globalisation, vertically integrated transnational corporations relied on proprietary information systems and hierarchical control to extend their global reach. In trade-based globalisation, the operations of transnational corporations were decentralised and firms in different parts of the world allied with each other to form global value chains that involved horizontal rather than vertical co-ordination, and resembled spider webs more than pyramids (Reich, 1991: chapter 7). These value chains are shaped by the same kind of informational logic found in vertically integrated companies, but in a weaker form. The new digital era of globalisation is characterised by a dramatic increase in connectivity that is melting the informational glue that holds corporations and global value chains together.

Competition in the global economy is forged by the interaction of three broad sets of factors: technological, institutional and organisational innovations; the enterprise networks that emerge out of and increasingly move beyond national business systems; and the regulatory powers vested in regional, national and local governments. These patterns of competition change over time and across industries, and they are embodied in the organisation of global value chains (Gereffi and Korzeniewicz, 1994; Gereffi and Kaplinsky, 2001)[1].

Governance has particular importance in global value chains (Humphrey and Schmitz, 2001). It refers to the key actors in the chains who determine the inter-firm division of labour and shape the capacities of participants to upgrade their activities. Initially, only two types of governance structures predominated. Global value chains were either producer-driven or buyer-driven (Gereffi, 1994). A third form, oriented around the internet, began to emerge in the mid-1990s. The differences between these value chains reflect major changes in how international production and trade systems are organised over time, the emergence of new actors and economic roles in the chains and a continuing shift in the locus of power from producers to retailers to consumers. The concept of governance is neither static nor exclusive as a defining feature of global industries.

The governance structures in global value chains must be understood in historical perspective. Technological, institutional and organisational innovations, as well as changes in regulatory environments, transform the structures of industries and the power of the leading firms within them. Governance structures in global value chains evolve in conjunction with the forces that shape industry structures. Thus, at a particular time or within a given industry new governance structures co-exist and interact with earlier forms. The second section of this article highlights the origins of producer-driven and buyer-driven governance structures in global value chains, and the third focuses on the current emergence of internet-oriented value chains. The paper concludes by outlining several scenarios that explore the degree to which the internet challenges or sustains existing governance structures.

An Evolutionary Perspective on Global Value Chains

Two fundamental changes in the international arena profoundly shape our contemporary perspectives on global value chains. First, a widespread shift has occurred in national development strategies from import-substituting industrialisation (ISI) to export-oriented industrialisation (EOI) throughout the developing world (Gereffi and Wyman, 1990). Buttressed by the policy prescriptions of powerful international economic organisations such as the World Bank and the International Monetary Fund, as well as the US government, this preference for EOI rests heavily on the experience of the East Asian "miracle economies" from the 1960s to the mid-1990s. During this period, Japan and a handful of other high-performing Asian economies (most notably, the "four tigers" of Hong Kong, Chinese Taipei, South Korea and Singapore) attained booming exports and lofty per capita growth rates. They did so against the backdrop of relatively low income inequality, high educational attainment and record levels of domestic saving and investment (World Bank, 1993). EOI remains the development orthodoxy in much of the world, despite the financial crisis that wracked Asia in the late 1990s and increasingly strident criticisms among both academics and political activists (Gore, 2000) of the Washington Consensus that favoured EOI.

Second, a major transformation in the organisation of global production also occurred in the latter half of the 20th century. Under ISI development strategies, transnational corporations were the dominant economic actors. They were vertically integrated and had a global reach through the operations of wholly owned subsidiaries that extracted natural resources for export or engaged in local production for sale in domestic markets around the world. Exchange between core and peripheral areas has since become much more complex. The surge of imports in developed countries since the 1970s reveals that the centre of gravity for the production and export of many manufactures encompasses a very diverse array of newly industrialising nations in the developing world. As the relatively advanced East Asian and Latin American economies have moved toward more technology-intensive and skill-intensive exports, it has become clear that "cheap labour" alone no longer adequately explains Third World industrialisation. The recent expansion of global production and trade networks is propelled by both producer-driven and buyer-driven value chains.

There is an affinity between the transitions from ISI to EOI strategies and the shift from producer-driven to buyer-driven global value chains. The ISI strategy, which prevailed in Latin America for nearly five decades until the 1970s, was based on producer-driven value chains. Transnational corporations, which have actively tapped Latin America's oil, mineral and agricultural resources since the 19th century, were invited to establish more advanced manufacturing industries in the region, beginning with automobile assembly plants in large countries such as Mexico, Brazil and Argentina in the 1920s. By the 1950s and 1960s, a range of advanced ISI factories had spread throughout the region in diverse industries such as petrochemicals, pharmaceuticals, automobiles, electrical and non-electrical machinery and computers (Gereffi and Wyman, 1990). Output was destined mainly for local markets, although beginning in the 1970s more attention went to manufactured exports to offset the costly import bills associated with ISI deepening. Buyer-driven value chains, by contrast, were virtually ignored in most of Latin America until recently, because the transnational firms that established ISI were primarily interested in their local markets, not exports. This allowed exporters in the East Asian economies that pursued EOI to gain the lion's share of US and European markets for the profitable consumer goods supplied only via buyer-driven chains. With the onset of the Caribbean Basin Initiative in the mid-1980s and the North American Free Trade Agreement in 1994, Mexico, Central America and the Caribbean have become major players in US-oriented buyer-driven chains such as apparel (Gereffi *et al.*, 2002).

Economic globalisation is a kaleidoscopic fragmentation of production processes and their geographic relocation on a global scale in ways that slice through national boundaries (Dicken, 1998). Core corporations are shifting from high-volume to high-value production. Instead of a pyramid, where power concentrates in the headquarters of transnational firms with vertical chains of command, global production networks today are webs of independent yet interconnected enterprises. Core firms act as strategic brokers at the centres of the webs, controlling critical information, skills and resources needed for the overall global network to function efficiently (Reich, 1991). For countries and firms to succeed in today's international economy, they need to position themselves strategically within these global networks and develop strategies for gaining access to the lead firms in order to improve their positions.

The evolution of the organisational capabilities of leading firms in the global economy drives the emergence of new forms of value-chain governance. This organisational perspective is quite distinct from both the emphasis in neo-classical economics on pure markets as the key determinant of economic progress and that in political science on the role of the state in shaping national competitive advantage. While competitive markets and effective states are clearly important institutional features of successful modern economies, the global value-chain perspective highlights a different dimension frequently ignored by these other approaches. It reveals the shifting bases of power exercised by lead firms in global industries and the ways in which the governance structures of these industries shape the creation of markets as well as national development outcomes.

Producer-Driven Chains

Direct foreign investment by transnational corporations was central to the evolution of producer-driven value chains, given that these companies usually established international production networks to access raw materials and new overseas markets. Extending the multidivisional corporate structures pioneered by large US enterprises to tap the newly emerging American national market (Chandler, 1962), transnational firms in natural resource sectors such as oil, mining and agriculture set up international production networks throughout the world to gain access to vital and profitable raw materials. Breakthroughs in transportation and communication technologies (e.g. shipping, telegraph and telephone) made integrated production networks possible (Vernon, 1971), although their ultimate benefits for national development remain the subject of intense controversy (Barnet and Cavanaugh, 1994).

In the 1950s and 1960s, transnational corporations in the consumer durable and capital goods manufacturing sectors began to set up their own international production networks to penetrate overseas markets, especially in Latin America and Asia, which were regulated by national ISI policies (Gereffi and Wyman, 1990). These companies had access to the capital, technology and managerial resources essential for the development of new industries overseas. Because of their emphasis on locally owned subsidiaries, they had substantial control over the backward and forward linkages in the entire value chains of which they were parts.

Buyer-Driven Chains

Beginning in the late 1960s, direct foreign investment took a new tack. It supplemented its resource-seeking and market-seeking motives for globalisation with a global search for cheap labour. This "new international division of labour" (Fröbel *et al.*, 1981) relied on further improvements in transport and communication technologies to slice up the value chain so that the most labour-intensive stages of the production process could be spatially relocated to areas with the most abundant and productive low-cost labour. This strategy of firms coincided with the shift by developing countries from ISI to EOI, facilitated initially by the growth of export-processing zones in many parts of the developing world (Grunwald and Flamm, 1985).

Traditional accounts of the so-called new international division of labour do not go far enough, however. First, the transnational manufacturers involved in export-processing zones typically come from different industries than those involved in the producer-driven value chains associated with ISI. Export-processing zones tend to attract "light industries" (e.g. apparel, footwear, consumer electronics, toys), with relatively low barriers to entry. Second, the production-oriented frameworks — whether espoused by neo-classical economists, Marxist scholars, or the World Bank — miss the role of commercial capital in the globalisation process. This is the major feature of the distinction between producer-driven and buyer-driven global commodity chains (Gereffi, 1994, 1999). Third, global sourcing in buyer-driven chains is driven by intense competition among different types of developed-country retailers and marketers[2] who feel compelled to mimic each other's moves in two ways: in growing offshore sourcing networks and in using brands as sources of market power.

Particularly noteworthy in the shift to both buyer-driven and internet-oriented value chains is the growing importance of global brands, which can be created without proprietary links to specific manufacturers or distribution channels. "Brands are the information — whether real or imagined, intellectual or emotional — that consumers associate with a product" (Evans and Wurster, 2000, p. 11). For consumers, brand knowledge is simply a high-richness/low-reach stock of information that comes from advertising, reputation and especially prior experience, in contrast with the high reach and low richness of classic markets. For companies, brands are a way to resist commodification when value chains deconstruct. Sellers use brands to lock in customer relationships[3] and to compete when reach (choice) goes up. Thus, building brand awareness is a fundamental challenge and a major source of market power for firms in both buyer-driven and internet-oriented value chains.

One of the main sources of organisational innovation in the shift from producer-driven to buyer-driven value chains derives from the disarticulation of brands and the production process. Originally, leading manufacturers developed brands to differentiate their products from those made by competitors (e.g. General Electric light bulbs, Levi's jeans, Kodak film). Both retailers and marketers then decided to tap into the profitability enjoyed by branded manufacturers. To distinguish themselves from larger and more diversified department stores, emergent speciality retailers sold only one kind of product under the store's own brand name (e.g. The Limited, Victoria's Secret, The Gap, Benetton). Marketers like Nike, Reebok, Liz Claiborne, and Ralph Lauren took the branding concept one step farther by eschewing both factories and actual stores; their profitability derived solely from elaborate promotional schemes based on carefully crafted "lifestyle brands" associated with their products. Department stores fought back with private-label merchandise — i.e. stores' brands that competed with the top national brands on price but nonetheless had better quality and style than other products[4]. Today, brands are even dissociated from specific products and linked to the internet infomediaries that channel information to web-based consumers (America Online, for example, is one of the best known brands, even though it is only a web-based navigator).

Table 1.1 summarises a number of the evolutionary shifts alluded to above. Whereas producer-driven global value chains are characterised by vertical integration by transnational corporations based on ownership and control, buyer-driven chains highlight the global sourcing networks established by retailers and marketers that rely heavily on sophisticated logistics and performance trust among numerous contractors. Table 1.1 uses the dates when leading US retailers and marketers were founded, or went public, to trace the sequential entry into the global sourcing game of large retailers, pure marketers and speciality retailers in the 1970s, and private-label (store brand) programmes in the 1980s. In the 1990s, the information revolution motivated the

24

direction and pace of organisational innovation in the current shift to internet-oriented value chains based on virtual integration and an explosion in connectivity due to the open and almost cost-free exchange of a widening universe of rich information.

Electronic Commerce and the Reorientation of Value Chains

The economic transformation at the turn of the 21st century, driven by the often spectacular development and diffusion of modern electronics-based information technology, has a variety of names — innovation economy, knowledge economy, network economy, digital economy and E-conomy (Cohen *et al.*, 2000). Yet electronic commerce is not simply a creature of technology. It also involves profound changes in business organisation, market structures, government regulation and human experience. The internet already is beginning to have a significant impact on the structure and competitive dynamics of global value chains[5].

The two most important types of e-commerce occur in business-to-consumer (B2C) and business-to-business (B2B) markets[6]. The B2C market transfers goods and services to individual consumers (a retail model), whereas B2B entails procurement, logistics and administrative processes between firms (a supply-chain model). Electronic commerce is growing so rapidly that estimates of the magnitude of these two markets vary widely. For example, the Boston Consulting Group estimates total on-line retail sales of $34.2 billion in 1999. Forrester Research calculates on-line sales of $20 billion in the B2C market in 1999, but expects that figure to grow to $184 billion by 2004 (U.S. Department of Commerce, 2000, pp. 42-43; *The Economist*, 2000a, pp. 9-10). B2B transactions dwarf on-line retail sales, however. They account for as much as 80 per cent of all e-commerce. According to the Gartner Group, a Connecticut-based market research firm, the worldwide B2B market will grow from $145 billion in 1999 to $401 billion in 2000 and $7.3 trillion by 2004 (i.e. 7 per cent of the forecast $105 trillion in worldwide sales transactions) (Standard & Poor's, 2001, p. 2).

The internet has the potential to transform both buyer-driven and producer-driven chains because of two fundamental factors: *i)* its ability to create markets on scales and with levels of efficiency not previously possible[7]; and *ii)* a radical "pull" business strategy that substitutes information for inventory and ships products only when there is real demand from customers. The shift from manufacturer "push" to consumer "pull" appears to be a long-term trend in many industries. It places a premium on a "build-to-order" business model and reflects a focus on consumer satisfaction and convenience (see the discussions of AOL, Amazon.com, and Dell in Gereffi, 2001). The "pull" strategy in supply-chain management is embodied in popular business-school concepts such as mass customisation (Pine, 1992), lean production (Womack *et al.*, 1990) and lean retailing (Abernathy *et al.*, 1999).

Table 1.1. **The Historical and Institutional Origins of Changing Governance Structures in Global Value Chains**

Governance Structure of Global Value Chains	Leading Industries and Timing	Main Drivers	Form and Dominant Principles of Value Chain Integration	Institutional and Organisational Innovations	Corporate and National Pioneers[a]
Producer-Driven Chains	Natural resources: late 19th and early 20th centuries; Capital goods and consumer durables: 1950s and 1960s	Transnational manufacturers	Vertical integration (ownership and control)	Vertically integrated TNCs with international production networks; Mass production	Oil companies (1870s onward); Mining (early 20th century); Agribusiness (early 20th century); Fordism (1920s onward); Japanese TNCs (Toyota, early 1960s on)
Buyer-Driven Chains	Consumer nondurables: 1970s & 1980s	Retailers and marketers	Network integration (logistics and trust)	Lean production; Growth of export processing zones; Global sourcing by retailers; Rise of pure marketers; Rise of specialty retailers; Growth of private labels (store brands); Lean retailing	Mexico, the Philippines, Chinese Taipei, South Korea, etc. (mid-1960s onward); Sears, Kmart, Montgomery Ward, JC Penney (early 1970s onward); Liz Claiborne (1976), Nike (1976), Reebok (1979); The Limited (1969), The Gap (1976); JC Penney, Sears, Wal-Mart, Kmart (mid-1980s onward); Wal-Mart, JC Penney, Dillard's, Federated (late 1980s onward)
Internet-Oriented Chains (emerging)	Services (B2C) – online retailing – online brokerage; Intermediates (B2B) – autos (Covisint) – computers; 1990s & 2000s	Internet infomediaries (B2C market) and some established manufacturers (B2B market)	Virtual integration (information and access)	Rise of e-commerce; Mass customisation; Disintermediation: – Direct sales (skip retailers) – Online services (e.g. brokerage); New internet navigators	Amazon.com (1997); Dell (1988), Gateway (1993); E*Trade (1992), Schwab (1996); AOL (1992), Yahoo! (1996), Excite@Home (1999)

Note: a) Specific dates indicate when companies were founded, went public (The Limited, The Gap, Dell, Gateway, Amazon, AOL, Yahoo!), or became established as US firms (Nike, Reebok). Decades are used for the onset of trends.

The B2C Market

One of the early changes attributed to the internet is the emergence of a new breed of "infomediaries" — companies that turn on-line access to customers, and especially detailed information about their purchasing habits, into a highly valued asset. Although most infomediaries in B2C transactions currently represent the interests of consumers trying to get the most out of the web, internet navigators are also affiliated with producers, sellers and traditional value-chain intermediaries. This infomediary model is based on oligpolistic competition, in which dominant infomediaries like AOL or Yahoo! control portals[8] and other strategic entry points to the internet. They further leverage their power by becoming more integrated across the internet organisational chain through mergers, acquisitions and strategic alliances.

Table 1.2 shows the internet's organisational chain, composed of the main firms that make internet transactions possible. The internet is an interconnected global network of smaller networks that links millions of computers through thousands of servers. It is built on a complex hardware infrastructure of internet equipment providers, computer makers and component suppliers, integrated by software and services. Companies such as Cisco Systems, Nortel Networks, and Lucent Technologies dominate the market for internet equipment, such as routers and remote access concentrators. The main customers for the internet are businesses (B2B markets) and individual consumers (B2C markets), with B2B markets currently dwarfing B2C transactions in size.

Computer makers are an integral part of the internet chain because most businesses and individuals hook up to it with personal computers. Corporate clients look for "single solutions" to meet their increasingly complex computing needs, and thus the major computer companies have shifted their focus to three main areas of growth: servers, storage and services. The expected demand for global technology services, by far the largest of the three, will nearly double from $359 billion in 1999 to over $700 billion by 2004 (Standard & Poor's, 2000e, pp. 3-6). Firms such as Oracle, Ariba, Commerce One and i2 Technologies that develop software for on-line transactions are becoming key players in the rapidly emerging B2B marketplace. Other important links in the internet organisational chain are:

— *web browsers* (browser software permits on-line navigation by allowing users to view the text and graphics located on internet web sites);

— *internet service providers* (ISPs offer basic, flat-rate internet access to customers);

— *internet content providers* (ICPs use mostly original material to create internet destinations where people go for information, entertainment, or commerce).

In each segment of the internet organisational chain, the leading companies have dominant market shares. Cisco controls more than three-quarters of the global market for internet routers and switches. The top four personal computer vendors (Compaq, Dell, IBM and Hewlett-Packard) account for nearly 40 per cent of unit shipments worldwide. Microsoft controls about 90 per cent of personal computer

Table 1. 2. The Internet's Organisation Chain

Internet Equipment Suppliers[1]	Personal Computer (PC) Manufacturers and Component Suppliers[2]	PC and E-Business Software[3]	Web Browsers[4]	Internet Service Providers (ISPs)[5]	Internet Content Providers (ICPs)[6]	Customers[7]
Cisco Systems Lucent Technologies Nortel Networks Sun Microsystems	*PCs*: Compaq, Dell, Hewlett-Packard, IBM. *Microprocessors*: Intel, AMD. *Disk Drives*: Seagate, Quantum	*PCs*: Microsoft, Apple. *Servers*: Unix, Linux. *E-Business*: Oracle, Ariba, Commerce One, SAP	Microsoft Netscape/AOL	AOL Microsoft AT&T	AOL Microsoft Yahoo! Lycos Excite	Businesses (B2B) – Covisint (Autos) Consumers (B2C) – Amazon.com – Dell Computers

Notes and Sources:

1. Cisco controls more than 75 per cent of the global market for internet routers and switches (Hoover's *Company Profiles*, 2000). Sun Microsystems is the main supplier of the Unix server market with a 28 per cent market share in 1999, followed by Hewlett-Packard (23 per cent) and IBM (18 per cent) (Standard & Poor's, 2000e, p. 4).

2. Compaq had 13.1 per cent of third-quarter 2000 worldwide PC shipments, followed by Dell (11.5 per cent), Hewlett-Packard (7.8 per cent) and IBM (7.4 per cent). In the US market, however, Dell (20.2 per cent) pulled ahead of Compaq (16.5 per cent) as the leading PC vendor in third-quarter 2000 sales. More than 80 per cent of the world's personal computers include an Intel microprocessor (Standard & Poor's, 2000e, pp. 2-3, 18).

3. Microsoft's Windows operating system software is used in an estimated 85–90 per cent of PCs worldwide (Standard & Poor's, 2000e, p. 12). Unix and Linux power most web servers with proprietary and open-source software, respectively, while Oracle, Ariba, Commerce One, and Germany's SAP are among the largest providers of software for e-business transactions.

4. In June 2000, Microsoft's Internet Explorer had 86 per cent of the web browser market and Netscape's Navigator (now a part of AOL) the remaining 14 per cent (Standard & Poor's, 2000d, p. 9).

5. America Online had 43 per cent of the ISP market in 1999, followed by Microsoft (6 per cent), and AT&T WorldNet (5 per cent) (Standard & Poor's, 2000c, p. 3). This was prior to the merger of AOL with the cable giant Time Warner Inc., announced in January 2000 and finally approved one year later.

6. The most visited web properties in July 2000 (i.e. the percentage of web-active individuals who visited a site at least once during the month) were the AOL network (worldwide web and proprietary — 78 per cent); Microsoft sites (63 per cent); Yahoo sites (61 per cent); Lycos (40 per cent); and Excite (34 per cent) (Standard & Poor's, 2000d, p. 4).

7. Global B2B e-commerce is predicted to reach $4 trillion by 2003, a market 10 times bigger than the $400 billion forecast for B2C online sales to consumers in 2003 (The Economist, 2000b, p. 11).

28

operating systems, and two-thirds of the web browser market. America Online (AOL) had 43 per cent of the internet service provider market in 1999 and more subscribers than the next 20 ISPs combined. AOL, Yahoo! and Microsoft sit atop the internet content provider market as well. (See Table 1.2 for references.)

The B2B Market

The automotive industry leads in B2B e-commerce. It contains the world's largest on-line marketplace to date. *Covisint* is a newly formed joint venture that combines the purchasing activities of General Motors, Ford, Daimler–Chrysler, Renault, Nissan and their suppliers. Initially announced in February 2000 as a joint electronic supply agreement among General Motors, Ford and Daimler-Chrysler, Covisint subsequently added Renault/Nissan, and in October 2000, following US Federal Trade Commission clearance, the first on-line auctions took place (Standard & Poor's, 2000*b*, p. 5). The scope of the venture is staggering. In 1999, General Motors' total automotive purchases were approximately $87 billion, Ford's were $85 billion, and Daimler–Chrysler's were $80 billion. Each does business with about 30 000 suppliers. Estimated annual transactions on the exchange will exceed $240 billion, and the venture is expected to shave billions of dollars off procurement costs[9]. Commerce One and Oracle have been brought in as technology partners to help develop on-line software for the auto parts exchange.

Covisint promises lower prices, faster transaction turnarounds and other efficiencies, but many suppliers fear they could become losers because lower prices for buyers will mean lower margins for sellers. While Covisint strives for unprecedented collaboration among the world's leading automakers, other equally significant changes are occurring. The tight vertical structures that used to bind most parts suppliers to particular car manufacturers are loosening. The large, technologically sophisticated global suppliers (such as Bosch, Denso, Johnson Controls, Lear Corporation, TRW and Magna) are gaining strength, as they become preferred partners in all the major automakers' supply chains (Sturgeon and Florida, 1999). These developments, together with the emergent megadealers in automotive retailing[10], could lead to substantial realignments in the relative power and profitability of major segments in the automotive value chain.

Three Scenarios for the Internet's Impact on Global Value Chains

The internet remains in its early stages of development, but its impact on global value chains is already evident. While it may be premature to try to identify lasting changes on producer-driven and buyer-driven chains, three possible and not mutually exclusive scenarios are emerging. In the first, the internet will lead to the formation of new infomediary-based value chains, which implies a different set of organisational drivers. Although some spectacularly successful e-commerce ventures appeared in the late 1990s, the B2C market is still too small and volatile to establish a radically distinct and durable governance structure.

In the second scenario, the internet significantly extends the logic of buyer-driven chains as both information and power continue to shift inexorably from producers and retailers to consumers. Rather than serving as an alternative to buyer-driven chains, the internet intensifies a shift that makes all industries more "buyer driven" — in the sense that new consumer-oriented competitors undermine the power of manufacturers, retailers, and marketers that do not take advantage of the internet's ability to facilitate mass customisation.

The third scenario sees the impact of the internet in both B2B and B2C transactions captured and integrated into the business practices of leading manufacturers, retailers, and marketers. Pitting the so-called new economy against the old economy completely misses the point because the internet's major impact will be to improve the productivity of all parts of the economy, especially the old-economy firms. Established leaders in both producer-driven and buyer-driven chains are proving surprisingly adept at incorporating e-commerce in their business strategies (in popular jargon, these companies are moving from "bricks and mortar" to "clicks and mortar"). Thus, the biggest and most powerful companies co-opt and internalise the internet, and they force their rivals and suppliers alike to bear the costs of adapting to new information technologies.

While there is evidence to support all three scenarios, the third model currently seems dominant. Nonetheless, lead firms in major industries are adopting quite different strategies for key supply-chain issues such as vertical integration, outsourcing and globalisation. The impact of the internet on these business structures remains an open question.

Notes

1. Although the concepts of global value chains, global commodity chains and global supply chains are closely related, the term "global value chains" will be used in this paper to emphasise the flows of information, resources, goods and services along the full range of activities and organisations in the supply chain. For a more detailed discussion of the origins and use of these concepts, see Gereffi (1994), Kaplinsky (2000), and Raikes *et al.* (2000).

2. In the original distinction between producer-driven and buyer-driven commodity chains (Gereffi, 1994), the term "buyer" was used in an organisational sense to refer to retailers and marketers (in their pure form, marketers build and commercialise their own brand names but own neither factories nor stores). These organisational buyers are to be distinguished from the actual individual consumers who are the targets of much contemporary e-commerce.

3. Brand affiliation is surprisingly stable. Of the 25 top-selling consumer goods brands in 1960, 16 of them are still among the top 25 today (Evans and Wurster, 2000, p. 150).

4. This trend is most visible in apparel products (see Standard & Poor's, 2000a). In blue jeans, for example, JC Penney's Arizona jeans and Sears' Canyon River Blues go head-to-head with upscale jeans sold by Tommy Hilfiger, Calvin Klein and Donna Karan.

5. The material in the remainder of the paper is summarised from the more detailed discussion in Gereffi (2001).

6. If one were to complete the e-commerce matrix, the consumer-to-business (C2B) market would be represented by Priceline.com, the most popular of several reverse-auction sites, while the consumer-to-consumer (C2C) segment includes consumers' auctions, epitomised by the auction site eBay.com. See *The Economist* (2000a) for a fuller analysis of the e-commerce matrix.

7. A couple of familiar companies provide good illustrations of the extensive reach provided by the internet. Amazon.com, one of the first electronic retailers on the web, has no physical stores but offers an electronic list of 3 million books, 20 times larger than the holdings of Barnes & Noble, the largest chain bookstore. Dell's internet site offers over 10 million computer configurations (Evans and Wurster, 2000, pp. 61-62, 111).

8. Portals are web sites designed to be an internet user's initial entry point for exploring the web. They typically generate revenues by renting out advertising space.

9. The on-line exchange is expected to yield savings of $2 000-$3 000 on a $19 000 vehicle (Covisint, 2001).

10. AutoNation is the largest car dealer in the United States. It had sales of approximately $1 billion (about 46 000 vehicles) via the internet in 1999 (Standard & Poor's, 2000b, p. 5).

Bibliography

ABERNATHY, F.H., J.T. DUNLOP, J.H. HAMMOND and D. WEIL (1999), *A Stitch in Time: Lean Retailing and the Transformation of Manufacturing — Lessons from the Apparel and Textile Industries.* Oxford University Press, New York, NY.

BARNET, R.J. and J. CAVANAUGH (1994), *Global Dreams: Imperial Corporations and the New World Order*, Simon & Schuster, New York, NY.

BARNET, R.J. and R.E. MÜLLER (1974), *Global Reach: The Power of the Multinational Corporations*, Simon & Schuster, New York, NY.

CHANDLER, A.D., JR. (1962), *Strategy and Structure: Chapters in the History of the American Industrial Enterprise*, MIT Press, Cambridge, MA.

COHEN, S.S., J. BRADFORD DELONG and J. ZYSMAN (2000), "Tools for Thought: What is New and Important about the 'E-conomy'?", BRIE Working Paper No. 138, Berkeley Roundtable on the International Economy, Berkeley, CA.

COVISINT (2001), General FAQ's about Covisint [online]. http://www.covisint.com/info/faq_gen.shtml (down-loaded on Feb. 17, 2001).

DICKEN, P. (1998), *Global Shift: Transforming the World Economy*, 3rd edition, Guilford Press, New York, NY.

EVANS, P. and T.S. WURSTER (2000), *Blown to Bits: How the New Economics of Information Transforms Strategy*, Harvard Business School Press, Boston, MA.

FRÖBEL, F., J. HEINRICHS and O. KREYE (1981), *The New International Division of Labor*, Cambridge University Press, New York, NY.

GEREFFI, G. (2001), "Shifting Governance Structures in Global Commodity Chains, with Special Reference to the Internet", *American Behavioral Scientist*, Vol. 44, No. 10.

GEREFFI, G. (1999), "International Trade and Industrial Upgrading in the Apparel Commodity Chain", *Journal of International Economics*, Vol. 48, No. 1.

GEREFFI, G. (1994), "The Organization of Buyer-Driven Global Commodity Chains: How U.S. Retailers Shape Overseas Production Networks", *in* GEREFFI, G. and M. KORZENIEWICZ (1994).

GEREFFI, G. and R. KAPLINSKY (eds.) (2001), *The Value of Value Chains: Spreading the Gains from Globalisation*, *IDS Bulletin*, Vol. 32, No. 3.

GEREFFI, G. and M. KORZENIEWICZ (eds.) (1994), *Commodity Chains and Global Capitalism*, Praeger, Westport, CT.

GEREFFI, G., D. SPENER and J. BAIR (eds.) (2002), *Free Trade and Uneven Development: The North American Apparel Industry after NAFTA*, Temple University Press, Philadelphia, PA.

GEREFFI, G. and D.L. WYMAN (eds.) (1990), *Manufacturing Miracles: Paths of Industrialisation in Latin America and East Asia*, Princeton University Press, Princeton, NJ.

GORE, C. (2000), "The Rise and Fall of the Washington Consensus as a Paradigm for Developing Countries", *World Development*, Vol. 28, No. 5.

GRUNWALD, J. and K. FLAMM (1985), *The Global Factory: Foreign Assembly in International Trade*, The Brookings Institution, Washington, D.C.

HOOVER'S ONLINE (2000), *Company Profiles* [online]. http://www,hoovers.com.

HUMPHREY, J. and H. SCHMITZ (2001), "Governance in Global Value Chains", *IDS Bulletin*, Vol. 32, No. 3.

KAPLINSKY, R. (2000), "Spreading the Gains from Globalisation: What Can Be Learned from Value Chain Analysis?", *Journal of Development Studies*, Vol. 37, No. 2.

PINE, B. J. (1992), *Mass Customization: The New Frontier in Business Competition*, Harvard Business School Press, Boston, MA.

RAIKES, P., M.F. JENSEN and S. PONTE (2000), "Global Commodity Chain Analysis and the French *Filière* Approach: Comparison and Critique", *Economy and Society*, Vol. 29, No. 3.

REICH, R.B. (1991), *The Work of Nations: Preparing Ourselves for 21st-Century Capitalism*, Alfred A. Knopf, New York, NY.

STANDARD & POOR'S (2001), *Industry Surveys*, "Computers: Commercial Services", 25 January.

STANDARD & POOR'S (2000a), *Industry Surveys*, "Apparel & Footwear", 5 October.

STANDARD & POOR'S (2000b), *Industry Surveys*, "Autos & Auto Parts", 28 December.

STANDARD & POOR'S (2000c), *Industry Surveys*, "Computers: Consumer Services & the Internet", 16 March.

STANDARD & POOR'S (2000d), *Industry Surveys*, "Computers: Consumer Services & the Internet", 28 September.

STANDARD & POOR'S (2000e), *Industry Surveys*, "Computers: Hardware", 14 December.

STURGEON, T. and R. FLORIDA (1999), "The World that Changed the Machine: Globalisation and Jobs in the Automotive Industry", unpublished final report to the Alfred P. Sloan Foundation, 5 May.

The Economist (2000a), "Shopping Around the Web: A Survey of E-Commerce", 26 February.

The Economist (2000b), "Untangling E-conomics", 23 September.

US DEPARTMENT OF COMMERCE (2000), *U.S. Industry & Trade Outlook 2000*, McGraw Hill/ U.S. Department of Commerce, New York, NY.

VERNON, R. (1971), *Sovereignty at Bay: The Multinational Spread of U.S. Enterprises*, Basic Books, New York, NY.

WOMACK, J.P., D.T. JONES and D. ROOS (1990), *The Machine That Changed the World*, Rawson Associates, New York, NY.

WORLD BANK (1993), *The East Asian Miracle*, Oxford University Press, New York, NY.

Chapter 2

E-Commerce for Development:
A General Framework

Patrizia Fariselli

Introduction and Summary

Change and Models

Policies to overcome the digital divide or prevent its emergence in developing countries need grounding in a general view of the impact of the digital economy on development and growth — a view not yet clear or formalised into robust models. OECD work to analyse the contribution of information and communications technologies (ICTs) to macroeconomic performance requires the reconstruction of indicators and accounting frameworks. The interplay between the dynamics of socio-economic change — induced and/or altered by pervasive ICT infrastructures, services, and goods — and those of research and policy gives expectations, case studies and short-term analyses a prevailing and sometimes misleading role. Potential network effects make the measurement of impacts from application of new ICTs that much more difficult but at the same time more important.

Early attention to electronic commerce tended to focus on business-to-consumer (B2C) trading. Forecasts of phenomenal B2C growth proved exaggerated, sometimes in the extreme, and recent prognoses are more sober. More recently, much attention has gone to business-to-business (B2B) e-commerce and its potential, but once more the integration of B2B models within the supply chains of the so- called "old" economy has been slower than expected. Euphoric expectations of the contribution of electronic commerce to corporate profit growth produced over five years a gigantic investment bubble in dotcom start-up companies that has since been deflated. Looking at the new economy in this light raises the question of what if anything is really new. The change is not in investors' behaviour, which has always swung between optimism and pessimism, but apparently in how international capital markets function. It derives primarily but not exclusively from technological change — the pervasiveness of ICTs and the way they make the information and knowledge content of transactions transparent. The major impact is on the configuration of the networks (ICT infrastructure, financial and business organisations and research, education and policy networks). The possibilities both of becoming interactive and global and of decomposing and recomposing operations and supply chains strain the stability of established networks. The application of ICTs makes a network's boundaries and configuration extraordinarily flexible. ICTs perform an enabling function to the extent that they provide methods, tools and solutions to address increasingly complex computational and system organisation and implementation requirements.

Access to Networks and Access to Knowledge

The digital economy's boundaries go beyond the trading of intangible goods, typical of electronic commerce at its early stage, to encompass all business and community relations. The notions of the "knowledge economy" and the "net economy" become more appropriate than that of electronic commerce. The link between ICT and development is represented basically by *access to networks* — the global ICT infrastructure, business organisations, research and education communities and policy institutions — and by *access to information and knowledge*. Information and knowledge can be valuable resources that command a market price but they also have important public-good properties, with an inherent tension between their private and public aspects. Technologies of digital reproduction also make it ever easier to share information over the internet, causing certain industries — notably the music industry — to redouble efforts at strict copyright enforcement. This is a crucial economic and policy issue concerning the relationship between ICT and development. Beside the debate about IPRs on information and knowledge products currently in the market, the generation of new information and knowledge is influenced by the accessibility of those products as a means of producing new knowledge.

Countries and regions lagging behind in ICT diffusion can take advantage of business and policy experience accumulated in the developed world over the last several years, but that does not necessarily imply that they should replicate the same paths or sequences. The rich countries are experiencing a set of innovations — in technologies, in markets, in business organisations, in public administration and in socio-cultural environments — which open up multiple scenarios for the future. The end result in economic growth and social welfare is an open question. A digital divide between the haves and have-nots is perceived as a risk both between and within countries.

The components influencing the take-up of ICT and access to the digital economy may be grouped into the four categories listed below. How and how intensely these components are associated contribute to the occurrence, deepening or reduction of the digital divide.

— Physical Network → ICT Infrastructure and Systems
— Economic Network → Market and Business Organisations
— Resources → Information and Knowledge; Financial Capital
— Policy → Support and Regulatory Frameworks

The digital divide is evident in the short run from a comparison of ICT market indicators across countries or regions, and the reduction of transaction costs in business organisations based on e-commerce is measurable with currently available accountancy tools. Yet assessment of the contribution of digital technologies to development and growth remains a work in progress. Besides economic variables, it must also look at policies, because the role played by policy institutions in technology and infrastructure access deeply influences the divide and development prospects. Barriers to IC networks, exclusion from digital marketplaces or communities and exclusion from the generation and sharing of knowledge and innovation processes will all likely produce market fragmentation, loss of resources, reduction of pluralism and a slowdown of technical progress and innovation, in both developed and developing countries. Only policy actions can prevent these effects.

Developing countries or areas cannot reasonably be expected to follow entirely the same paths as the most developed ones in the transition to the digital economy. They can leverage the same catalytic components, particularly the policy components, but they cannot rely to the same extent on the prospect of reducing transaction costs in markets and organisations. The priority in the weakest economies is to build capacity and critical mass rather than reduce the use of resources. Except where resources get incorporated into supply chains under the control of large transnational corporations — which amounts to absorbing e-commerce practices passively — the problem usually involves just having in place a sufficient critical mass of local businesses to make electronic interrelations possible and effective.

On the other hand, the trend towards technological convergence offers underdeveloped areas the opportunity to leapfrog some phases of the development of telecommunications infrastructure in the industrialised world over the last century. Mobile telephony/internet and satellite communication networks can easily be set up where fixed networks in place are not capillary. New technology applications and a liberalised market for carriers allow bypassing the hurdles raised by bureaucratic incumbents — the old PSTNs — and facilitate less expensive mass access to the modern communication networks. Yet the pricing practices of broadband service and satellite network suppliers still represent a bottleneck to access to the global communications infrastructure. Public investment in telecommunications infrastructure becomes crucial, as it has been and still is in the most industrialised countries. There, a universal service philosophy and low-cost access to the internet have been supported by state administrations to the joint advantage of citizens, public and private carriers and the ICT industry.

Local Generation of Knowledge

Besides access to the physical infrastructure, access to knowledge is the major opportunity and challenge in the digital economy. The erosion of time, space and cost barriers, and the decentralised network model, make ICT extremely powerful in stimulating or accelerating growth. They allow knowledge resources to break the chains imposed by old and rigid business organisation models and favour creativity in exploring new application fields. The creation and trading of knowledge have become key objectives of economic activity everywhere. As global as the knowledge market is, however, knowledge has an essentially local dimension. Part of the reason for a digital divide, besides limited access to the physical network, is the limited quantity and quality of knowledge under local control. Good practices in electronic commerce from the most developed countries and markets must be adapted to local contextual requirements if they are to generate local development and growth and avoid the creation of islands connected to corporations based elsewhere but disconnected from the local context.

By decomposing and recomposing network components through the isolation and transfer of information and knowledge, ICT and the internet contribute to blurring geo-economic borders and shifting comparative advantage. While certain high-tech industries and activities remain highly concentrated in a few noteworthy agglomerations in the developed world, important new entrants include such traditionally marginal areas as Sweden, Finland, Brazil, India, Israel and perhaps South Africa. The same holds at the sub-national or regional level. The well established practice of outsourcing to India segments of data processing, software development and internet-related services by large US or Europe-based corporations is evolving toward the establishment of local business units (delocation) and the creation of new local enterprises able to compete in the global market. India's successes show the boost possible from a combination of policy support and private investment in physical infrastructure, business creation, human resources and education.

From Divide to Development

The extension of ICT and internet networks and access to them are preconditions for any form of electronic commerce and the uptake of the digital economy anywhere. The penetration of ICT and the cost of access are reshaping the global map. In the LDCs, the picture is differentiated.

Pro-active policies can make the difference. Public Administration (PA) can play a strategic role in piloting the transition to the information society and to the digital economy. Internet applications within government include PA-to-Citizens, PA-to-Business, and PA-to-PA. The internet can serve as a development tool that permits government simultaneously to address the needs of internal and international integration and faster and wider diffusion of public services such as education and training, health care and assistance to business creation and management. Systemic issues related to electronic commerce, whether legal (contracts, security, confidence, IPR), financial (e-payment, insurance, taxation), or technical (interoperability of systems and standards), have simultaneously a national and an international dimension. Adopting e-government frameworks and procedures enables LDC governments to participate effectively in the global forums setting international standards and the rules for international trade in the digital economy. PA can also play a significant role in supporting the development of economic institutions and of the knowledge resources needed to enable local economies to compete in global markets. Policies to build local capacity could be associated with measures (e.g. on-line procurement) to enhance effective local demand for internet services and to encourage the production of local content and local provision of internet-related services and applications.

What is E-Commerce?

Business-to-Consumers

A tide of new terminology floods current language, spreading from specialist disciplines through the mass communications media. Symbols, prefixes and acronyms such as @, *e*-, and B2B have become signposts to identify a largely uncharted territory. Indicators and models are still in process, so that examples often substitute for definitions and have an imprint on them. Widely accepted definitions of electronic commerce delivered by the European Commission (1997) and the OECD (1998) reflected a then prevailing view of electronic commerce as buying and selling consumer goods over the internet, particularly software, music, books, travel, culture, hobbies and advertising. The services to develop in that early stage were mostly electronic catalogues, electronic malls, and anything connected with the design, operation and maintenance of commercial web sites and related data bases.

At first, the global and decentralised internet unveiled the global market as a place that consumers and suppliers, individuals or companies, could access directly, bypassing intermediaries, taxes and bureaucratic hurdles. In a way, the nature of the interaction tool (internet) was transferred to the object of the interaction itself (commercial transactions). Yet the models required to implement electronic trading over the internet efficiently and effectively also include the (re)setting of manifold components involving technology and economics, business management and regulations, content and behaviour. All are usually listed as "barriers" to the uptake of electronic commerce. Local and international policies get launched to support and enhance the "readiness" for electronic commerce and its governance around the globe. In fact, the possibility of entering the global marketplace in a one-to-one relationship (consumer-to-producer and vice versa) endangers the role of traditional intermediaries, especially in retailing and wholesaling. It also creates, however, a wide population of new on-line intermediaries, as providers of equipment, network access and services, web-related services, data warehouses, business intelligence, content management, financial tools and services for on-line transactions, marketing, advertising and consulting.

Empirical studies provide mixed evidence on internet market efficiency properties (price levels, price elasticities and menu costs) compared with conventional retail channels for a number of products such as CDs, books, software, used cars and airline tickets. Price dispersion is never lower in internet markets. It is substantially higher (between 20 per cent and 33 per cent) for books, CDs and airline tickets (Smith *et al.*, 1999)[1]. Many factors contribute to the decision to shop on-line and to make specific purchases. Price appears to be only one of them, and the lowest price does not necessarily take priority in customers' preferences. The cultural and life-style profiles of internet shoppers and the marketing policies of suppliers both influence consumer behaviour. Time is a highly valued commodity in internet business[2], and the time efficiency that internet-enabled search offers to consumers may make some willing to pay price premiums in exchange for time savings. This partly explains the persistence of price dispersion. Information about consumers' profiles, tastes and preferences adds value to electronic transactions exceeding their market prices, because it becomes an input to the customer-oriented production of the goods, services and advertising delivered by suppliers. In a way, consumers participate in the process as both consumers and producers of information incorporated in the supply of goods and services. Research work on the *weightless economy* focuses on this interplay (Quah, 1999).

Business-to-Business

A greater appreciation of the importance of business-to-business applications has come more recently to balance the initial emphasis on e-shopping. Awareness of the potential impact of internet technologies on business processes behind the front office has grown apace. Business-to-business transactions represent by far the largest turnover in e-commerce markets. Since the mid-1960s, the adoption of ICT application systems has steadily increased in business management, along with the evolution of computer and component technology (Schiller, 2000). ICTs have become increasingly essential to the firm and its management as the complexity of the processes and relations underpinning the enterprise increases. The complexity derives from the web of interdependencies and the nexus of contracts within which the typical firm is situated. When internet technologies are coupled with ICTs, electronic commerce allows enterprises to do more with less (Kalakota and Whinston, 1997) by reducing the costs of managing the business processes underlying the enterprise's activities along the value chain.

E-Business

A number of business models have developed along with ICT-driven business processes and supply chain integration (Lefebvre and Lefebvre, 2000). The evolution of e-commerce from one-to-one applications (e-tailing) to one-to-many applications, such as enterprise and supply chain integration, e-procurement, e-auctions, e-marketplaces, collaborative commerce and virtual communities, is rendering virtual both the value-added activities of an enterprise and the enterprise itself. It reinforces the shift from the enterprise-centric vision to the multi-enterprise network or virtual enterprise[3]. The key implication is that ICT and internet use can not only reduce costs but also create value. Value is generated from brokering transactions and matching orders between companies as well as from the provision of additional services. Those services can include ASP (application and professional services for integrating companies' legacy systems into the e-marketplace), business services to support transactions (legal and financial, logistics, project and contract management), background services (market intelligence) and services to set up virtual private marketplaces for smaller and targeted e-business communities.

In an antidote to the vagueness of most data concerning internet commerce and particularly business-to-business dealings, *EITO 2001* provides a more precise definition of e-business. E-business is an umbrella term. It encompasses e-commerce and marketing/information web sites, as well as the concept of E-business services, i.e. the range of ICT support services associated with the customisation, implementation and ongoing running, hosting and maintenance of one-to-many e-commerce solutions and e-marketplaces, plus those associated with marketing/information web sites. The total European e-business services market was worth Euro 11.4 billion in 2000. The market for one-to-many e-commerce ICT services was Euro 6.2 billion (55 per cent of the total), distributed as follows: 45 per cent in implementation services, 41 per cent in application hosting, 8 per cent in other ongoing support services and 6 per cent in e-ordering-specific services (EITO, 2001).

The rate of penetration of one-to-many e-commerce applications is relatively high in the service sector (with finance/insurance reporting an e-ordering rate of 45 per cent of total orders) compared with manufacturing and the public sector. In manufacturing, the companies driving the buy-side e-commerce solutions are those with big supply chains and heavy procurement expenditures, such as automotive, aerospace, chemicals, engineering, metals, mining and energy/utilities firms. Large companies dominate in these branches, with the necessary resources to invest in e-procurement and e-marketplaces. They can adopt e-commerce with both suppliers and consumers. Marketing/information web site ICT services accounted for Euro 4.45 billion, 39 per cent of the total European e-business services market in 2000. Web site hosting took 79 per cent, web site design 13 per cent and other ongoing support services 8 per cent. Web site hosting and design are outsourced in two-thirds or more of the cases. The role of the government as party to business transactions involves it in electronic commerce practices as well. Besides the demand/supply for ICT services to support so-called on-line government, e-procurement adds a strong boost to the uptake of electronic commerce; public procurement is large relative to GDP in many European countries.

To sum up, the service sector — especially finance and insurance — and large manufacturing organisations lead in e-commerce applications. Small and medium-sized companies lag significantly behind, despite high interest in advancing their access to e-marketplaces. The barriers to entry, however, depend on the costs of adopting e-commerce applications and on the control of the knowledge to be traded along digital channels.

From E-Commerce to Digital Economy

Optimal Allocation vs. Dynamic Accumulation

Goods, services and coded information are the media for embodying, reproducing and transferring knowledge from one context to another. Markets, hierarchies and networks are the three basic knowledge-transfer mechanisms, co-ordinating the relationship between producers and users of knowledge (Grandinetti and Rullani, 1996). Transnational corporations were early users of information and telecommunications applications well before electronic commerce entered the mass media jargon and even before the adoption of the EDI standard. The wider the networks and the deeper the relationships between enterprises, the greater the need to ensure replication and smooth transfer of knowledge within and between firms. This calls for efficient, all-inclusive and wide-reaching information systems, shared languages and common semantics. Digital circuits, network technologies and HTML provide the best available means to that end.

Study of the economic impact of ICTs focuses on the effects of communications technologies on transaction costs and of electronic brokerage on co-ordination and search costs as they stimulate electronic integration within the firm and the supply chain (Malone *et al.*, 1987). That is consistent with a view of the information circulated and shared over electronic channels as a static component, to be appropriately packed and relocated within the electronic hierarchy or market in accordance with the principle of the optimal allocation of resources. Because of the philosophy of decentralisation and interactivity on which they are based, however, the internet and internet-related applications enhance the dynamism of the knowledge transfer and creation processes. By blurring the borders between producers and consumers, goods and services and markets and hierarchies, the internet produces feedback effects: resistance, adaptation, creativity and exit.

Network Instability

The effect of internet technologies integrated with ICTs does not fall exclusively on the reduction of costs associated with business management. It also touches on the reconfiguration of networks. This is not new. What is new is that ICT and the internet make knowledge accessible to individuals and organisations as soon as they interact (i.e. in real time), not exclusively after they have interacted. The market — as a set of transacting but not interacting individuals — cannot represent fully the dynamics of knowledge creation and re-creation, which have a fundamental relational nature independent of the information and communication platform but heavily influenced by it.

A deeper investigation of the implications of B2B electronic commerce for business models would include business process re-engineering in the value chain, complemented with two new models — of the *value network* and of *dynamic market configuration* — to introduce the concept of market process engineering (Timmers, 1999). Value networks, focused on deepening the internal relationships within enterprises by integrating information flows, and dynamic markets, focused on increasing value from flexible external relationships, have existed for a long time. Now, however, digital technologies affect how the value-creation process is organised, entry to and exit from networks and the evolution from one to another network configuration. The digital market for goods and services opens networks to companies or networks that are outsiders, without necessarily incorporating them into stable relationships. Typically, market dynamism enters into networks via ICT and the internet, changing their configurations but not their nature as intermediate forms of co-ordination between hierarchy and market. Access to dynamic networks is a precondition for the development of new businesses, but it is now assessed increasingly by the ability to compete in the market.

Access to the Digital Economy

The structural change brought about by ICTs and the internet is giving birth to the digital economy. By increasing information's divisibility, transportability and tradability, and by making possible on-line interaction between producers and consumers of knowledge, ICT and the internet permit a separation of the supply of technological information from the accumulation of technological competence. (Antonelli, 1999). That has an extremely important impact on economic development and growth, which depends increasingly on the quantity of knowledge incorporated into goods, services, business processes and organisations, and on the degree of "connectivity" in the socio-economic system.

The debate about what's new in the "new" economy and which new models will replace the old ones remains open, constrained by the difficulties of measuring the "new", and of interpreting change using "old" paradigms and parameters such as productivity. The OECD works on measurement, economists produce research hypotheses, institutions organise high level conferences and journalists stoke the fire. Some argue that the new economy is new only to mainstream economists (Antonelli *et al.*, 2000), because the disequilibrium nature of allocation and production processes and continuous structural dynamics are not new at all in economics. As the digital economy makes time and knowledge visible as key economic resources, we no longer face a problem of rational choice, but rather a process of learning (Pasinetti, based on a quote in IST, 2000).

The digital economy offers as many opportunities as challenges for development. Old and new players can either take economic advantage of the application of new information and communication technologies or be disadvantaged by their mis(sed)-application. ICTs do facilitate fast communications and circulation of information at a relatively low cost, but the economic impact depends on how technologies and communication intertwine with other resources, namely knowledge and financial capital.

Entering the digital economy requires a "gateway", a term that serves as both a metaphor for and a literal description of *access*. Access is needed to get into (or not be excluded from) networks — the ICT infrastructure, business organisations, supply chains, clusters of companies and virtual enterprises, the research community or policy institutions. It means having fast and low-cost connectivity in the free market, interoperable systems, user-friendly applications, open standards and programmes addressing pluralistic demand rather than requirements for adaptation to market-leading technological solutions. The characteristic interactivity of the new ICTs is a key quality that must be preserved. Global diffusion and accessibility of ICT tools (such as operating systems and basic applications) and exploitation of the full potential of ICTs are difficult to couple. A subtle confrontation is underway in the market between top-down pressures towards simplification — supported by policies for global market diffusion of integrated architectures and tool kits — and bottom-up pressures for open and flexible platforms, designed to address and capture complexity.

A dual relationship of co-operation and conflict characterises research and the markets. Market exploitation of research is indispensable to fuel investment in research, but the need to meet current demand and lead the market may divert research from innovative paths to replication and trigger lock-in. These effects generate a process in which technologies selected by the market are not always the best or most useful. Technology is not neutral. It participates in the social process of fulfilment and redefinition of users' requirements (Malerba *et al.*, 1999). Information technology, in particular, enjoys an extremely powerful role in shaping the market and social relations because it is simultaneously process, product and industry (Eischen, 2000). In the digital economy the contribution of ICT to development depends on access to all three, which in turn means access to:

—   network infrastructure built on ICT products and services;

—   knowledge generation, codification and trading; and

—   network dynamics.

Access to the ICT market

Both individuals and organisations provide the demand. Whatever the application, the purpose, the equipment, the services mobilised and the value of an e-transaction, an end-user somewhere clicks the icon "internet connection". Over 65 per cent of the 372 453 000 regular internet users in the world in 2000 inhabited a macro-area corresponding to 14 per cent of the world population, i.e. mostly the OECD countries. The same holds for internet host distribution (OECD, 2001). North America leads by far — 168.68 hosts per 1 000 inhabitants, compared with 59.16 in Oceania, 20.22 in Europe, 2.53 in Central and Southern America, 1.96 in Asia and 0.31 in Africa. Africa, with 780 million people, has about as many hosts on the internet as a small Eastern European country, Latvia, with a population of 2.5 million (Jensen, 2000).

A small number of American Internet Backbone Providers (IBPs) control access to the internet. They provide the gateways to about 90 per cent of total backbone traffic in the United States, where most internet traffic must transit. IBPs provide access to information located in the United States. They secure access to the core routing structure and to all internet addresses in the world (Foros and Kind, 2000). Such centralisation of control of an inherently decentralised network raises the costs of connection, particularly when there is empty space between end-users, local telecom operators and the IBPs, as in Africa. There, the high costs of local and international calls discourage local ISPs from entering the market and operating cross-border connections. This generates a large cash outflow for transit fees — estimated at $400 million per year — that reduces funds available for investment in local infrastructure (UNCTAD, 2000).

A look at the extremes of internet development and underdevelopment between the United States and Africa makes one appreciate the role of policy as the indispensable supporter of market maturation in the digital economy. The United States opened the internet to the market after it had grown up under the protective wing of the state and when it was ready to fly in a liberalised telecommunication environment. In Africa, the PSTN revenue transferred to governments has few available substitutes, making it difficult for them to contemplate wholesale liberalisation and competition.

Several forces should generate an impetus towards appropriate policies in the underdeveloped areas of the world. They include the fast development of alternative connection channels bypassing the fixed phone network and the widely perceived advantage of broad internet access in the less-connected world, together with the current concern about the digital divide. Policies can exert deep influence on investors' decisions. Interesting data (UNCTAD, 2000) show that, despite a strong correlation between the use of the internet and per capita income levels, income is by no means the sole determinant of use. Some countries with rather low per capita incomes have a large number of internet hosts.

Figures showing the penetration of ICT are usually taken as plain evidence of the digital divide, which is approached predominantly in terms of access to the ICT infrastructure. That is obviously a necessary precondition for any further exploitation of the potential of digital technologies, but not a sufficient one. Access to the infrastructure means having the opportunity, on the demand side, to click and use it, and, on the supply side, to participate in building networks, products and services. The share of ICT production in gross world product rose from 8.6 per cent in 1998 to 10.4 per cent in 2000. The ICT share of 2000 GDP was 13.3 per cent in Europe, 8.2 per cent in the United States, and 6.7 per cent in Japan. Studies on ICT investment in the G7 countries show that in 1990-96 the real growth rate of capital investment was 23.8 per cent in the United States and ranged from 11 per cent to 18.6 per cent in the other six countries. ICT may contribute to output and productivity growth not only in the ICT-producing sectors, whose economic weight is growing, but also in

ICT-using sectors. Exploratory investigations of the impact of ICT capital goods on the acceleration of multi-factor productivity (MFP) in non-ICT-producing industries are furthest advanced in the United States (Bassanini *et al.*, 2000).

The effects generated by equity investment in dotcom companies also deserve mention. Morgan Stanley, surveying 1 750 US companies, calculated that despite the sell-off over the past year (a loss of about $1 trillion), technology companies that have gone public since 1980 have created more than $2.5 trillion of value. Moreover, Morgan Stanley calculated the overspending on IT as a result of excess funding raised by dotcom companies in 2000 at around 6 per cent of total IT spending, "not as high as many believe" (*Financial Times,* 16 April 2001).

The past five years have seen a rush to reposition in the global market by both old-economy and new-economy corporations, trying to occupy the newly generated (or expected) ICT-driven markets through a wave of mergers, acquisitions and alliances, supported until 2000 by an extremely favourable stock market performance. The early movers' strategic priority has been to ensure competitive if not dominant market shares. The process has been remarkable in the telecommunications industry, leading to the re-formation of giants amidst deregulation in the United States and Europe.

US companies dominate the IT market. Of the 50 top IT firms, 36 are based in the United States, nine in Japan, four in Europe and one in Chinese Taipei (OECD, 2000). The supply side of the digital economy is well rooted and growing in the United States, Europe and Japan, based on large corporations extending the range of business activities from original core competencies to new ICT and internet-related competencies. They battle to control an increasingly global and innovation-led market. A trend towards business convergence is also underway, mirroring technology convergence and reflecting the need to ensure a critical mass to sustain rapid innovation. Fragmented dotcom businesses — those that do not die off — are being absorbed within the networks of large corporations. Meanwhile, partnerships among telecommunications companies, IT service providers and consulting companies configure dynamic networks as an alternative to all-inclusive corporations.

Access to the Knowledge Market

Possession and control of specialised knowledge (whatever the technological profile and the industry) is not sufficient to ensure competitive positioning in the market. To the extent that markets are global, the individual company or network of companies needs to control increasing amounts of information and knowledge to cope with global competition, even if hitherto it has been active exclusively in the domestic or regional market. In the interconnected, open market, businesses operating in the local market confront both local and international competitors, but access to the networks where market knowledge flows is not as free as the enhanced technical accessibility would lead one to expect, either for consumers or producers and traders of knowledge.

The information and knowledge are incorporated increasingly in intangibles delivered as final or intermediary products by the service industries (Windrum and Tomlinson, 1999). The impact of ICTs on knowledge transferability goes beyond the provision of broad, fast, interconnected channels to a logical structure for knowledge transfer embedded in network software (Eischen, 2000). Information and knowledge tradability by means of software codification implies:

— awareness of the information and knowledge in one's possession;

— control of the codification procedures and tools;

— compatibility through adoption of common interface standards.

Despite the trend towards market-led centralisation in leading networks and procedures, space remains for innovation and competition by players with valuable knowledge. Knowledge is the output of an accumulation process whose complexity is due to a pluralistic set of agents and components interacting over different temporal and social contexts. Micro-diversity and the interaction of different levels of co-ordination generate the microeconomic turmoil that underlies the "restless" process of knowledge accumulation. Economic growth can be seen as the evolutionary outcome of this process (Metcalfe *et al.*, 2001). Local knowledge — knowledge generated locally that is tacit or codified under different standards — provides indispensable inputs to the knowledge market, whatever its organisation. The critical testing point for the correlation between ICT and development lies at the crossroads between horizontal and vertical applications and standards. They either transform knowledge into information traded on networks interfacing the global market or re-aggregate it from local networks to access the global market.

Development in the Digital Economy

The digital economy is in early days. The potential of digital technologies to support the knowledge accumulation process remains far from full exploitation. The interplay between the dynamics of institutional resetting and those of micro-behaviour is an asynchronous, endless process. The most striking opportunity offered by current ICT development lies in the affordability or perceived accessibility of the digital infrastructure to an increasingly large portion of the world population, sharing different cultural and business models and living standards. The creativity bubbling behind the scene is certain to find its way toward the accumulation of knowledge along the digital net, as soon as there is a gateway to enter.

Digital Divide

The term *digital divide* was apparently coined at the World Economic Forum Annual Meeting in Davos in early 2000, after which the G8 Summit (July 2000) endorsed the *Global Digital Divide Initiative* in the *Okinawa Charter on the Global Information Society*. The G8 Summit in Genoa (July 2001) subsequently adopted a

Plan of Action to reduce the digital divide. The UN, World Bank and OECD have devoted resources to understanding the phenomenon and designing appropriate remedial policies (Analysys, 2000, UNCTAD, 2000 and OECD, 2001). The early vision of digital divide was mostly oriented to the gaps between individuals, households and businesses, within and between countries, in access to and usage of the internet (OECD, 2001). Its measurement involves comparisons of indicators related to ICT infrastructure (connectivity, geographic dispersion, telephone-internet charges, correlations of income, education, ethnic variables and business size with ICT penetration, etc.). A stress on the transversal dimension of the digital divide appears in comparisons between rich and poor countries and within the developed ones as well. The work of Dot Force (Digital Opportunity Task Force) leading up to the Genoa Summit stressed that synergistic policy actions must be put in place, targeted to improve both the status of connectivity and development of local physical and human capital (G8 Summit, 2001). The basic foundations of the information society and the digital economy are the same: access to and usage of network technologies.

Policy plays a key role in overcoming the digital divide wherever it exists. It involves not only capital investment and policy guidelines and regulations to improve access to the digital infrastructure, but also pro-active policies exerting a catalytic role on citizens' behaviour by moving administrative procedures and public services on-line. Public administration acts as a key lever to promote ICT and the internet, as both consumer and supplier of on-line services. Moreover, the use of ICT can even facilitate the solution of endemic problems in the less developed world, such as public administration transparency, health care, education, logistics and — particularly important — support policies for local knowledge development via business and network creation.

Local Development

Research on local clusters of firms emphasises their tight link with learning and innovation, to the extent that clusters support "firms … to collectively transform 'low tech' industries … into tacit knowledge intensive industries and internalise this competitive advantage within the cluster" (Mytelka, 2000, p. 27). The delocalisation of activities from developed to less developed countries driven by low labour costs, local business integration into the supply chains of foreign-based companies and the establishment of locally-managed subsidiaries by multinational companies are all potential channels of knowledge transfer and accumulation in the developing world. Other elements are necessary, however, to upgrade local activities into local development — elements such as market opportunities, capital investment, local capabilities and policy support.

The right mix cannot be summarised in a few "golden rules". Approaches differ in the ICT industry itself, where outsourcing of software development and ICT services from US, European and Japanese corporations to some less developed countries is a well-established practice. India, for example, differs from the Philippines or from Mexico (Lubeck and Eischen, 2000). India provides interesting evidence of ICT-driven local development as it migrates up the value chain from being a leading offshore software development centre to ICT services more lucrative than traditional code programming. The Indian software industry as a whole has grown about 50 per cent annually over the past decade. Besides its comparatively low costs, India has capitalised on available technically skilled and English-speaking manpower (it has the second-largest group of software professionals in the world after the United States) and on deep Indian roots in Silicon Valley technology and venture capital companies. All this makes India highly competitive *vis-à-vis* China, Russia, Eastern Europe and the Philippines for big corporations outsourcing software development and other services (*Financial Times Dossier India*, 2001). It has allowed the successful entry of Indian brands on the ICT market (four Indian companies are listed on the US Nasdaq and NYSE). The Andhra Pradesh region has revealed that it is possible to turn to innovation-led local development the same resources that are assets for competition in the global market. A farsighted government strategy and the integration of local and global networks at the highest level support local development. The strategy is not one of latecomer catch-up. It seeks to establish a local information society around a high-tech pole competitive on a global scale.

There is broad agreement on the existence of locational patterns in the ICT sector, based on either of two types. The first involves geographical concentration and clustering in critical metropolitan or intra-metropolitan areas; it has been observed in the United States, the United Kingdom and Sweden. The second reflects a tendency towards dispersal as the impact of ICT reduces the "friction of distance", especially within the spatial organisation of large companies. The shift from and to centralisation and decentralisation is a dynamic process, which depends on the nature of the activity and particularly the nature of the knowledge at stake. Many researchers observe that upper-tier activities (command and control of knowledge-intensive activities) tend to be spatially concentrated in nodal centres, while lower-tier activities (based on easily codifiable and replicable knowledge) may be delocalised to seize lower-cost opportunities in remote nodes of networks. The impact of delocalised ICT services on local development in host areas is not well understood.

Essentially, the correlation between digital inclusion and local development depends on the quality of access to the ICT infrastructure and of the knowledge to be traded over the digital infrastructure. The dynamics of this correlation may evolve over time as local activities upgrade technologically. That depends, however, not only on local human capital and other resource endowments but also on the mix of policy commitment and strategy able to direct the opportunities offered by the digital technologies towards social and economic value creation.

Conclusions

The ICT-driven changes currently underway in the economy and society raise questions for analysts, policy makers and the general public about the impact of ICTs on development. The questions stem from the perception that the innovations reshaping communications, business management, consumer preferences and social behaviour are radical, and their dynamics, still unfolding, can destabilise existing market structures and organisations. These changes have a dominantly but not exclusively technological nature, deriving from the pervasiveness of ICTs and highlighting the roles of information and knowledge creation and sharing in most economic processes.

The impact of digitisation on the global communication architecture and on knowledge transfer makes it sensible to introduce the notion of a *digital economy*. The extraordinary growth of supply and demand for goods and services related to the physical infrastructure represents a major propellant to growth in the countries where the ICT industry is based. The ICT market is global, but the industry remains based in the developed world, with some exceptions. The dominant software firms, telecommunications carriers, ICT equipment makers, e-commerce businesses and multimedia applications firms at the core of recent US economic growth are mostly in the United States, Europe and Japan. Nevertheless, the trend towards technology convergence, the shortage of skilled human resources in the OECD area and the need to address multicultural global demand give room to local businesses as either suppliers or brokers of ICT services all over the world.

The potential of ICT to alter business process organisation and network dynamics is very high and far from fully exploited. The most visible present impacts appear in adjustment oriented towards cost reduction in the service sector (mostly finance) and in big supply chains associated with heavy procurement expenditures, where large manufacturing corporations usually lead. Harder to measure, but nevertheless highly relevant, is the impact of new ICT in the information-based and knowledge-based activities that support virtual communities or virtual enterprises in multi-sector value chains. The worldwide diffusion of the service economy (including in the less developed world) makes the potential impact of ICT that much more extensive.

Barriers to ICT networks, exclusion from digital marketplaces or communities and interdiction from the generation and sharing of knowledge and innovation risk producing irreversible effects — market fragmentation, loss of resources, reduction of pluralism and slower technical progress and innovation — in both developed and developing countries. The digital divide is multiform. The link between ICTs and development depends on access to dynamic networks, to information and knowledge creation, codification and trading, and to financial capital.

However global the knowledge market, the sources of knowledge have an essentially local dimension aside from any global input. The correlation between digital inclusion and local development depends on the quality of access to the ICT infrastructure and of the knowledge to be traded over the digital infrastructure.

Policy institutions play a key role in piloting the transition to the information society and the digital economy. Both government and corporate strategies must address the new challenges as opportunities for development. Besides dealing with access to and governance of the digital infrastructure, policies can exert a deep influence on investors' decisions and play a significant role in supporting the local development of network and knowledge resources needed for effective competition in the global marketplace.

Notes

1. The literature review includes empirical studies carried out by the authors themselves and others from 1997 to 2000.

2. The centrality of time and preferences has been emphasised by the so-called *attention economy*. See Aigrain (1997).

3. "A virtual organisation is a goal-oriented enterprise (i.e. unit or function within a company) operating under metamanagement ", (Mowshowitz, 1999, p. 9).

Bibliography

AIGRAIN, P. (1997), "Attention, Media, Value and Economics", *First Monday*, 9 December, available at www.firstmonday.org.

ANALYSYS (2000), *The Network Revolution and the Developing World*, Final Report for World Bank and InfoDev, [http://www.infodev.org/library/working.htm].

ANTONELLI, C. (1999), *The Microdynamics of Technological Change*, Routledge, London.

ANTONELLI, G., N. DE LISO and R. LEONCINI (2000), *Innovation and Human Capital in the New Real Economy: Some Evidence and Interpretative Hints*, paper presented at the 40th Congress of the European Regional Science Association, Barcelona, 29 August-1 September.

BASSANINI, A., S. SCARPETTA and I. VISCO (2000), "Knowledge, Technology and Economic Growth: Recent Evidence from OECD Countries", OECD Economics Department working papers 259, OECD, Paris.

EISCHEN, K. (2000), "Information Technology: History, Practice and Implications for Development", CGIRS Papers Series 2000-4, Center for Global, International and Regional Studies, University of California, Santa Cruz.

EITO/EEIG-EUROPEAN INFORMATION TECHNOLOGY OBSERVATORY/EUROPEAN ECONOMIC INTEREST GROUPING, (2001), Frankfurt am Main.

EUROPEAN COMMISSION (EC) (1997), Communication to the European Parliament, the Council of Ministers, the Economic and Social Committee and the Committee of the Regions, COM (97) 157final, 15/04/97, at http://www.ispo.cec.be/Ecommerce.

Financial Times Dossier India, July 2001.

FOROS, Ø. and H.J. KIND (2000), "National and Global Regulation of the Market for Internet Connectivity", paper presented at the Third Berlin Internet Economics Workshop, 26-27 May.

G8 SUMMIT (2001), "Preparatory work, Report from Session 6 — Digital Divide and International Co-operation", 12 March.

GRANDINETTI, R. and E. RULLANI (1996), *Impresa transnazionale ed economia globale*, La Nuova Italia Scientifica, Roma.

JENSEN, M. (2000), *African Internet Status*, at www3.sn.apc.org/africa, accessed 19 December, 2000.

KALAKOTA, R. and A.B.WHINSTON (1997), *Electronic Commerce*, Addison-Wesley, Reading, MA.

LEFEBVRE, L.A. and E. LEFEBVRE (2000), "E-commerce and Virtual Enterprises: Issues and Challenges for Transition Economies", paper prepared for the United Nations Economic Commission conference on Global Electronic Commerce, Geneva, 19-20 June.

LUBECK, P. and K. EISCHEN (2000), "Silicon Islands and Silicon 'Valles': Informational Networks and Regional Development in an Era of Globalization", *in* N. KLAHN, P. CASTILLO, A. ALVAREZ and F. MANCHÓN (eds.), *Las Nuevas Fronteras del Siglo XXI/New Frontiers of the 21st Century*, La Jornada Ediciones, México, D.F.

MALERBA, F., R. NELSON, L. ORSENIGO and S. WINTER (1999), "'History-Friendly' Models of Industry Evolution: The Computer Industry", *Industrial and Corporate Change*, Vol. 8, No. 1.

MALONE, T.W, J. YATES and R.I. BENJAMIN (1987), "Electronic Markets and Electronic Hierarchies", *Communications of the ACM*, Vol. 30, No. 6.

METCALFE, J.S., M.D. FONSECA and R. RAMLOGAN (2001), "Innovation, Growth and Competition: Evolving Complexity or Complex Evolution", CRIC Discussion Paper 41, Center for Research on Innovation and Competition, University of Manchester.

MOWSHOWITZ, A. (1999), "The Switching Principle in Virtual Organisation", *in Organisational Virtualness and Electronic Commerce*, Proceedings of the 2nd International VoNet Workshop, 23-24 September, Institute of Information Systems, Department of Information Management, University of Bern, in www.virtual-organization.net.

MYTELKA, L. (2000), "Local Clusters, Innovation Systems and Sustained Competitiveness", INTECH Discussion Paper 2005, Institute for New Technologies, United Nations University.

OECD (2001), *Understanding the Digital Divide*, background documentation for the OECD Emerging Market Economy Forum on Electronic Commerce, Dubai, UAE, 16-17 January.

OECD (2000), *Information Technology Outlook 2000*, OECD, Paris.

OECD (1998), *A Borderless World: Realising the Potential of Global Electronic Commerce*, OECD, Paris.

PASINETTI, L., based on a quote in IST (2000), *The New Economy of the Global Information Society - Implication for Growth, Work and Employment*, Report of a workshop, Brussels, 6-7 April.

QUAH, D.T. (1999), "The Weightless Economy in Economic Development", Centre for Economic Performance Discussion Paper 417, London School of Economics.

SCHILLER, D. (2000), *Digital Capitalism — Networking the Global Market System*, The MIT Press, Cambridge, MA.

SMITH, M.D., J. BAILEY and E. BRYNJOLFSSON (1999), "Understanding Digital Markets: Review and Assessment", at http://www.ecommerce.mit.edu/papers/ude.

TIMMERS, P. (1999), *Electronic Commerce: Strategies and Models for Business-To-Business Trading*, John Wiley & Sons, New York, NY.

UNCTAD (2000), *Building Confidence - Electronic Commerce and Development*, Geneva.

WINDRUM, P. and M. TOMLINSON (1999), "Knowledge-Intensive Service and International Competitiveness: A Four Country Comparison", *Technology Analysis & Strategic Management*, Vol. 11, No. 3.

Chapter 3

E-Commerce for Development: Between Scylla and Charybdis

David O'Connor

Introduction

What do the internet and e-commerce mean for people living in developing countries? For the vast majority of rural people eking out an existence from the land, the answer is, "probably very little, at least in the near term". Certainly, for them, research into how to improve the productivity of their land or how to grow new crops that offer better nutrition or higher market returns matters much more. This does not mean that information and communications technologies (ICTs) are irrelevant to poverty reduction, but rather that the benefits they offer are often rather indirect and long-term. Arguably one of the most important contributions of ICTs has been to the productivity of the research process itself. From medical and pharmaceutical research to crop research, it is difficult to imagine returning to a world without powerful computers and rapid communications among researchers spread across the globe. Admittedly, few of the innovations facilitated by ICTs have brought tremendous benefit to the poor, but even a few major breakthroughs — e.g. low-cost malaria or AIDS vaccines — could yield enormous benefits.

The focus here lies not so much on these broad developmental applications of ICTs as on the technologies' potential contribution to business development and entrepreneurship in developing countries. In other words, the concern is with e-commerce[1] and what benefits it may offer developing countries, notably as suppliers of goods and services to the world market.

Digital Opportunities?

While much media attention has focused on the "digital divide" separating rich from poor countries, the costs of ICTs have fallen at historically unprecedented rates. Thus, while large income gaps between the richest and the poorest countries still pose major problems of ICT affordability, the prospects have never been so good for poor countries to acquire advanced technologies relatively early in their diffusion phase. Rather than widening the technology gap, rapid technological innovation at the frontier can actually hasten diffusion by inexorably driving down costs of computing power and communications. Technological innovation is, of course, only part of the explanation for the rapidly declining costs of telecommunications and internet use. Widespread deregulation of the telecoms sector in both developed and developing countries has also played a crucial role.

If the technology is becoming more affordable to developing country entrepreneurs, is it becoming more useful? The answer to this is a qualified "yes". The qualifications are several. First, for many entrepreneurs in developing countries, information needs are highly localised. Unless content providers have placed useful local information — on market prices, financing, weather conditions, pest prevention/eradication, veterinary health, etc. — on the internet, its usefulness is apt to be limited. Not all locally useful content needs to be provided locally (e.g. global satellite images and meteorological information downloaded from remote web sites can be useful to local fishermen or farmers). In localities where few people are educated and even fewer are literate in English, the usefulness of the internet will likely be very limited. Even here, however, the internet can be combined with traditional communications media such as AM radio to disseminate downloaded information over the airwaves. Other ICTs, notably mobile telephony, can also be valuable in this context, as the Grameen Phone experience in Bangladesh demonstrates.

D-evelopment E-conomics

Analysis of the economics of the internet in a developing country context ought to start from the recognition of the role of information in an economy, particularly in the functioning of markets. The literature on transactions costs (from Coase onwards) identifies information asymmetries as one important source. Likewise, Stiglitz and others have made plain how pervasive information incompleteness is, notably in insurance and financial markets. These imperfections in information flows and access have given rise to search costs, and they can result in a variety of compensatory mechanisms and alternative governance structures, e.g. the internalisation of transactions within a single firm when the costs of transacting through markets become prohibitive.

Information technologies raise the possibility of smoothing many of the information flows in any economy. They can make markets work more efficiently, and they can improve information management within organisations, whether firms, governments or others. Empirical work on the size of such cost savings is just in early days, but it is a potentially fruitful field of quantitative research, as internet-based transactions can generate rich databases at low cost.

A review of early empirical work on internet markets paints a mixed picture of their relative efficiency *vis-à-vis* conventional markets (Smith *et al.*, 1999). Four measures of efficiency are found in the literature: price levels, price elasticity, menu costs and price dispersion. The most consistent set of results relates to menu costs, which are found to be lower in internet markets, as reflected in the frequency and the size of price changes. With respect to price levels, the earlier studies found them to be higher in internet markets, while more recent ones found them to be lower. A possible explanation is the change in price behaviour with increasing entry into and maturity of these markets. On price elasticity, Goolsbee (2000) finds on-line buyers to be highly price-sensitive, as reflected in the significantly higher use of the internet in US states with high sales taxes. On the other hand, Lynch and Ariely (1998) find that providing better product information mutes price competition in an electronic wine market, making possible a better fit between buyers' tastes and the available supply. Similarly, some evidence on price dispersion suggests a significant degree of it in internet markets. A variety of explanations includes market immaturity, heterogeneity of on-line retailer characteristics (e.g. trustworthiness, brand name recognition), retailer market segmentation strategies and price discrimination. In short, precious little evidence yet shows that internet markets are consistently more efficient than conventional ones.

Information in Developing Economies

One factor differentiating developing from developed economies is that more serious information imperfections characterise their markets. Another, related to the first, is that transaction costs are higher. If this is a fair description of reality, then a reasonable working hypothesis is that ICTs can potentially yield larger cost economies in developing countries than in developed ones. This depends in part on the source of the transaction costs. It is possible that, in many cases, high transaction costs reflect fundamental institutional weaknesses for which ICTs cannot easily compensate. For example, the lack of codified regulations, procedures and protocols governing transactions and/or weak incentives for their enforcement can raise transaction costs. Each transaction takes on the character of a one-time event, with a low level of predictability and a possibly high opportunity cost in time spent to complete it. Of course, excessive but predictable regulations can also impose significant opportunity costs, but without an additional high probability of failure to complete the transaction.

Assuming that some incentive exists (in the form of competitive market pressures) to minimise transaction costs, then the availability of ICT to assist in cost reduction may itself provide a spur to the codification and documentation of information so as to make possible the technology's effective application. Without the incentive structure in place, ICT does not offer a quick technological fix. The importance of competitive pressures suggests that ICT adoption in developing countries may occur earliest in those sectors most heavily exposed to international competition — although strong domestic competition can have the same effect.

Depending on how broadly one defines transaction costs, some may be more amenable to reduction through the application of ICTs than others. For example, if the costs result largely from poor inventory management techniques, they may be more easily reduced through applying ICTs than if they result from poor transport infrastructure. In general though, the inventory cost savings potential in developing countries would appear to be large. Guasch and Kogan (2001) find that the costs of raw materials inventories in manufacturing are two to five times higher in developing countries than in the United States (see also Blond, 2001, for an India-US comparison of inventory-to-sales ratios in several manufacturing sectors).

The objection may be raised that, even if markets and other institutions manage information less efficiently in developing countries, there is less of it involved in most transactions, so poor information management matters less to overall economic efficiency. It is intuitively plausible that the information intensity of a largely agricultural economy is lower than that of a heavily service-oriented economy. Yet, to the author's knowledge, there is no good empirical measure of the information intensity of different markets or economic sectors, independently of a measure of ICT investment or use *per se*. Within given sectors, information-handling requirements may actually be greater in developing than in developed countries. Cement is an example. The Mexican cement maker, Cemex, faces stronger incentives than its major richer country competitors to computerise logistics and shift sales and distribution on-line, because it deals with many small distributors — a common pattern in developing countries — rather than a few large ones as is more typical in developed countries. (See "E-strategy brief", *The Economist*, 16 June 2001, pp. 85-86). If a less concentrated distribution sector is a general distinguishing feature of developing countries, then industrial enterprises not just in cement but across a broad spectrum of industries may face similarly strong incentives to automate logistics and sales.

One of the touted benefits of the internet and web-mediated e-commerce is the elimination of intermediate transaction layers between producer and ultimate customer for a particular good or service ("digital disintermediation"). Yet early evidence on internet markets (e.g. for used cars) in OECD countries suggests that they may not eliminate middlemen but merely alter their role and their way of doing business. Even with ICT, in some kinds of markets there may be reason for continued reliance on the services of middlemen. For instance, looking at even a 3D virtual model of an automobile on a computer screen is a poor substitute for test driving it.

The middleman is a pervasive response to information and other market imperfections in developing countries. What the internet may well do is put more information — on consumer tastes, prices of competing products, etc. — in the hands of small producers in these countries, so that their bargaining power *vis-à-vis* the middleman is enhanced. If there is continued need for such a market intermediary — e.g. to handle transport and logistics or financing — then at least s/he no longer stands to profit from imperfect information. Goldstein and O'Connor (2000) present some examples of this disintermediation in markets for handicrafts, but in several cases non-profit organisations acting as intermediaries ensure that a larger share of revenues stays with the producers. Intermediaries are not eliminated altogether.

Information in an Evolutionary Perspective

Industry structure and supply chain organisation are crucial determinants of information management requirements, hence of the likely benefits to be derived from ICT application. Structure and organisation are dynamic, however, so the information needs of a given industry and enterprise are likely to evolve over time. Industries tend to be rather concentrated when they are young, become less concentrated with new entrants eager to share in the high profits, then become more concentrated again in maturity, as economies of scale favour size and the more profitable either obliterate or absorb their competitors. Similarly, the degree of vertical integration not only varies systematically across sectors (in accordance for example with differences in transaction costs) but also can vary over time. When an industry is still relatively immature, it may not yet have a group of specialist supplier firms, so existing firms need to provide their own internal capacity — e.g. for component, tool and/or machinery making, which eventually can be spun off or contracted out to independent firms.

Does vertical dis-integration of the supply chain itself give rise to greater demand for ICTs and electronic networks? In all probability it does, since one common feature of dis-integration is the emergence of multiple independent suppliers of any system or component, increasing the number of potential information flows. Here again one might ask whether there is a systematic tendency for industries in developing countries to be more or less vertically integrated than their developed-country counterparts.

Path-Dependent ICT Evolution

Industrial technology, industry structure and their historical evolution shape the way in which ICT is used and how important it is to an industry's costs and competitiveness. Two contrasting examples illustrate the point: automobiles and personal computers (as epitomised by the "Dell direct model") (see Helper and MacDuffie, 2000). To begin with computers, several technical features condition the global organisation of production and the place of ICT and the internet in organising the supply and distribution chain. These include:

— discrete modules coterminous with sub-systems;

— standard interfaces;

— easy outsourcing of module production; and

— easy integration of modules in final assembly.

This implies that a personal computer can be customised at relatively low cost simply by re-specifying the combination of standard modules incorporated in the final product. If the customer prefers a more powerful processor or hard disk drive, or a CD-ROM instead of floppy disk drive, they can be readily substituted one for another, each fitting into the same standard slot.

In contrast, the auto industry model is built on the following technical considerations:

— distributed systems (e.g. the power train);

— only a few stand-alone modules (like the "cockpit");

— multiple components, many model-specific; and

— integral design.

This requires close co-ordination between the big assemblers (or OEMs — Original Equipment Manufacturers) and their major (tier-1) suppliers, who are often involved in module and/or system design. On the other hand, it implies less flexibility than with personal computers to configure the final product according to customer preferences. The "bespoke" vehicle is still too expensive for the mass market.

Even within the automobile industry, contrasting models of supplier relations may condition how auto companies make use of the internet. The models depend in part on national industry characteristics, in part on enterprise culture and in part on location within the vertical supply chain. In the spirit of Hirschman, Helper and MacDuffie (2000) refer to these as the "exit model" and the "voice model". The exit model is characterised by relatively low switching costs between suppliers, leaving them with weak bargaining power *vis-à-vis* a given OEM customer. The forward auction, in which suppliers bid against one another to offer the most attractive price, is associated with this model. The voice model is characterised by intensive information exchange between supplier and customer, with a correspondingly higher cost of switching suppliers. This gets manifested in long-term collaboration on joint vehicle design. In the exit model, the internet becomes the site for conducting parts auctions; in the voice model, it becomes the medium for intensive data interchange among collaborators.

Once more, the question arises of where developing-country entrepreneurs fit into the broader scheme of things. Between the personal computer industry and the auto industry, there would seem to be greater opportunities for outsourcing in the former, also greater opportunity for new entrants to produce standardised components for world markets. This is the case with semiconductors, disk drives, terminals and other PC components and peripherals. The quality requirements for participating in such markets are daunting, however, especially as suppliers to computer industry leaders. In the auto industry, national and regional market requirements are sufficiently varied (in terms of vehicle size, fuel-efficiency requirements, road conditions, etc.) that maintaining a "local" presence can be important. While a few large developing countries have strong domestic OEM and 1st tier supplier bases, in most countries these industry segments are heavily dominated by large multinationals. Local suppliers are mostly confined to tiers two and below, i.e. precisely those segments of the industry where the "exit model" can be most readily applied. For them, the arrival of the internet and on-line auctions poses the risk of diminished bargaining strength *vis-à-vis* their customers and diminished profit margins.

B2B2C

The union of B2B and B2C e-commerce is one of the most promising sources of efficiency gains the internet can offer. By rationalising inventory control and supply-chain management, the internet should permit better demand forecasting all along the chain, from final customer back to raw materials. In principle, this effect can be measured by reference to the variation in inventory-to-sales ratios of firms along a vertical supply chain.

E-commerce can, in theory, place greater power in the hands of consumers to customise products and services according to their own preferences. The evidence on internet prices *vs.* conventional market prices suggests that, rather than being solely or even principally a vehicle for price arbitrage, the internet is often used as a means of better matching supply to demand. The "customer as designer" model may not be equally well suited to all products and industries, but it is a tendency in many. The feedback from the customer interface should be valuable all along the supply chain, not only in inventory management as mentioned above but also in adapting to and anticipating changes in consumer preferences, incorporating new design features, planning more effective advertising and marketing campaigns, etc.

One of the principal challenges facing developing country export producers is keeping abreast of major OECD market trends. This is especially relevant for differentiated product markets such as textiles and clothing and footwear, but also for those in which product innovation is very rapid, such as semiconductors, PCs and other electronics. Having timely information on changing market conditions and having the R&D and/or design capacity to respond in a timely fashion to those changes are clearly not the same thing. Still, presence in a given market presupposes a certain technical capacity, one that the internet can help to enrich and update. Where the internet can be especially useful, however, is in providing the rapid feedback from customers visiting a B2C web site.

Alternative Internet Pricing Models

There are two basic approaches to pricing of goods and services on the internet. The first is fixed pricing, the on-line equivalent of the supermarket checkout counter, which is why it is appropriate for Amazon.com to provide a virtual shopping cart to its on-line customers. The other is dynamic pricing, with real-time price setting either through negotiation or an auction. The principal attraction of fixed pricing is for small, individual, low-value transactions in which economies of scale on the supplier side permit volume discounts on the buyer side. There may also be some cost shifting from the seller to the buyer, who must bear any search costs as well as the costs of providing information needed to complete the transaction. Presumably the purchaser's willingness to absorb these costs is bounded by the alternative cost of buying the same product in a "bricks-and-mortar" shop. The main attraction of dynamic pricing is for high-value transactions where negotiation costs are a small share. The high market liquidity in this case also permits a closer matching of demand and supply.

Instances of both pricing models can be found in developing countries, although casual empiricism suggests that the dynamic pricing model is far more pervasive across a broader range of markets than in OECD countries. The village market epitomises this; few prices are fixed and almost any purchase is the object of haggling — although clearly both buyer and seller have reservation prices. If the internet is indeed to become the marketplace of a "global village", the pricing model even for standardised products may need to move in the direction of a dynamic one. Moreover, in developing countries tight firm and household budget constraints normally mean that purchases are made in small quantities on an as-needed basis, rather than in *Costco* quantities to capture volume discounts. Given this fact, developing countries may well pioneer micro-payment schemes for internet micro-purchases.

Terra Incognita

Even if we should succeed in navigating between the Scylla of techno-pessimism and the Charybdis of unfounded optimism, researching the internet and e-commerce in developing countries takes us to a vast *terra incognita* waiting to be explored. The widespread use of the internet for e-commerce is a very recent phenomenon even in the OECD area, with only a few years of historical data on which to base any quantitative analysis. Given the low internet penetration rates and the low e-commerce turnover in most of the developing world, quantitative analyses of the type performed thus far mostly in the United States still lie some way in the future.

The internet is a global technology creating a global e-commerce marketplace. Developing countries have differing capacities to respond to the challenges and opportunities it presents. Public policy plays a role in the response, but mostly in providing a suitable regulatory framework to encourage private investment, both in the provision of the basic telecommunications infrastructure and in the operation of internet-related businesses such as web portals and internet service providers. The private sector has taken the initiative to deal in a virtual environment with many of the problems encountered by conventional businesses (for example consumer protection), plus new ones thrown up by the internet itself (e.g. security of transactions). Still, supportive government legislation and regulation (e.g. on litigation of disputes, recognition of electronic signatures, personal privacy) are needed to underpin private initiatives. Co-operation is also required among countries to address jurisdictional questions and potential conflicts in such areas as enforcement of contracts, tax liability and privacy protection. Given its longstanding involvement in crafting guidelines on various policy aspects of e-commerce for its Members, the OECD as an organisation is in a favoured position to offer guidance to developing country governments on issues of e-commerce readiness.

In parallel with policy guidance, empirical research is needed on the ways in which ICTs, including but not limited to the internet, affect the competitive environment in sectors where developing countries have traditionally enjoyed a comparative advantage. Garment manufacturers in Bangladesh, coffee growers and traders in Kenya, auto components suppliers in Brazil — all need to know what the internet and e-commerce will mean for them. Similarly, potential e-ntrepreneurs in developing countries would benefit from knowing how the internet is changing various service markets and what opportunities this may open for outsourcing to developing countries.

Notes

1.   The term e-commerce is used here to refer to all applications of electronic network technology (notably the internet) to a firm's business operations, whether to deal with customers, suppliers and other partners, or to organise internal management functions (the latter application is sometimes referred to in the literature as e-business).

Bibliography

BLOND, C. (2001), "Analysis of the Determinants of Transaction Costs", OECD Development Centre, Paris, mimeo.

BRYNJOLFSSON, E. and B. KAHIN (Eds.), (1999), *Understanding the Digital Economy*, MIT Press, Cambridge, MA.

GOLDSTEIN, A. and D. O'CONNOR (2000), *E-Commerce for Development: Prospects and Policy Issues*, Development Centre Technical Paper No. 164, OECD, Paris.

GOOLSBEE, A. (2000), "In a World Without Borders: The Impact of Taxes on Internet Commerce", *Quarterly Journal of Economics*, Vol. 115, No. 2.

GUASCH, J.L. and J. KOGAN (2001), "Inventories in Developing Countries: Levels and Determinants — A Red Flag for Competitiveness and Growth", Working Paper 2552, World Bank, Washington, D.C.

HELPER, S. and J.P. MACDUFFIE (2000), "E-volving the Auto Industry: E-Commerce Effects on Consumer and Supplier Relationships", prepared for *E-Business and the Changing Terms of Competition: A View from Within the Sectors*, Roundtable sponsored by the Berkeley Roundtable on the International Economy and Haas School of Business, U.C. Berkeley, 12 September version.

LYNCH, J.G., JR. and D. ARIELY (1998), "Interactive Home Shopping: Effects of Search Cost for Price and Quality Information On Consumer Price Sensitivity, Satisfaction with Merchandise, and Retention", at *Marketing Science and the Internet,* INFORM College on Marketing Mini-Conference, Cambridge, MA, 6-8 March.

SMITH, M.D., J. BAILEY and E. BRYNJOLFSSON (1999), "Understanding Digital Markets: Review and Assessment", at http://www.ecommerce.mit.edu/papers/ude.

PART TWO

SECTORAL ANALYSES

Chapter 4

The Prospects and Challenges of E-Business for the South African Automotive Components Sector: Preliminary Findings from Two Benchmarking Clubs

Sagren Moodley

Introduction

The South African automotive components industry currently finds itself under threat from three directions. First, rapid and sweeping liberalisation of the national trade policy regime[1] has increased international competition. Second, the domestic market has become stagnant. Third, local sourcing by South African original equipment manufacturers (OEMs) is eroding rapidly as they become increasingly integrated into the global strategic operations of their parent companies. According to Barnes (2000*b*, p. 70), "(U)ncompetitive firms with poor international linkages will disappear from the (components) industry, but those firms that improve their competitiveness and create appropriate linkages with international firms could benefit from burgeoning export sales". The industry thus urgently needs to reposition itself in global-scale value chains in order to consolidate relationships with OEMs and facilitate exports. Transnational companies' (TNCs) control of international production and trade networks makes it extremely difficult for domestic component firms to export independently. Hence, the issue of connection to OEMs or to TNC 1st tier component suppliers has become fundamentally important for long-term survival and growth.

From a development perspective, export growth prospects for the components industry hinge increasingly on leveraging information and communication technologies (ICTs) to promote industrial upgrading within global-scale value chains. In the global automotive industry, TNCs are moving quickly to integrate global supply chains electronically. Most are setting up procurement and supply chain systems. The South African components industry will need urgently a capability to use the internet to take part in these global production networks. In a few years' time, its firms may find themselves bidding for business within a global, internet-connected automotive industry.

The industry's need to enter export markets and compete with new entrants in the domestic market has become critical to its long-term survival and growth. Information flow is one critical mechanism through which firms could improve or consolidate their positions within the value chain. Gaining access to global-scale trade networks is crucial, and digitally connecting to advanced markets has critical importance, whether through complex sourcing relationships or the export of finished products. The use of the internet to co-ordinate production through domestic and cross-border, inter-firm networks will likely have a significant impact on the industry's competitiveness.

The internet's potential to create seamless, collaborative supply networks has recently come under academic scrutiny (Gereffi, 2000). Network-oriented ICTs, by compressing space, time and knowledge, allow for unprecedented reach, speed and complexity in the management of the automotive supply chain. Theoretically, the internet holds great potential for revamping traditional supply chains to improve data flow and streamline operations. The challenge for South African component firms is to position themselves within the evolving internet-connected global supply chains in order to gain competitive advantage and capture value. Drawing on evidence from 19 component firms in the Eastern Cape (ECBC) and KwaZulu-Natal (KNBC) Benchmarking Clubs, this paper explores the uptake, potential and challenges of e-business for the sector.

The paper aims to provide a preliminary analytical foundation to help focus the policy debate. Section two, a synopsis of the key challenges facing the industry, stresses the importance for survival of an outward orientation, global connectedness to transnational production and trade networks, the generation of export volumes and industrial upgrading. Section three introduces the two benchmarking clubs, the research population for the study. It provides an overview of the clubs and flags some of the members' supply-chain problems, which give scope for e-business to streamline the supply chain and reduce information-related uncertainties. Section four presents a conceptual definition of e-business and discusses its importance for the sector. Section five speculates on the internet's likely impact on the components value chain, especially for supply-chain management. E-business is still in an early stage of development and the current research base is quite thin. With the theoretical foundation for the empirical research thus established, section six reviews the empirical findings from a survey of the 19 firms in the two benchmarking clubs. Section seven concludes the study.

The South African Automotive Components Sector: An Overview

Except for the German-owned OEMs and their global lead-source component suppliers, the South African automotive industry generally has weak global networking links. The inward orientation of its components sector reflects a history of state protectionism and import-substitution industrialisation (ISI) during the apartheid era (Joffe *et al.*, 1995). Trade isolation, disinvestment and economic sanctions during the 1980s and early 1990s reinforced this inward focus. Nationally based producers were long insulated from the cut and thrust of international competition. Since the transition period (post-1994), however, the twin pressures of globalisation and rapid trade-policy liberalisation have substantially altered the industry's landscape. In September 1995, the government launched a Motor Industry Development Programme (MIDP) to promote greater integration of the domestic automotive assembly and component industries into the global automotive market. It aimed primarily to improve the international competitiveness of the sector and to expand it, especially through exports.

The industry involves multiple players in logistically complex supply chains. It can best be described as a "producer-driven" supply chain with multi-layered production systems organised hierarchically into tiers (i.e. OEMs and 1st, 2nd and 3rd tier component suppliers) (Gereffi, 1999). Figure 4.1 clearly shows that except for a few independent aftermarket suppliers, seven OEMs largely control the industry, namely Toyota SA, Volkswagen SA, BMW SA, Mercedes Benz SA, Samcor, Automakers and Delta. The domestic aftermarket currently provides enough scope and volume to sustain a number of independent component manufacturers of relatively stable-technology products such as air filters and batteries. Relationships within and between the automotive value chains tend to be fixed, linear and clearly demarcated. Enormous potential exists, therefore, to create an environment of more direct, cost efficient and interactive relationships.

Figure 4.1. **South African Automotive Value Chains: A Schematic Overview**

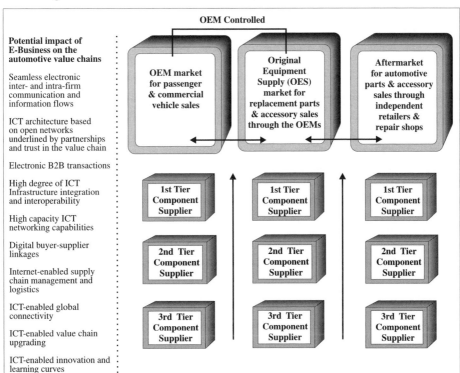

The South African automotive industry is the 18th largest in the world but accounts for less than 1 per cent of the world market. It employs about 82 000 people and accounts for 6.4 per cent of manufacturing GDP (Barnes, 2000b). About 180 component firms primarily supply the industry, with another 200 secondary suppliers (Barnes and Kaplinsky, 2000a). The components sector is being forced to adjust to fundamental changes taking place in the assembly industry. Locally owned and controlled domestic assemblers are re-incorporating under global ownership, and the OEMs are integrating increasingly into their parent companies' global manufacturing operations (Barnes and Kaplinsky, 2000a)[2]. Toyota SA and the Delta Motor Corporation, the two exceptions, still have majority local ownership and are still largely inwardly focused[3].

Vehicle and component manufacturers are becoming increasingly dependent on exports. In 1999, vehicles, parts and accessories comprised 6.5 per cent of total exports; this category did not even feature in 1990 (*Finance Week*, 27 October 2000). The liberalised trading environment has effectively set the domestic OEMs free from local purchasing requirements, and they now operate under a more or less duty-free tariff structure. The net effect has been a recent trend for domestic OEMs to import components previously sourced domestically (Barnes and Kaplinsky, 2000b). Survival of the components industry will depend to a large extent on finding a space in increasingly international production networks, largely controlled by TNCs. Thus, greater connectivity of domestic firms to TNC component firms, which effectively control design, marketing and technology for high value-added products, is critical (Barnes and Kaplinsky, 2000a,b; Barnes, 2000a,b).

The Benchmarking Clubs

The Eastern Cape (ECBC) and KwaZulu-Natal (KZBC) Benchmarking Clubs have as their prime objective the continuous improvement of their members' operational competitiveness through the generation of comparative domestic and international benchmarks. They are effectively joint partnerships between the Department of Trade and Industry through the Sector Partnership Fund and local automotive component firms. Club members seek to improve their competitiveness through a learning network. Figure 4.2 provides an indication of how important the component manufacturers are as a source of employment in both KZN and the Eastern Cape. It shows the average employment figures for 13 of the 19 club members[4]. Average employment peaked in 1996 (at 455 for the Eastern Cape and 263.5 for KZN), then steadily declined to lows of 216.04 in KZN and 335.0 for the Eastern Cape in 1999. Figure 4.3 shows average turnover figures and hints at the potential contribution that the clubs make to the regional and national economies[5]. Average ECBC turnover peaked in 1997 (at R 99 737 000), and deteriorated steadily thereafter. By contrast, average KZNBC turnover improved continuously from 1996 (R 47 345 922) to 1999 (R 60 779 499).

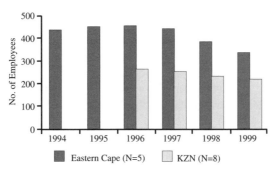

Figure 4.2. **Average Number of Employees**
(Component Manufacturers)

Eastern Cape (N=5)   KZN (N=8)

Source: IRP Database.

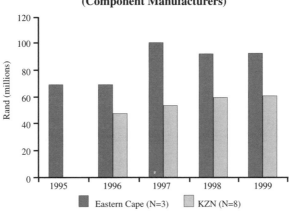

Figure 4.3. **Average Turnover**
(Component Manufacturers)

Eastern Cape (N=3)   KZN (N=8)

Source: IRP Database.

Inventory-level measurements provide a rough proxy for the level of integration in the supply chain. Figures 4.4-4.7 compare the inventory performance of firms belonging to the two clubs with their international counterparts, to present an outline of the variance in inventory performance. The comparison is based on close benchmarking of like-for-like component manufacturers. The key inventory control measures considered are total inventory (Figure 4.4), raw materials inventory (Figure 4.5), work in progress (Figure 4.6) and finished goods inventory (Figure 4.7).

Figure 4.4 clearly shows that while improvements in the number of days of total inventory have been significant, the general performance of club members remains well below that required for international competitiveness. Moreover, while raw materials (Figure 4.5) and work in progress (Figure 4.6) inventories have on average improved significantly, finished-goods holdings (Figure 4.7) have significantly deteriorated at many firms. In most cases, however, this reflects increased export growth rather than actual inventory deterioration; many club members need increased finished-goods stock to meet monthly or biweekly shipping schedules to foreign customers. Nonetheless, the figures clearly show that club members have a supply-chain management (SCM) problem, in that they lag behind their international counterparts in inventory performance[6]. Inventory, excess capacity and stock-outs are the key consequences of information-related uncertainties in the value chain. E-business, in theory, offers club members the possibility of closer synchronisation of the supply chain. They can reduce inventory and shorten cycle times as firms jointly manage inventories across the supply chain, forecast sales together and plan collaboratively to keep levels of component and completed product inventory down to a bare minimum.

Figure 4.4. **Number of Days of Total Inventory: Club Members vs. International Counterparts**

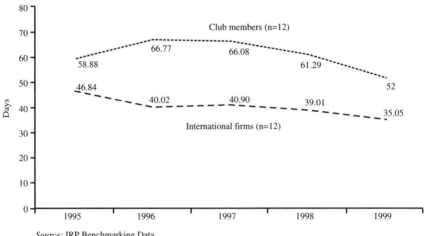

Source: IRP Benchmarking Data.

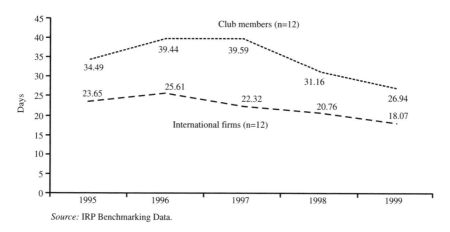

Figure 4.5. **Raw Material Inventories:
Club Members vs. International Counterparts**

Club members (n=12)

39.44 39.59

34.49

31.16

23.65 25.61

22.32

20.76 26.94

International firms (n=12) 18.07

Days

45
40
35
30
25
20
15
10
5
0

1995 1996 1997 1998 1999

Source: IRP Benchmarking Data.

Figure 4.6. **Work in Progress: Club Members vs. International Counterparts**

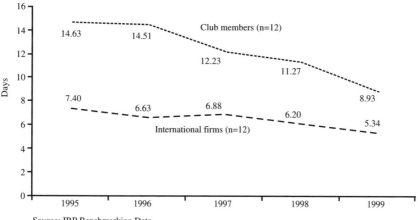

Club members (n=12)

14.63 14.51

12.23

11.27

7.40

6.63 6.88

6.20

8.93

International firms (n=12) 5.34

Days

16

14

12

10

8

6

4

2

0

1995 1996 1997 1998 1999

Source: IRP Benchmarking Data.

73

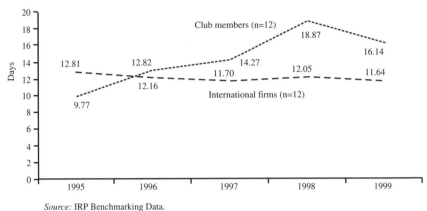

Figure 4.7. **Finished Goods Inventory:**
Club Members vs. International Counterparts

Source: IRP Benchmarking Data.

E-Business: Towards a Definition

Pervasive ICT use, deregulation, the opening of markets and global trade expansion drive economic globalisation (Cohen *et al.*, 2000; Dicken, 1998). ICTs now form an integral part of its accelerated pace, linking nations into complex webs of transnational exchanges (Castells, 1996; Gereffi, 2000)[7]. The internet is becoming a key enabler of the global, digitally networked economy, with economic progress becoming increasingly knowledge-driven, and information and knowledge becoming primary wealth-creating assets (Castells, 1996; Evans and Wurster, 2000; Fine, 1998). Although the internet's precursor appeared in the late 1960s, e-business is primarily a product of six significant transformations in the global economy:

— the globalisation of markets;

— the shift towards an economy based on knowledge and information;

— the growing prominence of ICTs in the economy;

— innovations in business organisation and practice (just-in-time production, total quality management, knowledge management, etc.);

— the liberalisation of the telecommunications sector, primarily in OECD countries;

— technological innovations such as email, the world wide web, internet browsers and the expansion in the volume and capacity of communication networks (*viz.* optic fibre, digital subscriber line technologies and satellites).

The term "e-business" has no widely accepted definition. In a very broad sense, it means doing business over the internet. This paper defines e-business as *any form of commercial or administrative transaction or information exchange that takes place via an internet-based, computer-mediated network.* E-business thus entails the application of the internet to the complete value chain of business processes. It places a premium on openness, transparency and trust. The internet offers a wide spectrum of potential commercial activities and information exchange (Figure 4.8). The paper focuses exclusively on business-to-business (B2B) internet interactions (the shaded block in Figure 4.8), for two main reasons. First, the concern is primarily with the potential of the internet for enhancing inter-firm supply-chain management, and, second, because current trends indicate that B2B e-commerce will far outstrip business-to-consumer (B2C) e-commerce (*Intelligence*, "Business in the Internet Age", May 2000). One reason for the exponential growth anticipated in B2B e-commerce in the automotive industry is the expected migration of supply-chain management from relatively expensive, proprietary (i.e. closed) electronic data interchange (EDI) networks to the open network communication system of the internet.

Figure 4.8. **E-Business Matrix**

	Government	Business	Consumer	Employee
Government	G2G	G2B	G2C	G2E
Business	B2G	**B2B**	B2C	B2E
Consumer	C2G	C2B	C2C	C2E
Employee	E2G	E2B	E2C	E2E

B2B e-commerce refers to procurement, logistics and administrative processes occurring between firms. Companies use the internet to integrate the value-added chain, which can extend from the supplier of raw materials to the final consumer. Inter-business e-commerce can be divided into two categories: *open, marketplace-based trade* and *direct trade between business partners*. The former occurs in various internet-based auctions or exchange sites (e.g. Covisint), while the latter occurs either through a firm's web site with an on-line purchasing function or an EDI-type network. Some argue that B2B e-commerce will likely spread globally and grow rapidly primarily because of its potential for: *i)* controlling business costs (associated with inventories, sales, procurement and distribution); *ii)* connecting to markets through greater geographical reach; *iii)* value creation; *iv)* productivity and systemic efficiency gains in the value chain; and *v)* advanced supply-chain management (Cohen *et al.,* 2000; IBM, 2000). It appears, therefore, that the South African automotive components industry could, in theory, benefit substantially from adopting e-business.

Potential Impact of E-Business on the Automotive Component Value Chain: Theoretical Evidence

In the simple, physical value chain, the flow of goods is linear. The traditional value chain is a series of arms-length, value-adding links from raw materials to end customers. It consists of a sequence of activities with clearly demarcated points of input and output. This value-chain model (Figure 4.9) deals with information as a support to the value-adding process and not as a source of value itself. Contrast this with the internet-enabled value chain (Figure 4.10) where the value-adding steps are performed through and with information. The internet-enabled virtual value chain is non-linear (Figures 4.10 and 4.11). Rayport and Sviokla (1994, 1995) argue that firms compete in both the physical world of goods (the marketplace) and the virtual world of information (the marketspace). The virtual value chain consists of "a matrix of potential inputs and outputs that can be accessed and distributed through a wide variety of channels" (Rayport and Sviokla, 1995, p. 83). Information can be captured in real time at all stages of the chain, analysed electronically to improve performance at each stage and co-ordinated across the chain. In a completely networked value chain, the internet connects every node (i.e. the "pull" system becomes operational) (Figure 4.10). Materials are pulled through the supply chain ultimately by customer request. The logic implies that firms should hold minimum inventory and make just what is needed when it is asked for and not before.

Figure 4.9. **A Simple Physical Value Chain**

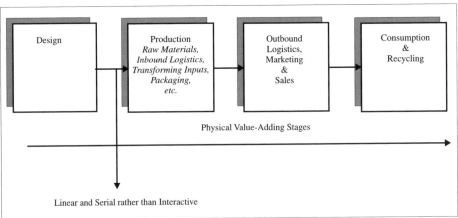

Figure 4.10. **A Virtual Corporate Value Chain**

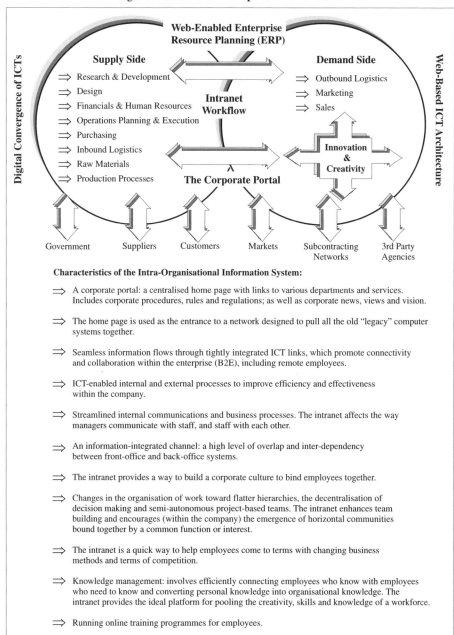

Characteristics of the Intra-Organisational Information System:

⟹ A corporate portal: a centralised home page with links to various departments and services. Includes corporate procedures, rules and regulations; as well as corporate news, views and vision.

⟹ The home page is used as the entrance to a network designed to pull all the old "legacy" computer systems together.

⟹ Seamless information flows through tightly integrated ICT links, which promote connectivity and collaboration within the enterprise (B2E), including remote employees.

⟹ ICT-enabled internal and external processes to improve efficiency and effectiveness within the company.

⟹ Streamlined internal communications and business processes. The intranet affects the way managers communicate with staff, and staff with each other.

⟹ An information-integrated channel: a high level of overlap and inter-dependency between front-office and back-office systems.

⟹ The intranet provides a way to build a corporate culture to bind employees together.

⟹ Changes in the organisation of work toward flatter hierarchies, the decentralisation of decision making and semi-autonomous project-based teams. The intranet enhances team building and encourages (within the company) the emergence of horizontal communities bound together by a common function or interest.

⟹ The intranet is a quick way to help employees come to terms with changing business methods and terms of competition.

⟹ Knowledge management: involves efficiently connecting employees who know with employees who need to know and converting personal knowledge into organisational knowledge. The intranet provides the ideal platform for pooling the creativity, skills and knowledge of a workforce.

⟹ Running online training programmes for employees.

⟹ Focus is on getting information to key decision makers.

Figure 4.11. **An Integrated Value Chain**

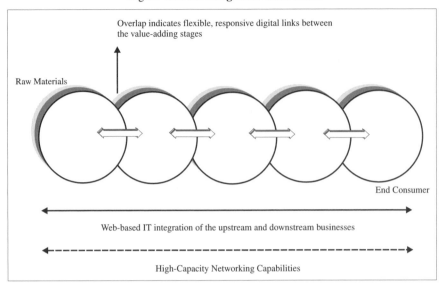

Gereffi (2000, p. 2) argues that "The new digital era of globalization is characterized by an explosion in connectivity that is melting the informational glue that holds corporate value chains and global value chains together". With virtual integration, the links no longer stand alone. Instead, strategic, information-defined inter-relationships proliferate between the various players in the value chain (Figure 4.12). Cross-enterprise virtual integration blurs the traditional boundaries and roles of the players in the value chain. The linkages between firms tend to become more fluid, interactive, pervasive, customised, spontaneous and potentially mutually beneficial. Further, the digital links enable the firm to become more flexible and responsive to change. The virtual value chain is an integrated system (Figure 4.11) rather than "a set of discrete though related activities" (Figure 4.9) (Rayport and Sviokla, 1995, p. 78). Firms use the internet to integrate the value-added chain, which can extend from the supplier of raw materials to the final consumer (Figure 4.11).

Figure 4.11 illustrates how an integrated internet-based system enables a firm to visualise its value chain from end to end, as an integrated whole. The firm can add real value by focusing on what it does best and then collaborating with other firms involved in the overall supply chain. The internet facilitates collaboration both within and between firms by dynamically sharing information in real time (Figure 4.12). Figure 4.11 also shows how the internet enables the networked or virtual organisation to connect, dynamically and in real time, the supply and demand sides of the company. Companies use intranets to link their employees, providing them with a new communication platform and a new way to access up-to-date information relevant to them. The next step would be an extranet, to give suppliers and customers access to real-time and relevant information by linking into an enterprise's internet system. This makes it easier for the company and its constellation of suppliers, customers and partners to work together more effectively (Figure 4.12).

Figure 4.12. **E-Business-Enabled Extended Enterprise**

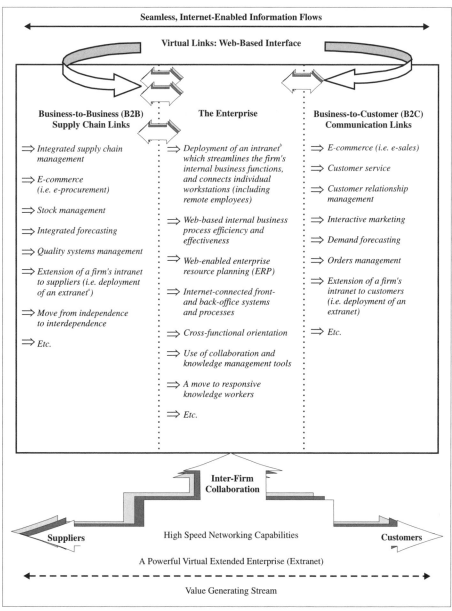

Notes:
a) Internet-based network for use by a company and its business partners.
b) Internet-based network for company use only.

The firm focuses on its distinctive capabilities, then forms strategic alliances with others in the value chain. Increased dependence upon suppliers thus becomes a requirement and has a major impact on the buyer-supplier relationship. In the global automotive industry, this relationship, traditionally arm's-length and adversarial, is now moving towards closer collaboration as a defence against the complexity and uncertainty of markets (Humphrey, 1999).

The internet holds great promise for the South African automotive components sector in three key areas: *i)* increasing the efficiency of internal processes (Figure 4.10); *ii)* streamlining inter-firm linkages (systemic efficiencies); and *iii)* connecting to markets (Figure 4.12). Dell Computer's internet-enabled build-to-order business model, for example, illustrates the power of a fully integrated internet-based assembler production system (www.dell.com; Magretta, 1998). Apart from improving intra-firm and inter-firm process efficiencies, the internet can also play a key role in facilitating supply chain learning and innovation. B2B internet-based collaborative interaction and real-time communication are likely to sharpen the competitive edge of the participating firms, reduce information asymmetries and improve the quality of information embodied in business relationships.

There are also risks associated with e-business, i.e. cost cutting, price-based supplier relationships and competitive switching. Electronic links theoretically make it easier for buyers to begin and end supplier relationships. Component suppliers will lose the protection afforded by familiar inter-firm relationships and their customers' incomplete information about alternative supply sources. The pursuit of short-term price advantages and the concomitant "factory hopping" and "competitive switching" on the part of assemblers and 1st tier component manufacturers is, of course, at odds with upgrading the positioning of South African component manufacturers in local and global value chains. Therefore, building trust, loyalty and reciprocity to reduce the threat of opportunism and make it difficult to break long-term network relationships is important.

Empirical Evidence

Several key findings emerged from the survey of 19 South African component manufacturers. Table 4.1 shows that all club members have access to the Internet, but only 63.2 per cent have web sites. Connection with the internet, however, does not mean that its use is extensive. Nonetheless, club members claimed to be using it for a wide variety of purposes. They are only just beginning to do so for supply-chain management. Current use is most extensive for intra-firm and inter-firm communication and for marketing, rather than for inter-business transactions. Respondents cited inadequate ICT systems integration and a lack of standards for sharing B2B e-commerce data as the main barriers to fully-fledged e-business.

Table 4.1. **Uptake of E-Business**
(19 respondents)

E- Business Technology:	
Internet	100.0 per cent
EDI	73.7 per cent
Website	63.2 per cent

The internet is used mainly for:	
Communication	Sales
Order Processing	Marketing
Production	Procurement
Engineering/Technical applications	Services and support
Inventory management	Management of distribution channels
Logistics	Research

The researchers conducted an internet survey of club members' web sites, the results of which show that they are invariably not much more than front ends, on-line catalogues with orders being e-mailed, faxed and/or taken over the telephone. Customers cannot use them to check, for example, on service call status, order shipping status and delivery information. Four firms use their sites to take orders and deliver products but have not added capabilities such as customisation or interactivity to distinguish the service from other types of direct selling. This does not really constitute e-commerce because the firms have not developed fully transactional internet sales channels. Apparently, too much emphasis goes on establishing a web presence and too little on ensuring that the ICT infrastructure can support on-line procurement, trading, marketing and sales. Most club members are at the stage of basic on-line "brochureware". The web sites have static information, with minimal ability for interaction beyond e-mail, company background and, in a few cases, placing orders.

A substantial 73.7 per cent of club members have an EDI system in place. EDI entails considerable investment in dedicated software and proprietary networks. For effective inter-firm communications, buyers and suppliers need matching software and hardware, a common language for communications, a standard layout for documents and a common communication network. A major limitation is the one-to-one nature of EDI transactions. Therefore EDI is not suitable for companies engaged in occasional (or *ad hoc*) purchases, or even regular low-volume business — exactly the kind of business that SMEs do. EDI's major drawback is that it is uneconomical to link small suppliers into the system. Its cost and supply-chain management advantages create a tendency for large companies to purchase from suppliers with existing, compatible EDI links.

These forces tend to narrow and concentrate supply chains within a quasi-co-operative framework, which could, in principle, limit the scope of a firm's sourcing options. Nevertheless, companies with experience using EDI will probably make the transition to internet-based e-business to streamline the supply chain faster than companies with no such experience. In this sense, B2B e-commerce via the internet is an extension of the existing EDI network. In contrast to the private interactions of the EDI structure, the new virtual, open marketplace will likely increase competition among suppliers and push down purchasing prices.

Box 4.1 indicates the key drivers of e-business in the South African automotive component sector, as identified by the club members themselves. Box 4.2 lists what club members perceive to be the major benefits of the internet. Club members apparently are, by and large, quite positive about the need for e-business, especially regarding the strong forces promoting its rapid uptake (Box 4.1) and the expected benefits of internet use (Box 4.2). Table 4.2 reveals that internet-enabled supply-chain management is very much in its infancy in the benchmarking clubs. This sluggishness reflects the caution with which enterprises view an ICT tool that is still developing. Many club members feel that a misplaced step into the B2B space will result in more than the loss of substantial investment; they fear that they are also "betting the firm" on the move.

Box 4.1. **Key E-Business Drivers in the ECBC & KZNBC**

✓ Globalisation
✓ Trade liberalisation
✓ Customer requirements
✓ Closer integration with customers & suppliers
✓ Increased competitiveness
✓ Connectivity
✓ Agility/business flexibility
✓ Joint ventures
✓ Market expansion
✓ Customer retention
✓ Improved efficiencies
✓ Cost control
✓ Customer & supplier information exchange
✓ Accelerated speed to market
✓ The need to streamline business processes
✓ Spread of the internet

Box 4.2. **Benefits of the Internet According to the ECBC & KZNBC**

✓ Reduces the cost of information
✓ Improves inventory management
✓ Greater geographical reach: increases domestic and international market access
✓ Gives the firm a competitive edge
✓ Reduces transaction costs
✓ Shortens order-ship-bill cycles
✓ Speed combined with flexibility

Table 4.2. **Internet-Enabled Supply Chain Management**
(19 Respondents)

	Percentage of Respondents Replying "Yes"
Use of the internet for SCM	31.6
Do your suppliers have access to real-time information on your company's sales and stock levels?	10.5
Do your customers have access to real-time information on your company's stock levels?	31.6
Are your firm's internal operations electronically integrated with those of your customers?	21.1
Are your firm's internal operations electronically linked with those of your suppliers?	15.8
Does your company have the e-business capacity to access your suppliers'	
Production capacity?	21.1
Available inventory?	21.1
Lead times?	21.1
Delivery flexibility?	21.1
Are your front-office and back-office systems electronically integrated?	31.6
Does your company require suppliers to make use of e-business technologies?	26.3
Does your company have a supply-chain development programme?	0.0
Does your company use e-business technology for B2B procurement?	78.9
Does your company use e-business technology for B2B sales?	47.4

Integrating functions across businesses, such as workflow arrangements in a supply chain, is predicated on working, integrated internal systems. Table 4.2 reveals that many component manufacturers do not have fully automated and integrated back-office and front-office systems. The sector faces a major challenge to converge legacy ICT systems with the internet. The supply-chain efficiencies promised by the internet depend on full internet-based integration of the value chain, to offer a broad range of collaboration and integration between trading partners. Reaching this ideal will be expensive and require industry-wide co-operation not generally prevailing in the industry today. Component suppliers embarking on fully internet-enabled systems at this early stage in the development of e-business might find the return on investment quite low. The benefits might not justify the costs in the short term. Yet as more suppliers and customers use the internet to web-enable their front-office and back-office systems (internal functionality — Figure 4.10), and to connect with their trading partners (collaboration functionality — Figure 4.12), the benefits of B2B e-commerce will likely become more pronounced. E-business must be placed in a relative context. How fast is adoption compared to competitors? A B2B uptake rate lower than that of competitors may result in declining value added and market share. Until sufficient numbers of their main domestic and foreign customers and suppliers participate in e-business initiatives, individual firms have little incentive to develop a web-based customer and supplier interface and engage in e-business themselves.

Unlike the TNC 1st tier suppliers, domestic ones do not take responsibility for upgrading and co-ordinating their own supply chains. In his survey of 46 South African component suppliers, Barnes (1998) found very little supply-chain development activity from 1st tier suppliers down to the 2nd and 3rd tiers. Moreover, Barnes and Kaplinsky (2000a) describe the supply-chain upgrading activities of the South African OEMs as "modest". This means that possibilities for upgrading the ICT capabilities of component suppliers, especially lower-tier firms, remain very limited. This is likely to constrain the widespread diffusion of e-business in the components sector.

The issue of on-line B2B trading exchanges has recently received a great deal of attention in the automotive industry; especially with the launch of Covisint, the giant Detroit-based global virtual marketplace for procuring car components, supplies, services and information[8]. Only 36.8 per cent of club members are currently part of an on-line B2B trading hub (Table 4.3), but note that actual trade via the hubs has thus far been very limited. Nonetheless, club members listed a number of benefits likely to emerge from these networks. They also recognised a number of possible risks and stressed three main conditions for a trading hub to be successful: openness and transparency, trust and loyalty, and a critical mass of value-chain participants.

Table 4.3. **Internet-Based B2B Trading Hubs**
(19 respondents)

⟹ Is Your company linked to an Internet-based B2B trading exchange?
       Yes   36.8 per cent
       No   63.2 per cent

⟹ What are the benefits of the B2B trading exchange?

- ✓ Set standards
- ✓ Cut costs
- ✓ Speed: Internet-based transactions are instantaneous, interactive and rich
- ✓ Supply chain efficiency: enables direct interaction between manufacturers and suppliers, eliminating the need for intermediaries. This is likely to reduce procurement costs
- ✓ Market transparency: by being brought into one open platform, suppliers will be able to bid for contracts they may not previously have known about
- ✓ Improves operating efficiencies
- ✓ Economies of scale: the system should enable buyers with similar requirements to link together to order large quantities of inputs jointly, creating economies in production that will be reflected in lower purchasing prices

⟹ What are the disadvantages of the B2B trading exchange?

- ✓ Rationalisation of the supplier base
- ✓ Potential oligopolistic control and manipulation by transnational assemblers and TNC 1st tier component suppliers
- ✓ Privacy concerns
- ✓ Pressure on prices
- ✓ Threat to established partnerships, relationships & alliances

⟹ What are the main conditions for a successful B2B trading hub?

- ✓ Openness & transparency
- ✓ Trust & loyalty
- ✓ A critical mass of participating firms

Box 4.3. **Barriers to the Adoption of E-Business (ECBC & KZNBC)**

> ✓ Low use of e-business by customers & suppliers
> ✓ More pressing corporate priorities
> ✓ Security concerns
> ✓ Lack of standards
> ✓ Senior executives who do not support e-business
> ✓ Uncertainty over the returns which e-business will deliver
> ✓ Lack of e-business skills
> ✓ A lack of clear understanding of the potential of the Internet on
>   the part of top management

E-business is not yet a strategic imperative in the South African automotive components sector. Most firms in the industry cannot support e-business ventures because they do not have the integrated customer and supplier ICT interfaces in place (Table 4.2). Box 4.3 lists the barriers to the adoption of e-business that club members have identified. The author believes that the primary impediments are:

— the arm's-length and adversarial nature of current relationships between value-chain participants, both vertically and horizontally;

— the overwhelmingly cost-driven rather than knowledge-driven nature of the automotive value chain;

— a pervasive "wait and see" mindset among club members; and

— evolutionary path dependencies that have locked firms into an insular, inwardly oriented way of thinking. This manifests itself in firms' reluctance to bring their customers, suppliers and business partners inside the "corporate machine".

What is needed therefore is a new strategic direction in the industry, which is likely to entail a sea change in business mindsets. The progression of component firms to higher levels of e-business capabilities will likely be slow and incremental. Two critical success factors in e-business centre on the networking of internal and external business interactions. Component suppliers will need to seize and rapidly exploit them in order to be globally competitive. First, strengthening the bonds between an enterprise and its value chain through an internet-based system is important. Second, firms need to focus on their intra-organisational connectivity in order to tie transactional flows together within the organisation. Currently, most of the component firms still focus primarily on a functional orientation (Level 1 in Table 4.4) or on operational efficiency in the enterprise (Level 2). None of the firms uses e-business to increase the organisation's effectiveness outside the enterprise by linking across the internet with suppliers and customers to create virtual supply chains (Level 3).

Table 4.4. **Levels of E-Business Integration**

Levels	1	2	3
Sphere	Functional orientation	Integrating across functional departments	Cross-enterprise involvement
Rationale	Departmental focus, for example: EDI — purchasing & sales department; individual departments developing specific Internet applications, e.g. a marketing website.	Integrated business activities via internet/intranet applications.	A virtual ecosystem that connects employees, suppliers and customers by extending existing EDI. The extranet aims to: build trust and increase customers satisfaction; increase collaboration and knowledge sharing between customers and suppliers; and maximise synergies to lower costs, improve efficiencies and increase quality.
Levers	Technological infrastructure and software applications	Business processes (process efficiencies within the firm)	Cultivating knowledge workers; developing and exploiting intellectual capital to create opportunities; and building relationships

Conclusion

The critical mass needed to reap positive network externalities is not yet present in the South African automotive components sector. It requires leadership by several of the powerful OEMs and the large 1st tier suppliers to define e-business standards for all value-chain participants and create incentives that attract more companies. The catalytic role that early adopters can play is also critical. The following four additional factors will potentially lead to quicker adoption of e-business in the sector:

— a defensive reaction to competitors engaging in e-business;

— pressure by OEMs and 1st tier suppliers on all of their suppliers to link into their e-business systems as a condition of trade;

— on-line trading portals achieve a critical mass of members and become established as trading platforms of choice; and

— the cost-reduction and value creation potentials of the internet begin to be realised in practice.

The components sector critically needs an outward orientation to generate the economies of scale and scope required for global competitiveness. Significant and sustainable growth of the South African automotive industry is contingent upon its ability to compete in a global operating environment. Moreover, as TNCs integrate the internet into their cross-border business operations, South African firms run the risk of exclusion from global value chains if they cannot establish electronic ties with the major players. The policy challenge for the components sector, therefore, is how to use the internet to:

— leverage, consolidate and deepen its links with the global economy;

— access global internet-based trading portals;

— take advantage of the potentials of globalisation; and

— exploit the systemic and productivity-enhancing possibilities inherent in e-business.

E-business might well become an order-qualifying criterion for producers as a prior condition for participating in global markets. It could be seen as an advantage when competing for global supply contracts, and an e-business capability will likely become influential in determining export success. E-business is still at a very early stage in its development. The notion that internet application may lead to a sustained higher level of economic efficiency, still very much at the level of theory, will need rigorous exploration in practice. Achieving such efficiency gains depends on a number of factors, including access to e-business systems and the needed skills, firms' willingness to open their internal systems to suppliers and customers and, more generally, firms' evolutionary path dependencies. By not making the transition to internet-based business, component firms may be placing themselves at risk of becoming less competitive in the globally interconnected market, impacting on both their current market positions and long-term viability. If this were to happen, it would have adverse development implications for the country, such as job losses, a decline in revenue growth and an eroded export base.

The pressure on automotive component firms to reorganise to tap the advantages of e-business is currently not high. This is likely to change soon, as e-business becomes a powerful competitive tool for component suppliers to maintain what Sturgeon (2000) calls "geographic agility" and "output agility". The internet holds great potential for integrating the backward and forward linkages in the automotive components value chain, and digitally connecting all phases of the value chain from raw material supply to design, production, marketing, distribution, consumption and finally recycling (Figures 4.10 and 4.11). Hence, e-business could play an important role in facilitating network-based, dynamic learning and innovation curves in the value chain and improving the ability of automotive component firms to move to more profitable, knowledge-intensive, higher value-added economic niches in international trade networks. Industrial upgrading could take place through harnessing and exploiting the information flows and learning potential associated with internet-based buyer-supplier links. Thus, the internet-connected digital network could, at least in theory, be used to create a new source of competitive advantage for the sector in export-oriented development. All these benefits are still only potentials. They must be sought for and released.

Automotive component firms will have to weigh the importance of protecting existing relationships, which account for most of their current revenue, against the advantages of establishing future strategic positions and revenue streams through e-business. Internet impact can be fully examined only as a long-term phenomenon.

Initial assessments, especially at such an early stage of e-business development, are at best inconclusive. A need exists for long-term analytical studies by independent researchers.

OEMs developing long-term obligations and investing in their suppliers' ICT capabilities are critical for crafting a knowledge-intensive value-chain upgrading path for automotive component manufacturers in South Africa (Sako, 1992). OEMs need urgently to adopt a conscious policy of building stable, long-term relationships with their suppliers based on the transfer of complex information across the inter-firm link. Stronger inter-firm "informational" and "knowledge-based" relationships between OEMs and their suppliers are essential for component suppliers upgrading into quality-driven market segments which offer high returns. The upgrading challenge appears to be tightly bound with the e-business challenge of creating dynamic, high performance networking between buyers and suppliers to cope with the "new competition" (Best, 1990; Porter, 1990).

The ideal situation occurs when a company's internet-based infrastructure supports all aspects of the extended electronic enterprise, enabling the firm to inter-operate and collaborate with any number of business partners (Figure 4.12). In South Africa, fully internet-enabled supply chain models are a long way off. There is no blueprint or silver bullet that firms can use to be ready for e-business. They need to go beyond the traditional view of just looking at their own corporate capabilities and understand that their growth and profitability will increase by managing and improving the end-to-end process that delivers products to customers. The internet is not in itself a panacea or a quick-fix solution for all supply-chain difficulties. The idea is to use the technology's reach and ubiquity to enable firms to get closer to their employees, customers, suppliers and business partners.

E-business capabilities will not, by themselves, automatically lead to greater domestic and export sales volumes for South African component manufacturers. The future of the domestic automotive components industry also depends heavily on achieving international competitiveness through revitalising internal performance capabilities in conformity with world-class manufacturing principles. Nevertheless, a failure by domestic component manufacturers to adopt e-business will undermine their ability to survive the onslaught of global competition and further squeeze them into the low value-added manufacturing segment of the automotive value chains, where the barriers to entry are low and price-based competition is most intense.

Notes

1. At a rate much faster than that required by WTO regulations.

2. This is especially true of the German OEMs, i.e. BMW, Mercedes Benz and Volkswagen.

3. Toyota SA is 72.2 per cent locally owned, and the remaining 27.8 per cent is owned by the Toyota Motor Corporation of Japan. Delta, on the other hand, is 51 per cent locally owned, and 49 per cent is owned by General Motors (Barnes and Kaplinsky, 2000*a*).

4. Twelve KZN club members and seven Eastern Cape club members.

5. Recall that the data do not include six component manufacturers. Some club members regard turnover figures as private. Hence, the missing cases.

6. SCM examines how information can be used to change *how* and *when* products are moved to increase efficiency. Companies use SCM to link sales, marketing, distribution, manufacturing processes, and customers, suppliers and business partners together for a more unified approach to the market. The establishment of these links means that firms are able to build relationships with customers, suppliers and carriers more effectively to reduce operating costs, improve customer service and expand into new markets.

7. Castells (1996), for instance, writes about a globalised and networked "informational" capitalism.

8. Covisint has been developed by General Motors, Ford and DaimlerChrysler, and has recently been joined by Renault-Nissan (www.covisint.com).

Bibliography

BARNES, J. (2000a), "Changing Lanes: The Political Economy of the South African Automotive Value Chain", *Development Southern Africa*, Vol. 17, No. 3.

BARNES, J. (2000b), "Global Trends in the Automotive Industry: Their Likely Impact on South African Automotive Assembly and Component Manufacturers", *Transformation*.

BARNES, J. (1998), "Competing in the Global Economy: The Competitiveness of the South African Automotive Components Industry", CSDS Research Report 13, School of Development Studies, University of Natal, Durban.

BARNES, J. and R. KAPLINSKY (2000a), "Globalization and the Death of the Local Firm? The Automobile Components Sector in South Africa", *Regional Studies*, Vol. 34, No. 9.

BARNES, J. and R. KAPLINSKY (2000b), "Globalisation and Trade Policy Reform: Whither the Automobile Components Sector in South Africa", *Competition & Change*, Vol. 4.

BEST, M. (1990), *The New Competition*, Harvard University Press, Cambridge, MA.

CASTELLS, M. (1996), *The Information Age: Economy, Society, and Culture. Vol. I: The Rise of the Network Society*, Blackwell, Oxford, UK.

COHEN, S. J., B. DELONG and J. ZYSMAN (2000), "Tools for Thought: What is New and Important about the 'E-Conomy'", BRIE Working Paper 138, University of California, Berkeley.

DICKEN, P. (1998), *Global Shift: Transforming the World Economy* (3rd edition), Paul Chapman, London.

EVANS, P. and T.S. WURSTER (2000), *Blown to Bits: How the New Economics of Information Transforms Strategy*, Harvard Business School Press, Boston, MA.

FINE, C.H. (1998), *Clockspeed: Winning Industry Control in the Age of Temporary Advantage*, Perseus Books, Reading, MA.

GEREFFI, G. (1999), "A Commodity Chains Framework for Analysing Global Industries", Background Notes for IDS Workshop on the Spreading of the Gains from Globalisation, Institute of Development Studies, University of Sussex, Brighton, UK, 15-17 September.

GEREFFI, G. (2000), "Beyond the Producer-Driven/Buyer-Driven Dichotomy: An Expanding Typology of Global Value Chains with Special Reference to the Internet", unpublished paper, 14 September, http://www.ids.ac.uk/ids/global/bella.html.

HUMPHREY, J. (1999), "Globalisation and Supply Chain Networks: The Auto Industry in Brazil and India", *in* G. GEREFFI, F. PALPACUER and A. PARISOTTO (eds.), *Global Production and Local Jobs*, International Institute for Labour Studies, Geneva.

IBM (2000), *Making E-Business Deliver: Business Guide*, Caspian, London.

JOFFE, A., D.E. KAPLAN, R. KAPLINSKY and D. LEWIS (1995), *Improving Manufacturing Performance: The Report of the ISP*, UCT Press, Cape Town.

MAGRETTA, J. (1998), "The Power of Virtual Integration: An Interview With Dell Computer's Michael Dell", *Harvard Business Review*, March-April.

PORTER, M. (1990), *The Competitive Advantage of Nations*, Macmillan, London.

RAYPORT, J.F. and J.J. SVIOKLA (1995), "Exploiting the Virtual Value Chain", *Harvard Business Review*, November-December.

RAYPORT, J.F. and J.J. SVIOKLA (1994), "Managing in the Marketspace", *Harvard Business Review*, November-December.

SAKO, M. (1992), *Prices, Quality and Trust: Inter-Firm Relations in Britain and Japan*, Cambridge University Press, Cambridge, UK.

STURGEON, T. (2000), "How Do We Define Value Chains and Production Networks?", IPC Working Paper 01-005, MIT, Cambridge, MA.

WEB SITES:

www.covisint.com

www.dell.com

Chapter 5

Local Entrepreneurship in the Era of E-business: Early Evidence from the Indian Automobile Industry

Andrea Goldstein*

Introduction

Few statements are as often heard in management circles as "Supply chains face fundamental change because of electronic commerce" (Cohen and Agrawal, 2000). The integration of mass production and mass distribution late in the 19th century heralded the era of the giant corporation run by professional managers. The upcoming second supply-chain revolution, structured around web-based exchanges and hubs, interactive trading and advanced optimisation mechanisms, and matching algorithms to link customers with suppliers for individual transactions, will have profound implications for corporate organisation and industry structure. Thanks to open architecture, supply chains will become trading communities (supply webs) where rich amounts of information can be shared easily and inexpensively (Box 5.1)[1].

Completed on-line transactions are just the tip of the trade iceberg. Less visible but not necessarily less important are the efficiency gains from using internet technology as an enabler to optimise common business processes in the whole value chain, including product development, procurement and supply-chain management. Potential productivity gains expected from business-to-business (B2B) electronic commerce include cost efficiencies from automation of transactions, the probable advantages of new market intermediaries, consolidation of demand and supply through organised exchanges and changes in the extent of vertical integration of firms (Lucking-Reiley and Spulber, 2001).

* The author thanks Fiat Auto, Fiat Group, Fiat India, and their executives for kind assistance and co-operation and Anthony D'Costa, Mahrukh Doctor, John Humphrey and seminar participants at the International Conference on "E-commerce for Development: Reviewing Early Experiences, Comparing New Ideas", the OECD Development Centre and IE-UFRJ for precious comments and suggestions on an earlier draft.

Box 5.1. Supply Chains and Electronic Commerce

Products reach customers through chains of retailers, distributors, wholesalers, manufacturers and component suppliers. Supply-chain management is intended to accelerate the flow of goods, information and capital in both directions along the chain's entire length and to help companies monitor that flow. This includes sourcing and procurement, production scheduling, order processing, inventory management, transportation, warehousing and customer service. Importantly, it also embodies the information systems necessary to monitor all of these activities. Successful supply-chain management co-ordinates and integrates all of these activities into a seamless process. It embraces and links all of the partners in the chain. In addition to the departments within the organisation, these partners include vendors, carriers, third-party companies and information systems providers. The OECD Information, Computer and Communications Policy (ICCP) Committee defines electronic transactions as "...the sale or purchase of goods or services, whether between businesses, households, individuals, governments and other public or private organisations, conducted over computer-mediated networks. The goods and services are ordered over those networks, but the payment and the ultimate delivery of the good or service may be conducted on or off-line" (OECD, 2000). Because the costs of managing the supply chain — inventory, the warehouse and distribution centre and freight — can represent 10 per cent to 15 per cent of sales in most industries, the savings that B2B exchanges promise could have a genuine impact.

This paper documents the use of e-business solutions for supply-chain management in the automobile industry in India and its consequences for the interactions between foreign and local companies[2]. The choice of this sector responds to various factors. First, the car industry has traditionally pioneered in the incorporation of new management and organisational techniques, from mass production Taylorism in the 1920s to lean manufacturing and just in time (JIT) in the 1980s. In very recent years automotive manufacturers have reached a high level of sophistication in outsourcing the design, manufacture, and assembly of increasingly complex systems (e.g. Antiblocking Brake Systems, ABS) and modules (e.g. the vehicle cockpit), thereby shrinking the immediate supply base to sets of so-called Tier I suppliers. Ideally these assume responsibility for modular assembly and the on-line final module assembly into the vehicle, take an investment stake in the operation and manage the module supply chain. While transaction costs may have decreased, the co-ordination of competencies and knowledge has become more complex. Second, car assemblers are among the largest multinational companies in terms of assets located outside their home markets — indeed five of them count among the world's top 11 (UNCTAD, 2000). Third, and obviously related, producers of motor vehicles consistently rank among the largest investors in developing countries. In India, since the liberalisation process began in 1991, the auto sector has received 7.81 per cent of the total foreign direct investment inflow, the highest share in manufacturing. Fourth, the industry is an early adopter of e-business and e-commerce. Transport equipment occupied first place in the 1999 ranking of on-line sales in the United States, with

20.8 per cent of shipments originating in e-commerce[3]. Finally, the technical talent for setting up e-business systems is probably more widely available in India than in most other emerging economies.

The challenges for firms in developing countries are daunting, especially as the increased pace of technological and organisational change is accompanied by the liberalisation of trade barriers (such as minimum domestic content requirements, limits on the imports of second-hand cars, non-tariff barriers and investment incentives) that shielded them for most of the post-war period. On home markets, competition from imports and from foreign investors located in the developing world has increased very substantially, while firms selling into external markets are forced to compete with sophisticated producers to attract the loyalty of increasingly discerning customers[4]. The destiny of developing-country enterprises, however, is not cast in stone. In a business environment dominated by global competition and rapid technological change, firms show a surprisingly great heterogeneity in their (idiosyncratic) reactions to changes in the global incentive regime. For automotive components firms, competitive requirements include strength in core competencies, willingness to invest in new technologies and R&D, success in quality control and synergistic relationships with Original Equipment Manufacturers (OEMs). Yet while upgrading to achieve world standards may be within the reach of individual companies, sustaining this competitive process requires a systemic effort both downwards and upwards (there is indeed strong empirical support for the hypothesis that customers' demand is the strongest factor pushing firms to improve their performance). Realising efficiency gains from supply management will not result naturally from routine interaction among firms — not least because of the large network and co-ordination economies that cannot be appropriated at the level of the single firm. Lead-firms, usually large and (at least in developing countries) most often foreign-owned, can play an important role in tutoring smaller local suppliers (SDS, 2000). Government policies are also crucial in fostering development of domestic entrepreneurship. The process of opening is showing, perhaps paradoxically, that the firms better positioned to operate in the new environment are those that made better use of public intervention in the past (Tewari, 2001).

The paper starts by examining some major trends in the global automotive industry, then speculates in some detail on the implications of e-business for market structure and small and medium-sized enterprises (SMEs). It then sketches the evolution of the Indian car sector in the 1990s, following the progressive removal of most policy barriers and the entry of foreign OEMs. A case study follows, of Fiat and its strategy to produce in India the same "world car" that it developed in Brazil and now sells in other large, emerging markets. How do the speed and timing of business processes change? How do communications patterns shift — both within the firm and with external parties (suppliers, customers, alliance partners, etc.)? What are the social and technological factors that facilitate and constrain transitions to electronic modes of operating? The limitations of a case study are clear, but they are largely offset by the richness of the insights from focusing on a single firm, especially when it represents the larger universe of foreign investors in India. The paper concludes by indicating implications for policy makers and avenues for further research.

Major Trends in the Automotive Industry

After decades of operating a classic push system of manufacturing, building cars in huge numbers at costly and vertically integrated plants with highly unionised workforces (co-ordination inside the firm), the world's leading carmakers have found themselves saddled with over-capacity and declining profit margins. In the 1990s the business has become increasingly global, with emerging markets now representing a quarter of world supply. In some countries (e.g. Indonesia) the indigenous industry was basically intended to restrict foreign currency outflows, whereas in others (e.g. Brazil) it eyed participation in the world market from the beginning (Mukherjee and Sastry, 1996). The divide nowadays seems more a function of the degree to which countries on the OECD periphery are being incorporated into the productive structures of MNCs, with Mexico and Eastern Europe on the one hand and China, India and Mercosur on the other (Humphrey, 1999). A second challenge involves developing costly new fuel technologies to meet ever-tougher emissions legislation and vehicle recycling targets while also incorporating new electronic technologies. Another shock, whose real impact is still unclear, has been the arrival of the internet, a tool that all carmakers hope to harness in areas ranging from purchasing to in-car equipment to retailing.

OEMs are adapting through three different but closely intertwined strategies[5]. The first includes the restructuring of assembler-supplier relations and the adoption of the modular assembly system. In the old business model characterised by low levels of trust and high transaction costs, production was internalised and individual components were awarded on short-term contracts to multiple suppliers selected solely on the basis of price. Today, Tier I suppliers have become increasingly involved with customers in the provision — and sometimes design — of complex sub-systems such as dashboards, rear axles, body panels, seats, etc[6]. Modularity is preferred because it requires less investment, reduces time-to-market, allows more flexibility to change the body type and leads to higher performance in resistance and energy absorption. As OEMs spread their activities around the globe, suppliers have developed policies of "follow sourcing", producing components and complete functions wherever their customers set up bases. OEMs do indeed try to source production of all components on an exclusive basis to a reduced number of suppliers, which design and therefore own the specifications. These organisational linkages find their physical counterpart in suppliers conducting operations around or inside the car-manufacturing factory. Obviously the likelihood of trading different components internationally differs, reflecting both transport-to-value costs and tooling and set-up costs (Barnes and Kaplinsky, 2000).

The second strategy is to reduce the number of vehicle platforms OEMs rely on, while trying to satisfy consumer demand for a multiplicity of new model variants — from lifestyle vehicles to sports utilities, from urban two-seaters to people carriers — which have a shorter life span. A facet of this rationalisation trend in vehicle platforms is the design of "world cars" adapted to the particular operating environment of emerging economies, including weather conditions, environmental considerations, road infrastructure, personal tastes, etc. (Barnes, 1999). This phenomenon too is at play on a global scale, with identical cars produced around the world (so-called "follow design").

96

It is increasingly evident that only the very largest and financially muscular carmakers — which in many cases are, or have remained until recently, controlled by founding families (e.g. Ford, Fiat, Peugeot, Volvo, BMW) — will survive on a global basis. Cash flow considerations are important because the cosy tradition of captive dealers and exclusive distribution arrangements is doomed, while the margins made from selling finance and insurance are much higher than from making and selling cars. Modular assembly also puts a premium on companies that master competency in a range of related products, a capacity that is achieved faster through joint ventures, mergers and acquisitions than by organic growth. Hence the third response is a "great mating dance" of alliances and acquisitions. OEMs, moreover, have spun off their in-house component activities, first by encouraging them to compete for business and then by severing ownership links. Increasingly globalised itself, the components industry is following the same route and, in consolidating, the largest firms take over the most competitive companies in emerging markets.

The Impact of E-commerce in the Automobile Industry

General Features

One can hardly overestimate the importance of managing the supply chain in the automotive industry. On average, automobiles contain some 5 000 parts sourced from some 300-500 companies. The industry is a heavy user of materials such as steel, non-ferrous metal, rubber, plastics, glass and fibre. Design and production demand competence in areas as diverse as aerodynamics, fluid dynamics and various engineering skills. Far from filling an absolute void, web-based technologies are an evolution of existing technology initiatives — which have often failed to deliver returns in line with the huge amounts of goodwill, trust and credibility invested by suppliers (OSAT, 2000). Since the 1960s, systems such as proprietary electronic data interchange (EDI), a standard format for transmitting business documents between trading partners, have allowed efficient but only point-to-point communication of large amounts of data[7]. Many large companies rely on EDI, but in its traditional form it offers limited functionality and has not been standardised worldwide. For instance, EDI does not easily accommodate various paper and envelope sizes. As a consequence, only an estimated 5 per cent of the value chain (mainly Tier I suppliers) is connected to EDI (Deutsche Bank and Roland Berger, 2000). Another application is enterprise resource planning (ERP) software, used most often to automate companies' internal business processes such as tracking orders, planning production schedules and managing inventories. Overall, the lack of high-quality information that can be exchanged among all players in the industry still produces various forms of inefficiencies. Suppliers and dealers build huge inventories because they do not have accurate data on their customers' demand. Delays and associated costs are rampant in vehicle development because different CAD/CAM proprietary systems are not perfectly integrated and information has to be delivered manually between parties[8].

The diffusion of XML (extensive markup language[9]) makes it possible to switch from discrete information and data exchange through EDI to continuous web-based flows. The real gains from on-line B2B commerce may come not from trading but from better access to and sharing of information (Berryman and Heck, 2001). This information might include supply and demand forecasts, reports of inventory levels at points along the supply chain and market-tested predictions of the effect that the price of futures and other options will have on the availability of particular supplies, such as electricity and paper. Significant opportunities for productivity enhancement arise because networked communication lowers the costs of implementing changes, reduces the cost threshold of quality improvement, decreases direct and opportunity costs of communication and decision-making and makes the whole product development cycle faster and more frequent (Fine and Raff, 2000). Collaborative dealings are made possible by the development of internet-enabled manufacturing research planning (MRP) systems to facilitate collaborative product design of complex components or modules through new engineering, production and training techniques, called visualisation tools (Sturgeon, 2001). "Building-to-order", i.e. the customisation of car design and production according to clients' needs, is the (problematic) vision of where the internet may take the car industry in the long term (Helper and MacDuffie, 2000). The paradigm is the Dell Computer Corporation's business model and its zero inventory and retail costs[10]. In the industry jargon, such additional opportunities can be classified as:

— E-information management (activities associated with knowledge management, research and development, and marketing);

— E-documentation (configuration management and maintenance, repair and overhaul — MRO — activities); and

— E-collaboration (engineering and planning activities).

On the B2B side, the internet is posited as promoting both market-like and collaborative dealings with suppliers. For the former, arguably the most significant deal has been the decision of GM, Ford, and DaimlerChrysler to establish the world's biggest e-business purchasing joint venture — Covisint (Cupertino, Vision and Integration) — with two information technology firms, Commerce One and Oracle[11]. This is a "many-to-many" B2B supplier exchange on a single global internet portal designed for supplier auctions and to organise supply chains and plan logistics. The venture's core offerings will include services to assist in product design, supply chain management and procurement functions performed by auto manufacturers and their direct and indirect suppliers[12]. Alternatively, "private" on-line exchanges built by individual companies to connect their suppliers and customers often are complemented by resort to third parties, who conduct on-line auctions and vet bidders on behalf of big companies[13]. Its executives expected Covisint's growth to be spectacular, but in the first four months of operation (from October 2000 to January 2001) Covisint saw only some 100 auctions accounting for about $350 million in products traded. This was paltry, even in comparison with the private exchange run by Volkswagen, whose traded volume hovers around $1 billion, let alone the $210-220 billion bought annually by Covisint's shareholders[14].

Marketplaces have yet to focus on improving business processes to unlock additional value, since their founders typically focused on the "classical" benefits of an efficient marketplace: the ability to clear the market quickly and cheaply, to aggregate the orders of buyers and thus to achieve lower prices. Applications such as shipper and logistic assignment and tracking are nowhere near implementation for the Covisint portal — but they are almost routine for established dotcoms. Suppliers, especially in Tier II and below, have yet to be convinced of the benefits of e-business, which they see mostly as a tool put in place by OEMs to reduce their margins. Sceptics also say that most e-commerce forays are driven by nervousness about being left behind, as opposed to a credible cost-benefit analysis. There is also a feeling that the auto industry's current business model is far from appealing, as testified by its lacklustre stock market performance, and that executives have announced internet initiatives simply to benefit from the positive effect on equity prices[15].

Other than the general conditions needed for internet markets to function, moreover, car industry portals require a rather radical modification in the way automobiles are designed and produced, shifting from the integral/closed architecture to a modular/open one. To accomplish this, components should be standardised across products and companies, present common interfaces and have specifications widely known and accessible to a wide range of suppliers. A rather long list of engineering arguments question the benefits of modularisation, however (Helper and MacDuffie, 2000 and Sako and Murray, 2000). Moreover, a movement in this direction must by definition be made collectively; no assembler is willing to act alone. Another obstacle to the efficient application of internet-based solutions is that, no matter the speed of information exchange, its accuracy may remain insufficient. The information might include erroneous production forecasts, faulty release notices, inappropriate delivery schedules, etc., whether from OEMs or other suppliers. This is a serious concern because early automation efforts suffered from the rote implementation of "islands of automation", nicely automated portions of a process that were then embedded in an existing system. Such efforts often had little pay-off, sometimes because they addressed minor portions of the system, sometimes because their apparent improvements came from simply shifting problems elsewhere in the process. Similar rote "infomating" of the current system will yield at best little improvement.

Consequences for Market Structure

Fears that exchanges in which rivals come together might encourage collusion or price fixing have prompted anti-trust regulators on both sides of the Atlantic to examine B2B exchanges closely — including Covisint. The Federal Trade Commission opened its investigation of whether the formation of Covisint violates Section 7 of the Clayton Act in June 2000, concluding in September that "Because Covisint is in the early stages of its development and has not yet adopted bylaws, operating rules or terms for participant access, because it is not yet operational, and because its founders represent such a large share of the automobile market, the Commission cannot say that implementation of the Covisint venture will not cause competitive concerns. In view of this, the Commission reserved the right to take such further action as the public interest may require"[16]. Brussels authorities had provided official support for B2B ventures of this type in August 2000 when they approved MyAircraft.com, an e-marketplace serving the aerospace sector established by i2 Technologies, Honeywell, and United Technologies.

Although cutting through the hype has been rather difficult so far, there is an emerging trend for OEMs to conduct sourcing of components over the internet. That has caused considerable unease among suppliers, many of whom fear another attempt to screw down costs. In principle, insofar as it reduces transaction costs, B2B also removes entry barriers to smaller suppliers disadvantaged by the high costs of proprietary IT systems. In theory, nothing prevents a maker of components based in, say, Bangladesh, to bid to source, say, GM — although of course assets complementary to e-commerce are not widely available in developing countries (Goldstein and O'Connor, 2000). In practice, for the local firm in developing countries, a lot will hinge on the wider industrial organisation implications of e-procurement, particularly the mode of supplier relations that will dominate (Helper and MacDuffie, 2000). Reliance on the "voice" model (co-ordination through co-operation), characterised by a high density of contacts and information flows between the automaker and the original supplier, may rise if modular design is increasingly outsourced, or if vehicle design remains integral but the production of OEM-designed components is extensively subcontracted. In this case, e-procurement won't proceed by auction and the benefit from exchanges like Covisint will rather accrue from the provision of timely and accurate information, in turn aiding co-ordination and collaboration. Firms in the developing world are unlikely to derive much benefit from such a situation, in view of their weak capabilities in scheduling and logistics[17], poor levels of trust and relational knowledge and behavioural models hardly conducive to anything more than minor, incremental innovation.

If, however, modular design advances and is kept vertically integrated, outsourced production of relatively simple components may reinforce the "exit" model (co-ordination through the market), where OEMs interact with suppliers by replacing them when problems emerge.

> "The internet can facilitate this model by reducing the transaction costs of doing business with many suppliers, and with smaller firms that can't afford proprietary IT software. It is possible that internet auctions could lead to a reversal of recent trends toward sourcing from fewer firms, and from 'full-service' firms that can do design and sub-assembly as well as build to the automakers' print" (Helper and MacDuffie, 2000, p. 35).

While suppliers in general will likely see their bargaining power reduced, those that have not invested in design and modular production capabilities (certainly most firms in developing countries) may find their competitive positions relatively stronger *vis-à-vis* competitors with far higher sunk fixed costs.

These factors are likely to have even greater importance in emerging markets, where the costs associated with e-commerce may be higher than in the assemblers' home countries, and the benefits of leap-frogging technologies might conversely be lower. It is also plausible, however, that introducing e-commerce may be easier when establishing a supply chain from scratch, as is usually the case in emerging markets[18]. A parallel can be drawn with the simultaneous implementation of modularisation and outsourcing in the context of greenfield investment projects in non-traditional automotive regions, such as Mercedes-Benz's plant in Alabama[19]. Finally, in view of the different propensities of firms to modularise according to their nationality — higher in Europe and the United States than in Japan (Sako and Murray, 2000) — domestic firms may derive different benefits according to the origins of their automotive customers.

Recent Trends in the Indian Automotive Industry

The Indian automobile industry has been extensively regulated — in terms of imports, collaborations, equity ventures, capacity and technology transfer — since the country's independence in 1947. In a country characterised by extreme poverty, government planners considered the passenger car a luxury item and imposed very high tariffs. Behind the wall of high tariffs, technology was outdated, suppliers were fragmented and uncompetitive and assemblers maintained an inefficiently high degree of vertical integration[20]. Against the US vehicle population of 760 units per 1 000 people, India stood at a mere ten. Seeing a niche for a "people's car", Indira Gandhi's son Sanjay set up Maruti Udyog Ltd. (MUL) in 1981. The state-owned firm soon floundered and was rescued in 1990, when Japan's Suzuki, the first MNC to enter the local market, took a minority stake, which in 1992 rose to 50 per cent[21]. Its little 800cc car commanded a market share of some 80 per cent in 1996, more even than its technical annual production capacity of 250 000[22]. A programme of market liberalisation was started in 1991 and extended to the car industry two years later, luring many MNCs to enter the Indian market in various forms (Table 5.1)[23].

Although price still largely dominates quality in consumers' preference criteria, and new entrants initially imported a large proportion of components in the form of CKD/SKD kits, more modern manufacturing and organisational routines, such as lean production, have become increasingly common[24]. At least initially, the Indian state has played an important and supportive role in this process of industrial upgrading (D'Costa, 1995)[25]. To increase indigenisation[26], MUL has largely mimicked the JIT, TQM, and *kaizen* strategies of leading Japanese companies (D'Costa, 1995), and has successfully created linkages with local small and medium-size producers of car components (Okada, 1998 and 2000), sometimes taking equity positions in them. Gulyani (2001) documents how Maruti and Ford have tailored lean manufacturing to the Indian context. She stresses in particular how poor transport infrastructure, by introducing inefficiencies and unreliability in the supply chain, has created at least two distinct auto clusters — one in Delhi and another in Chennai — where "assemblers reduce their vulnerability to and demand for transportation services and therefore reduce both the direct costs and the external diseconomies associated with poor transportation systems" (p. 16).

Table 5.1. **The Indian Automotive Industry**

Company	Established	Foreign Ownership (percentages)	Installed Capacity	Sales[a]	Employees	Models	Plants
M&M[b]	1945						
Telco	1945		345 000[c]	74 595	n.a.	Indica, Estate, Sumo, Safari	Pune
Maruti	1981		350 000	336 276	5 719	800, Alto, Zen, Omni, WagonR, Esteem, Baleno, Altura, City	Gurgaon (near Delhi)
Daewoo	1994	91	72 000	47 825	2 319	Cielo, Matiz	Delhi
Mercedes	1994	86	9 000	634	338	E-Class, S-Class	Pune
Peugeot	1994[d]	32		0		--	Closed
Honda	1995	90	30 000	10 051	820	City	Pune
Mitsubishi	1996			7 889		Lancer	Tiruvallur (near Chennai)
Hyundai	1996	100	120 000	79 795	1 465	Accent, Santro	Near Chennai
Toyota	1997	70	50 000	23 576	502	Qualis	Bangalore
Fiat	1998[e]	100	60 000	10 329	2 352	Siena, Siena Weekend, Uno	Kurla (near Mumbai)
GM	1998[e]	100	25 000	7 952	555	Astra[f], Corsa	Halol (near Baroda)
Ford	1999[e]	100	100 000	17 506	608	Escort[g], Ikon	Near Chennai

Notes: a) March 2000-February 2001; b) Mahindra and Mahindra; c) includes vehicles other than passenger cars; d) exited India in 1997; e) as wholly owned subsidiary; f) joint venture with the Birla group; g) joint venture with the Mahindra group

Source: Society of Indian Automobile Manufacturers (2000), *Profile of the Indian Automobile Industry* and *Autocar India*, April 2001.

At a broader level, Tewari (2001) documents the transformation of the automotive supply base in Tamil Nadu following the arrival of three international assemblers: Ford, Hyundai and Mitsubishi. OEMs strove to adopt world-class standards in areas such as the rationalisation and narrowing of the supply base, focus on full-service and full-package component delivery. Although many local firms are falling behind, a fair number of them have been able to upgrade their production systems and compete with some success[27]. For example, several suppliers reported bidding for contracts and receiving requests for quotations (RFQ) from global buyers. Sundaram Fasteners has even become the world's biggest suppliers of metal radiator caps to GM (Box 5.2)[28]. As documented by Narayanan (1998), even in an era of capacity licensing, development of competitive skills crucially depended upon the ability to build specific technology trajectory advantages and complement imported technology with in-house technological efforts.

Box 5.2. **The TVS Group**[29]

With sales exceeding $1.7 billion, Chennai-based TVS is India's largest automotive component group and one of the country's largest business conglomerates. Its main subsidiaries are Sundaram Fasteners Limited (SFL), manufacturing fasteners, cold extruded parts, powder metal parts, iron powder, radiator caps and gear shifters, and Sundaram Clayton Ltd. (SCL), producing air brake actuation systems and pressure die castings. The group is owned by the Srinavasan family and directed by the founder's son, an engineer who received his MBA in the United States.

In the mid-1980s, TVS was India's first company to embrace Total Quality Management (TQM). With support from two Japanese consultants and a few Indian business scholars in foreign universities, SCL integrated TQM's ten core parameters into its quality practices of total employee involvement, policy deployment, standardisation, *Kaizen* (continuous improvement) and training. It set up an *ad hoc* quality policy room, where top managers meet at least once a week, and created a programme to familiarise all staff with statistical tools of quality control (such as the checksheet, the cause-and-effect diagram and histograms). SCL has 67 quality circles, some 250 of whose suggestions are implemented every month. By reorganising product-development teams along cross-functional lines and accompanying every process by continuous data analysis, time-to-market has been reduced from 24-30 months to 12-14 months. In 1998, SCL became Asia's first-ever winner of the Deming Prize for Company-Wide Quality Control in the Overseas Companies category, awarded by the Union of Japanese Scientists and Engineers. In the same year it implemented ERP and in 2000 it put on-line an intranet to combine documents and data and reduce paperwork.

On the basis of SCL's success, other TVS companies have achieved world class competitiveness. SFL was the first Indian company to obtain ISO 9000 Certification, and it received the Total Productive Maintenance (TPM) Excellence Award given by the Japanese Institute of Plant Maintenance in 1998. It is a global supplier for GM, which awarded SFL its best supplier award for the years 1996-99. To satisfy JIT requirements, SFL has established warehousing arrangements with EDI capabilities in the United States.

Islands of excellence, however, cannot conceal the generally low competitiveness of Indian small and medium-sized autoparts makers. Response times are long and defect rates are on average ten times higher than those in Japan[30]. Increasing competition translates into the necessity of reducing time-to-market — and therefore mastering concurrent engineering — and trimming costs. Consolidation is expected to occur in coming years, as the most competitive firms get bought by foreign investors and only a handful of domestic ones survive.

With the introduction of stricter environment norms ("Bharat Stage II") in 2000 and the phasing out of remaining trade protection in April 2001[31], auto manufacturers have started experimenting with the internet (Table 5.2). Improving after-sale service is emerging as a differentiating strategy and all OEMs maintain B2C sites with general information on the vehicles and the dealership network. Supply chains distributed over the vast geography of India could be enhanced by enabling smoother virtual communication. As summarised in Box 5.3, some large-scale local companies have already started e-procurement. While India is well known for its fast-growing software industry (Arora, 2001)[32], however, net-based business remains largely uncharted territory for corporate India. A survey of e-commerce use in 116 Indian companies found that, while at more than half of them e-commerce constitutes a substantial part of corporate strategy and internal e-mail is used by all companies, less than a tenth use the net for accepting customer orders (KPMG, 1999). The mean value of e-commerce deals, for the quarter of the respondent companies that do track their trades through the net, amounts to a microscopic 0.025 per cent of average turnover[33]. The lack of a standard payments infrastructure and the many suppliers and channels that are not net-enabled prevent companies from extending their e-commerce links to span the entire supply chain. While the government is rapidly privatising the phone system, few of the 28 states support internet connections[34]. In May 2000 Parliament passed the IT Act, amending laws to facilitate e-commerce. It provides a legal framework for electronic contracts and digital signatures, to enable the conclusion of contracts and creation of rights and obligations through the electronic medium, and to prevent computer crimes. It allows 100 per cent foreign equity in B2B e-commerce, while no FDI is allowed in retail e-commerce.

Table 5.2. **E-Commerce Initiatives in the Indian Automotive Industry**

Initiative	Description
All OEMs	Websites offer general information on characteristics of vehicles and location of dealers.
Automartindia.com	Second-hand vehicles web site launched by Mahindra and Mahindra.
Autowebex.com	Launched by Satyam Infoway, the country's largest ISP, which also manages B2B exchanges in such fields as agriculture and pharmaceuticals.
India Auto Exchange	Launched in mid-2000. It will include the entire automotive community from truckmakers to drivers, provide everything from auto parts to mapping services, and sell cars online.

A Case Study

Fiat's Global Strategy

At the turn of the 1980s, Fiat was dogged by its high dependence on small, low-margin cars and on the Italian market. Following the principles detailed in section two, its strategic response has been to streamline the supply chain, reduce the number of platforms and form an alliance. To raise productivity and in place of heavy reliance on automation and robotics in the 1980s, it has emphasised organisational interdependencies and co-ordinating mechanisms in the last decade (Camuffo and Volpato, 1994; Buratti, 2000). It has cut the number of direct suppliers from 700 to 340, introduced platforms, simultaneous engineering and process re-engineering and increasingly involved producers of auto components at early stages in the design and production cycle (Calabrese, 2000). In the mid-1990s, it opened a new "integrated factory" at Melfi, in Southern Italy[35]. Outside the gate is an industrial park of suppliers of parts, which roll in on electric trucks as the assembly line's computers order them. Stocks are counted in minutes and so flexible are the robots and the assembly lines that new models get phased in without stopping the lines. In the footprints of Melfi, which now has one of the best productivity records in the world, Fiat has made similar huge investments in Brazil, Argentina, Turkey and Poland to make its "world car", the smart and rugged little Palio (Box 5.4). In 2000, Fiat and GM agreed to exchange equity participation and to pool some of their activities.

Box 5.4. The Palio[36]

While most products are launched in manufacturers' home markets, Fiat developed its world car in Brazil, to enter emerging markets with an appropriate car designed with the correct consumers in mind. The car's origins date back to 1992, when the firm faced two challenges — to replace the best-selling but ageing Uno in Brazil and to reduce the firm's long dependence on the crowded West European market, especially Italy. Having decided on a new Third-World car, Fiat began to refine its strategy for "Project 178", the effort to produce a range of cars that would be modern, sufficiently flexible to suit local conditions and easy to build in volume. The Palio family includes three models: a hatchback, the Weekend estate car, launched in Brazil in March 1997, and the Siena saloon.

The task of designing the car was given to a 300-strong team, which assembled in Turin during 1993 and 1994. Among them were 120 Brazilians, ranging from engineers to shop-floor workers, as well as Argentinians, Turks and Poles. This group insisted that the new car should also have some non-European features[37]. Although the Palio broadly resembles the Punto, a success in Europe, it was designed as slightly bigger, to serve as the sole family car for many of its buyers. The Palio is also stronger and structurally more robust than the Punto, designed for the rough roads of the Brazilian interior. For Fiat, whose cars had a long-standing reputation for lightweight tinniness, this big change meant equipping the car with a higher and more flexible suspension and using materials appropriate to combat noise, dust and water. Fiat also aimed to give customers a few frills. Even the basic Palios come with safety features such as ABS, while optional extras include electronic locking, car alarms and air bags (then a first for a Brazilian-made car).

During 1994-95, Fiat sent 290 workers and engineers from Betim in Minas Gerais to Turin to set up a pilot Palio production line and build a prototype. After careful study, the company decided to automate only those parts of the line at Betim where precision and quality were vital. The renovated factory was not antiquated. The Palio assembly line uses rotating cradles that tilt the car body to convenient angles, improving both quality and job satisfaction. The firm has moved further towards just-in-time production. Under a previous policy known as *minarização*, Fiat had encouraged many of its principal suppliers to set up plants in Minas Gerais. For the Palio, it took this system further. Eschewing a new factory elsewhere, the firm squeezed the most out of its investment at Betim, while the Palio's huge potential production volume allowed Fiat to negotiate worldwide contracts with its chief suppliers. It persuaded some, such as Britain's BTR, to make big investments in developing components for the car and building new factories for them. Compared with around 200 component suppliers for the Uno, the Palio has just 130, the most important with factories close to Betim and some 40 linked by computer to Fiat's assembly line. Dealer groups have been cut from 420 to 335, of which the 248 main ones are connected by a satellite link so that customers can specify the accessories they want and get the finished product about 30 days later.

Fiat's Strategy in India

At the start of the 1990s, Fiat sold only 140 000 cars outside Europe; in 2000 it sold more than 800 000. The Palio has given Fiat the lead over Volkswagen in the Brazilian market, which accounts for 70 per cent of all South American car sales. The main plank of the strategy now is to build as many cars as possible on the same basic chassis to yield the economies of scale enjoyed only by the likes of Toyota, with its Corolla model. Although the Palio family model is produced in ten countries, and more than 1.5 million cars have been sold to customers in 41 countries in four years, Brazil still accounts for 80 per cent of total production[38]. The Palio family was designed to be flexible, and details such as colour schemes and manufacturing techniques can be adjusted to suit local needs. Brazil is a rather sophisticated market as emerging economies go. In India, well-off consumers who can buy a car can often also afford a chauffeur to drive it, so the specifications are different. For example, electric windows are in the rear rather than the front (Humphrey, 1999, p. 9) and there is more legroom in the back.

Fiat has been present in India indirectly since 1944 through a licensing agreement with Premier Automobiles Ltd. (PAL), owned by the Walchand group of the Doshi family[39]. In the 1960s PAL started production of the Padmini, an indigenised version of the glorious Fiat 1100 launched in Europe in 1962 and still in production in the early 1990s. The PAL factory at Kurla in Northeast Mumbai, however, was a typical *baniya* operation, milking the assets without major reinvestment and retooling (D'Costa, 2000). When the local market opened in the 1990s, Fiat decided to follow a dual strategy. First, it granted a licence to PAL to assemble CKD Uno kits in Kurla and set up IAL, a joint venture. Second, Fiat India Automobiles Ltd. (FIAL), a wholly owned subsidiary, signed a memorandum of understanding with the Maharashtra government in 1997 to build a plant in Ranjangaon, 60 km from Pune. The project involved transplanting the modular supplier park to India, with suppliers building their own dedicated facilities close to the OEM to produce modules (Magnabosco, 1999), and sourcing 65 per cent of the Palio's components locally by 1999 and 80 per cent by 2000[40].

Introduced in India in 1996, the Uno generated much interest. Over 290 000 bookings were received, but production problems quickly emerged and dissatisfied customers cancelled their orders[41]. Poor management and internal family squabbles made it impossible for the Doshis to put any more cash into the business. Fiat was compelled to refund to customers who had cancelled their orders, acquire majority control in the Kurla operations and incrementally increase its shareholding in IAL to the current 93 per cent[42]. The Uno sold around 1 800 units per month in 1999 but, although both the petrol and diesel versions had long waiting lists, the company could not increase domestic content and suffered from poor marketing and sales efforts[43]. Fiat came to the conclusion that it made little sense to pursue its plan for a separate greenfield facility in Ranjangaon, as there was adequate capacity at the Kurla plant to make the Palio Siena.

Fiat has invested $600 million in India, completely revamping the Kurla plant, especially to improve the welding and integrated paint shops. Domestic content of the Siena rose from 30 per cent at the time of launch to 60 per cent by end-2000. Given the low cost of the Indian workforce, the firm has not installed robots, even in the stamping area and the paint-shop. Fiat brought down manpower at Kurla, famous for labour unrest, by a little over 1 000 and reduced the number of hierarchical levels to seven. An internal union backed by management has overtaken the traditional unions. Team leaders, or supervisors, were appointed, and about 80 of them were sent for a month to the Fiat plant in Turkey[44]. Despite the introduction at Kurla of one of the basic organisational features of the integrated factory model — the so-called elementary technological units (UTE) — fully implementing lean manufacturing has been very difficult. Because of labour market regulations, Fiat has been unable to substitute a younger workforce for PAL workers and has found it hard if not impossible to adopt concepts such as continuous improvement, total employment involvement and quality control circles, and to change the value system[45]. Logistics posed further limits. Kurla is a dense urban area of Mumbai, with very high estate prices although slums surround it. As a result (and also because production volumes have remained rather modest) the scope for realising JIT has proved limited. Table 5.3 shows the geographical distribution of Fiat's suppliers. While those located in the Mumbai area represent more than a third of the total and supply more than half of total items, they account for only 10 per cent of the car's total value. The most important suppliers are located around other OEMs in the Delhi, Pune and Chennai auto clusters, although transport takes between one and five days. Because of poor logistics, the inventory is kept at three days. Another cost associated with a geographically spread supply chain is that the tax burden is 2 to 3 per cent higher in Mumbai (especially on account of the *octroi*, an entry tax charged by the municipality of final destination).

Table 5.3. **Fiat's Indian Suppliers**

Cluster	Distance from Kurla (kms)	Transit Time (days)	Number of Suppliers	Number of Items	Percentage of Total Value
Delhi	1 408	5	29	124	34
Chennai	1 367	5	11	53	19
Bangalore	1 033	4	7	22	3
Nagpur	861	3	2	6	0
Indore	600	3	1	1	3
Baroda	500	2	1	9	9
Aurangabad	400	2	1	1	3
Pune	200	1	25	146	20
Mumbai	100	1	43	386	10

After struggling in 1999-2000, Fiat completely restructured its 50-dealer network, which was set to go up to 90 by year-end 2001.The launch of the full Palio line in late 2001 is expected to raise Fiat's market share to 15 per cent by 2005. On the back of strong commonality with the Siena version, the other Palio models are expected to roll out with a localisation of 70 per cent and to allow full use of the Kurla assembly line. If the new cars prove a success, Kurla could be decommissioned and Ranjangaon finally opened. The company also intends an increase in the export of components and is considering the possibility of developing India as a competitive pole for global sourcing of skins and metal sheets.

Box 5.5 **Helping Local SMEs to Grow**[46]

Magneti Marelli and UNIDO launched a Partnership Programme in 1999 aimed at raising the production capability of Indian auto parts suppliers in the western region of the country. In its initial phase, the Programme targeted 20 small and medium-sized companies for non-capital changes induced through intensive shop-floor interventions, seminars and workshops on manufacturing methods, and marketing and study tours. The expert assistance was delivered in three rounds with a minimum of three weeks between them to allow enterprises to assimilate lessons learned and adapt them. The shop-floor interventions were supported by a workshop on lean manufacturing methods and marketing, plus three study tours (two national and one international) designed to help augment the knowledge gained. Early results in increased productivity, cleaner production methods, better use of technology and growing awareness of the need for continuous improvement appear to be positive. During the first demonstration phase, over just nine months, the average lead-time required for product completion was reduced by 52 per cent. The amount of shop floor training grew from near zero to 238 hours per month. Absenteeism dropped by 39 per cent. The application of standard operating procedures rose by 54 per cent, and production space grew by 25 per cent with the introduction of single-flow lines and better control of stocks, waste and scrap. The UNIDO-Fiat programme is considered one of the best projects currently running as a test case of involving multinationals to help in development.

The Internet and Supply-Chain Management at Fiat India

Like other global carmakers, Fiat has launched a number of e-business initiatives and expects to derive one third of its revenue from services offered over the internet by 2003 (Fusignani, 2001). More than a dozen different initiatives have also been launched to optimise supply-chain management, enhance design collaboration with other firms and improve internal operations related to knowledge and human resources management (Table 5.4)[47]. Fiat India has made a substantial ITC effort since 1998, implementing Baan, an enterprise resource planning (ERP) package, and successively introducing applications such as material requirements planning, EDI, manufacturing execution systems, CAD, customer relationship management, intranet[48], and, in 2001, the internet. Not surprisingly, Fiat does not operate solutions such as supply-chain management and enterprise application integration, which are standard requirements for e-commerce in OECD countries. Individual internal operating systems differ markedly in their degree of integration with external electronic networks. In design[49] and production, e-mail is used to exchange specifications for components with suppliers, although Fiat's increasing reliance on co-design arrangements means that drawings cannot always be transferred. While most suppliers are equipped with CAD systems such as Computer Vision, Fiat operates CATIA workstations, so communication has to be translated into other languages such as I-deas. Tellingly, in Italy all suppliers have CATIA[50].

Table 5.4. **Fiat Group's Projects in E-Business**

Objective	Initiative	Firm(s) involved
Optimise the supply-chain		
Dealerships	Spare parts (on-line orders for repair shops)	Fiat Auto
	Health Check Dealer Management System (network to connect all dealers)	Fiat Auto
	Internet SAP	Ferrari
	e-CRM (integrated offer for dealers)	Iveco
Suppliers	e-Procurement (direct portal)	Fiat Group (open to non-Fiat)
	Phase I (under launch): commodities, indirect materials, IT	
	Phase II (project in progress): direct components	
	Fast Buyer	Magneti Marelli
Improve internal processes	CWW-MYFIAT (knowledge management portal)	Fiat Auto
	HR portal (management of HR processes)	Iveco
Lengthen the supply chain	Worldwide Financing (on-line sale finance)	Fiat Auto
	Fidis fornitori on-line (home factoring)	Fidis
	Savarent on-line (fleet administration)	Sava
	Targa.com (assistance, infotainment)	Fiat Auto
Generate value	Fast Buyer (portal for e-procurement of raw materials)	Business Solutions
	Ciao Web (generic portal)	Fiat and IFIL
	OnTruck.com (vertical marketplace)	Iveco

Source: Fiat.

In procurement, the internet is hardly used, although e-mail serves for negotiation and billing. A new system has been introduced, however, to send material requisition planning orders to suppliers by e-mail, with potentially high savings on phone calls[51]. Payment is supported on EDI. Fiat expects its suppliers to have e-mail addresses, if possible one for sales and one for production, but does not require it — contrary to what seems to be the case at Maruti[52]. Aggregated information on the degree of e-awareness among suppliers shows a high correlation between foreign ownership, quality, size and e-mail availability. Suppliers in the Mumbai area, in particular, are smaller, produce goods of relatively lower quality and are less likely to have their own internet sites[53].

Fiat India has never considered procuring through auctions, although management expects no less than 80 per cent of its purchasing operations in India to be put on the internet by 2005. Lack of convincing evidence on the real benefits of B2B combines with the perception that, in India at least, business confidence has to be built over time through face-to-face interaction. An interesting finding is that one supplier — admittedly a member of India's largest business group and probably the first local firm to participate in an automotive auction — submitted a bid for a component on a Europe-based site, and to management's surprise discovered that its price is internationally competitive. This company thinks that assemblers' reluctance to share more information with potential suppliers is a limit on web bidding, since drawings are available only as image files and do not allow a precise understanding of components' specifications[54].

All white-collar employees have intranet and e-mail, although only managers have internet access. Not surprisingly, e-business is having a much greater impact on the internal organisation of the firm, although probably at a slower pace than in other Fiat subsidiaries, partly reflecting low production volumes. In procurement, for example, process audits of suppliers by the quality team go on the intranet and are accessible in other subsidiaries as well through a dedicated bulletin board (*bacheca di localizzazione*). Imports of knocked-out kits of complex systems are electronically co-ordinated through the company's headquarters in Italy, and Fiat India will eventually become a full participant in the Global Sourcing System, Fiat's private exchange. Shipments, orders, and operational plans can be traced in real time through the World Material Flow System, although follow-up calls are common. In marketing, Fiat put a considerable emphasis on the development of the internet ahead of the Palio launch. The nine zonal representatives are armed with a mobile phone and a laptop to ensure that they remain effective while roaming among the dealer outlets in the country. The dealers are connected to Fiat through the dealer on-line system (eDos), which allows full sharing of information on stock levels. More generally, communication flows with the headquarters and other subsidiaries are now conducted mostly through e-mail, and the intranet is used for trouble-shooting, often on the basis of previous experiences in other foreign plants. A starting-kit pool of application systems, aggregating legacy systems in use elsewhere in the Fiat universe and some India-specific applications, which was developed a few years ago, is now proposed for the new Fiat subsidiary in Thailand.

Conclusion

This paper embarked on an analysis of the use of e-business in the Indian car industry, taking Fiat India as a representative case study and looking in particular at the effects on (domestic) companies in the supply chain. As the research progressed, it became clear that the focus had to be broader. While net-based solutions are expected to streamline the automotive supply chain, they are necessarily of lesser importance than progress in implementing lean manufacturing. In this sense the choice of Fiat India may not be optimal for the present research because the company has struggled, for different reasons detailed above, to put supply-chain management principles into operation. At the same time, Fiat represents an ideal case study because it produces a homogeneous product for emerging markets in eight countries, including India, and has been very successful in optimising supply-chain management in Brazil, where it operates one of the largest non-OECD car factories[55]. Moreover, and despite much lower production volumes, there is no reason to expect Fiat India to be less internet-savvy than its local competitors. The other contextual element of great importance is the upgrading of local firms, SMEs in particular. Here again, the focus on a single company has allowed access to a rare source of information, and suppliers at any rate also sell to other OEMs.

The broad picture emerging from this research is one of deep transformations. The auto business in India, and supplier-OEM relationships in particular, are not immune from global pressures, including over-supply, industry consolidation, modular assembly and the increasing use of the internet. Internet use now appears to be a core element in the internal organisation of OEMs, *a fortiori* of a global company like Fiat, and to be taking an increasingly important role in organising inter-firm relationships. On the other hand the use of the medium is still very limited in intra-firm relationships. Such effects on the supply chain are clearly more tangible in terms of e-information management (knowledge management, research and development and marketing) than in procurement. These results appear to be in line with those of other studies (e.g. Hawkings and Prencipe, 2000). There also seems to be a high correlation between size and digital awareness, with SMEs around the world showing a lower propensity to using the internet. In short, almost regardless of the industry and the geographical region, early research has hinted that the impact is still minor. Companies are not putting in place necessary measures to reap potential cost savings and efficiency improvements, and neither customers nor suppliers are applying real pressure — despite strong theoretical arguments that the internet allows efficiency improvement by exchanging information and developing collaborative approaches all along the supply chain[56].

From a development perspective, one disquieting conclusion is that the much-awaited rebirth of local components manufacturers on the basis of lower entry barriers is still well down the road. While Fiat may not be able fully to achieve the efficiency goals of lean manufacturing, its suppliers are certainly representative of a wider universe. Hard data show that their insertion into global supply chains has hardly augmented in recent years, and evidence gathered during the fieldwork confirms that small-scale suppliers do not export through the internet. That the only firms credited with bidding on the internet belong to diversified business groups confirms that they still represent the backbone of industry in emerging markets (Khanna, 2000). It remains to be seen whether the fact that e-business does not modify relative bargaining positions in the automotive supply chain reflects country-specific or industry-specific peculiarities.

On the other hand, in view of the evolutionary nature of e-business and of the impact it is having on corporate organisation, the scholarly and policy implications are probably much clearer. Research should focus on how net-based applications change organisation routines, modify the pool of corporate resources and interact with strategy in firms of different size, nationality, ownership and industry. Given the lack of knowledge about the drivers of corporate growth, the value of aggregate analysis is probably very low. Policy makers should aim at solutions capable of increasing the general use of ICT and the internet, starting with the removal of existing barriers, and refrain if possible from targeted initiatives on e-commerce whose value is limited, at least in the short term. The upgrading programme in Tamil Nadu run by Fiat, Magneti, Marelli and UNIDO does indeed support the conclusion of Tewari (2001) that "innovative programs of support by the government could go a long way in diffusing 'successful' processes more widely".

Notes

1. See Goldstein and O'Connor (2000) on the implications of e-commerce in the productive sectors of developing countries.

2. The focus is on the interaction between corporations along the supply chain rather than on the implications of "clicks" for "bricks" — the so-called business-to-consumers (B2C) segment. One of the earliest studies on internet car retailing in the United States finds a rather minor, although positive, effect on prices: buyers who use an internet referral service save about 2 per cent on their average new car purchase (Scott Morton *et al.*, 2000).

3. According to US Commerce Department figures reported in "E-business to Business Soars", *Financial Times*, 8 March 2001.

4. The propensity to source components from local firms is also a function of the extent to which adaptations are made for the local market and the resource intensity of the parts involved (Barnes and Kaplinsky, 2000).

5. This section tries to summarise in a few paragraphs a body of literature that could fill various storehouses, so the author asks forgiveness for being selective if not inaccurate.

6. Similar dynamics are clear in other industries producing complex systems, such as aircraft, with manufacturers of components intervening as risk-sharing partners.

7. EDI requires users to purchase a value-added network (VAN) connection using leased lines.

8. In the case of Fiat, for example, Calabrese (2000) reports that 70-80 per cent of communication among people involved in product development takes place through face-to-face interaction, and only 10 per cent is via computer.

9. A mark-up language is a tool to identify structures in a document. Structured information contains both content (words, pictures, etc.) and some indication of what role that content plays (for example, content in a section heading has a different meaning from content in a footnote, which means something different from content in a figure caption or content in a database table, etc.). Almost all documents have some structure. The XML specification defines a standard way to add mark-up to documents.

10. Precisely because Dell Computer derives a competitive advantage from its exclusive collaborations and from the proprietary sharing of information with its suppliers, it has avoided public B2B marketplaces and exchanges (Cohen and Agrawal, 2000).

11. Renault-Nissan, Toyota and Peugeot joined later. Elsewhere in the motor sector a variety of B2B operations are being established. Partstrade.com is a UK-based site e-marketplace that brings together companies in all areas of the aftermarket. Buyers are able to request quotes for parts and services which are distributed to Partstrade.com's network of registered suppliers. Another area of B2B potential is seen in the procurement of raw materials. A third example is Bluecycle.com, a B2B site supported by the insurance group CGNU that offers auto salvage that has been cleared through the insurance claims process.

12. Independent marketplaces also exist that charge a small fee for matching up buyers and sellers. Most of them, however, failed to generate enough liquidity to become sustainable ventures.

13. GM had previously created TradeXchange and Ford had set up AutoExchange.

14. "Big Business Gets to Grips with Net Savings", *Financial Times*, 6 March 2001.

15. In late 1999, OEMs' total market capitalisation was one-third of their total turnover, while it was 22 times Microsoft's annual sales.

16. See http://www.ftc.gov/opa/2000/09/covisint.htm. A buyer-dominated B2B exchange need not overtly fix prices in order to engineer the results it wants. A dynamic price discovery mechanism — in which the buyer chooses a reverse auction, declares up front the desired quantity of a component to procure and makes suppliers compete in a downward price spiral — leads to a rent transfer with no need of price fixing.

17. However, insofar as the quality of developing countries' physical infrastructure remains low, OEMs may find it difficult to reduce rush orders by increased sourcing via the web. Treacherous roads and poor communications infrastructure may constitute an incentive for the adoption of modular forms of production organisation.

18. As Fine and Raff (2000) put it, "present practices and possibilities are often partly determined and highly constrained by past choices and historical events" (pp. 3-4).

19. Volkswagen, for instance, is developing its Net 2000 e-procurement system in Brazil in view of its later adoption in the rest of the world ("Metamorfose Digital", *Exame*, 6 September 2000). It is interesting to note that many OEMs experiment in Brazil with some of the world's most advanced modular assembly plants, such as VW's Resende and GM's Gravatai.

20. In other words, they chose to "make" rather than "buy".

21. Under the terms of the joint venture, Suzuki and the government take turns in nominating MUL's managing director, for five years at a time.

22. "Local hero", *The Economist*, 14 August 1997.

23. Under the present norms, foreign car manufacturers have to invest a minimum of $50 million over three years, increase domestic content to 50 per cent by the third year and 70 per cent over five years, and attain minimum levels of export earnings.

24. Other factors that have made upgrading necessary have included obligations to install catalytic converters, seat belts and laminated safety glass.

25. Relationships between the Indian government and Suzuki, however, have become increasingly bitter. In 2000, Suzuki agreed in principle to the government's divesting its 50 per cent stake and expressed its desire to see this stake sold to the public. The move might not find favour with the government, as it was unlikely to fetch the desired price. Suzuki is believed to have asked the government for a veto power on the possible sale of the latter's stake to a new partner.

26. By 1993, the Japanese content of Maruti fell from over 90 per cent to 5-6 per cent ("Cars by the million", *Financial Times*, 30 September 1993).

27. In 1999, roughly half of the 360 largest suppliers had ISO 9000 certification, although only 20 also had QS 9000-status (DREE, 1999).

28. Similar stalwarts exist in other emerging markets, such as Brazil's Sabó Retentores — a global supplier of oil rings, rubber hoses, and gaskets for Volkswagen — or San Luís — a Mexican firm that supplies suspension systems to Detroit's Big Three.

29. This box is based on "Total Quality Ltd.", *Business Today*, 22 November 1998.

30. According to a study by A.T. Kearney cited in "Steering in uncertain territory", *Business Standard*, 21 November 2000.

31. At present, auto firms have to balance the actual c.i.f. (cost including freight) value of imports of SKD/CKD kits and components and the f.o.b. (freight on board) value of exports of cars and components. The United States, the European Union and Japan had said this condition violated World Trade Organisation (WTO) rules. The European Union had even filed a petition before the dispute settlement body of the WTO. Foreign exchange neutrality norms have not applied since 31 March 2001, when all QRs were lifted.

32. DaimlerChrysler set up a 50-strong Research Centre-India in Bangalore, which focuses on encryption technology for security and communication and passive sensing mechanisms for detection of traffic and road conditions. Delphi, a global Tier-1 supplier, inaugurated a software development centre in Bangalore in November 2000, to programme software for engine-control computers. Fiat Group company Comau has a facility in Pune to source software elements of project engineering.

33. In the fourth quarter of 1999, e-commerce accounted for 0.6 per cent of US retail sales.

34. There are just 2.6 phone lines for every 100 Indians, compared with a world average of 15 per 100. Existing bandwidth meets only 60 per cent of current demand. India's first set of private ISPs, ending the three-year monopoly of the government-run telecom operators Videsh Sanchar Nigam Limited (VSNL) and the Department of Telecom (DoT), were set up in 2000. There are no limitations to the number of allowable licences, licence fees would be levied for the first five years, and only a token fee of about two cents a year would be due from the ISPs over the first ten years. More than 175 licences have already been issued to ISPs operating in national, regional and city-specific areas (see "Startup Fever in India", *Siliconindia*, February 2000).

35. See the proceedings of the International Workshop "Lean Production and Labour Force in the Car Industry" held at the Università della Calabria on 25-27 March 2000 (http://www.sociologia.unical.it/convdottorati.html).

36. This box is based on "A car is born", *The Economist*, 11 September 1997, Borges *et al.* (2000), and "Fiat cruises along Brazil's difficult roads", *Financial Times*, 4 April 2001.

37. Over the same period Ford invested $1.1 billion in a new assembly line at its factory in São Bernardo, a São Paulo suburb, installing scores of expensive robots. Its aim was to produce exactly the same car, in exactly the same way, as it does in Western Europe. But the launch was troubled: delays and two recalls because of minor defects dented Ford's Brazilian sales and profits in 1996.

38. "Brazil Launch for New World Car", *Made in Fiat*, October/November 2000.

39. Fiat's entry into India occurred around 1906 via an ambitious Englishman, D'Arcy Baker, who organised bus rides for journalists around Bombay at a then illegal 14 mph, and a race for the first taxi drivers. Between 1929 and 1934, around 800 Fiat 509 cars, commercial chassis, and taxicabs were imported into India. Fiat's commercial vehicle subsidiary, Iveco, is also present through Ashok Leyland's engine plant, a joint venture with the Chennai-based company. See "The Indian Connection: 90 years of Fiat in the Sub-Continent", *Made in Fiat*, August/September 1999.

40. "Fiat India Signs MoU for Car Project in Maharashtra," *Financial Daily*, 7 December 1997.

41. PAL also set up a plant in Kalyan in Northeast Mumbai with Peugeot, an equally beleaguered joint venture.

42. The firm's name changed to Fiat India Ltd. (FIL) in September 2000, although members of the Doshi family still hold management responsibilities.

43. The Uno's indigenisation level has risen from 52 per cent in 1997 to 70-plus per cent now.

44. "Italian Lady Injects Fresh Lease of Life into PAL Kurla Plant Work Force", *Financial Express*, 1 March 1999.

45. Fiat is indeed the only OEM that does not operate from a greenfield; Ford started with a joint venture but, after meeting initial resistance in putting new organisational measures in force, decided to move to southern India.

46. This box is based on "Impact of the UNIDO/FIAT Partnership", 10 February 2000 (http://www.unido.org/doc/f330871.htmls) and "UNIDO Embarks on a Policy Shift", *The Hindu*, 2 November 2000.

47. In Italy it entered internet sales with a "dealer-centric" OBS (on-line buying service) approach in June 2000, first with the Fiat brand (Buy@Fiat), adding Alfa and Lancia in September. In October 2000, Fiat and Alfa opened web sales sites in the UK and in November used cars were added in Italy. See "Testore details Fiat's future with GM", *Automotive News Europe*, 20 November 2000.

116

48. Intranets are designed to give a group of trusted employees access to a set of resources within one organisation. Fiat India does not have an extranet, i.e. a private business community that uses the internet as the backbone to extend mission-critical resources to partners, suppliers, customers and other individuals outside the physical walls of an organisation.

49. Fiat India obviously does not design new cars, but rather adapts, restyles, and remodels existing ones.

50. Other firms employ a similar set of ICT tools. Maruti in particular has a rudimentary MRP, uses EDI in dealing with suppliers, does not trade on-line and enjoys no inventory visibility along the production pipeline. Interview with Arindam Bhattacharya, A.T. Kearney, 19 April 2001.

51. Managers report that telecom prices in India are very high and that excessive red tape has prevented Fiat from maximising the use of dedicated phone lines to communicate with Italy.

52. Interview with Krishnan Arora, VP Purchasing, Fiat India, 16 April 2001.

53. As predicted on the basis of India's comparative advantage in electronic engineering, Fiat already outsources work in 3D modelling, although not for simulation or software development.

54. Interview with Raghu Mayya, Tata Auto Plastic Systems, 19 April 2001.

55. Not to mention that, for a variety of reasons, other OEMs could not prove as co-operative as Fiat.

56. In India these savings are estimated to total $400m (interview with Clifford Patrao, PricewaterhouseCoopers, 19 April 2001).

Bibliography

ARORA, A. (2001), "The Globalization of Software: The Indian Software Industry", presented at the Sloan Globalization Conference, Napa Valley, February.

BARNES, J. (1999), "Globalisation and Change: Major Trends in the International Automotive Industry and their Likely Impact on South African Assembly and Components Manufacturers", School of Development Studies Working Paper 23, University of Natal, Durban.

BARNES, J. and R. KAPLINSKY (2000), "Globalisation and the Death of the Local Firm? The Automobile Components Sector in South Africa", *Regional Studies*, Vol. 34, No. 9.

BERRYMAN, K. and S. HECK (2001), "Is the Third Time the Charm of B2B?", *The McKinsey Quarterly*, No. 2

BORGES, L., C. MAURO, C. DINIZ, F. BORGES TEIXEIRA DOS SANTOS, M.A. CROCCO and O. CAMARGO (2000), "O Arranjo Produtivo da Rede Fiat de Fornecedores", Nota Técnicas 17, Project "Arranjos e Sistemas Produtivos Locais e as Novas Políticas de Desenvolvimento Industrial e Tecnológico", UFRJ, Rio de Janeiro.

BURATTI, N. (2000), "New Product Development as Knowledge Management: How Many Goals Have Been Scored?", prepared for the 5th International Conference on Competence-Based Management, Helsinki, 10-14 June.

CAMUFFO, A. and G. VOLPATO (1994), "Making Manufacturing Lean in the Italian Automobile Industry: the Trajectory of Fiat", *Actes du GERPISA*, No. 10.

CALABRESE, G. (2000), "Reorganising the Product and Process Development of an Italian Car Manufacturer", *in* U. JURGENS (ed.), *New Product Development and Production Networks*, Springer-Verlag, Berlin.

COHEN, M. and V. AGRAWAL (2000), "All Change in the Second Supply Chain Revolution", *Financial Times, Mastering Management Supplement*, 2 October.

D'COSTA, A. (2000), "Capitalist Maturity and Corporate Responses to Economic Liberalization in India: the Steel, Auto, and Software Sectors", *Contemporary South Asia*, Vol. 9, No. 2.

D'COSTA, A. (1995), "The Restructuring of the Indian Automobile Industry: Indian State and Japanese Capital", *World Development*, Vol. 23, No. 3.

DEUTSCHE BANK and ROLAND BERGER (2000), *Automotive e-Commerce. A (Virtual) Reality Check.*

DREE (1999), "Le marché des composants automobiles en Inde", mimeo, Embassy of France in India.

FINE, C. and D. RAFF (2000), "Internet-Driven Innovation and Economic Performance in the American Automobile Industry", prepared for the conference "The E-Business Transformation", Washington, 26-27 September.

FUSIGNANI, F. (2001), "Esperienze Fiat", prepared for the conference "Next Business", Turin, 23 January.

GOLDSTEIN, A. and D. O'CONNOR (2000), *E-Commerce for Development: Prospects and Policy Issues*, Development Centre Technical Papers No. 164, OECD, Paris.

GULYANI, S. (2001), "Effects of Poor Transportation on Lean Production and Industrial Clustering: Evidence from the Indian Auto Industry", *World Development*. Vol. 29, No. 7.

HAWKINS, R. and A. PRENCIPE (2000), "Business-to-Business E-Commerce in the UK: A Synthesis of Sector Reports Commissioned by the Department of Trade and Industry", mimeo, SPRU, University of Sussex.

HELPER, S. and J. MacDUFFIE (2000), "E-volving the Auto Industry: E-Commerce Effects on Consumer and Supplier Relationships", prepared for the conference "E-Business and the Changing Terms of Competition", Berkeley, 12 September.

HUMPHREY, J. (1999), "Globalisation and Supply Chain Networks: the Auto Industry in Brazil and India", *in* G. GEREFFI, F. PALPACUER and A. PARISOTTO (eds.), *Global Production and Local Jobs*, International Institute for Labour Studies, Geneva.

KHANNA, T. (2000), "Business Groups and Social Welfare in Emerging Markets: Existing Evidence and Unanswered Questions", *European Economic Review*, Vol. 44, No. 4-6.

KPMG (1999), *E-Commerce Survey of Corporate India*.

LUCKING-REILEY, D. and D. SPULBER (2001), "Business-to-Business Electronic Commerce", *Journal of Economic Perspectives*, Vol. 15, No. 1.

MAGNABOSCO, M. (1999), "Dalla fabbrica integrata alla fabbrica modulare: le nuove frontiere competitive della Fiat Auto", *in* G. SIVINI (ed.), *Oltre Melfi*, Rubattino.

MUKHERJEE, A. and T. SASTRY (1996), "Automotive Industry in Emerging Economies", *Economic and Political Weekly*, 30 November.

NARAYANAN, K. (1998), "Technology Acquisition, De-Regulation and Competitiveness: a Study of Indian Automobile Industry", *Research Policy*, Vol. 27, No. 2.

OECD (2000), "Summary of the Methodology for Accessing the Dynamics and Impacts of Electronic Commerce", WPIE Ad Hoc Technical Expert Group, Paris.

OKADA, A. (2000), *Workers' Learning through Inter-firm Linkages in the Process of Globalization: Lessons from the Indian Automobile Industry*, Doctoral dissertation, Department of Urban Studies and Planning, MIT.

OKADA, A. (1998), "Does Globalization Improve Employment and the Quality of Jobs in India? A Case from the Automobile Industry", mimeo, IMVP-MIT.

OSAT (Office for the Study of Automotive Transportation) (2000), *The Automobile Industry: Moving @ eSpeed*, University of Michigan Transportation Research Institute.

SAKO, M. and F. MURRAY (2000), "Modules in Design, Production and Use: Implications for the Global Automotive Industry", mimeo, Said Business School, University of Oxford.

SCOTT MORTON, F., F. ZETTLEMEYER and J. SILVA RISSO (2000), "Internet Car Retailing", NBER Working Paper 7961, National Bureau of Economic Research, Cambridge, MA.

SDS (School of Development Studies) (2000), "Supply Chain Management: Assisting South African Industry to Upgrade", Policy Brief 3, University of Natal, Durban.

STURGEON, T. (2000), "How Do We Define Value Chains and Production Networks?", IPC Working Paper 01-005, MIT, Cambridge, MA.

TEWARI, M. (2001), "Engaging the New Global Interlocutors. Foreign Direct Investment and the Re-shaping of Local Productive Capabilities in Tamil Nadu's Automotive Supply Sector", mimeo, Harvard University, Center for International Development, India Program.

UNCTAD (2000), *World Investment Report*, Geneva.

Chapter 6

The World's First Internet Coffee Auction: Design, Implementation and Lessons Learned

Morten Scholer

Behind every success lie hard work, substantial risks, sleepless nights and — not least — the bit of luck that can make the whole difference. This brief paper looks at elements that turned into a success the world's first internet coffee auction, held in December 1999. Lessons are described here for others to learn, but also to avoid false expectations among the many who say, "Getting my coffee on the internet would change everything — for the better".

The Internet Auction of Brazilian Coffees

Coffee people still talk about the Brazilian coffees that were offered simultaneously on four continents. The auction was a success in at least two ways:

— the *technology* worked; and

— the coffees sold at *prices* substantially above expectations.

In October 1999, 315 coffees from different regions in Brazil participated in the "Best of Brazil" coffee quality contest. In the final round with 24 coffees, a group of internationally recognised coffee experts, so-called "cuppers", selected ten coffees to be offered at the auction. A total of 900 bags of 60 kg each were made available for sale. A Brazilian exporter was appointed to represent all ten participating farms. The auction was announced on a web site well known within the coffee trade, that of the Specialty Coffee Association of America (SCAA) (www.scaa.org). SCAA's staff and their webmaster helped prepare the live website that would be used for the auction. Twenty-three applicants qualified as bidders. They received samples of all the coffees, detailed instructions on the event and a password for on-line participation. In the days leading up to the auction, they had the opportunity to participate in a trial bidding just to get familiar with the system — sitting at their screens in the United States, Brazil, Europe and Japan. The auction started on 15 December 1999 in the American morning and lasted for 48 hours. The ten coffees were introduced one by one, every five minutes. The auction also closed coffee by coffee every five minutes, 48 hours later. To no surprise, the real "fight" for each of the coffees took place during the last hour of the auction.

Brazilian coffees normally sell at prices below the New York C-price, a common benchmark in the coffee trade. The auction coffees attracted an average price of $1.73 per lb. at a time when the New York C-price was approximately $1.00 per lb. Two coffees went at prices above $2.00 per lb.

Why Sell Coffee via the Internet?

The idea of selling coffee at an internet auction developed from two independent rationales. The first turned out to be right, but the second was only partially vindicated. The two notions were:

— a wish to see the spirit of competition among the coffee growers extended to subsequent links in the chain from field to cup — obviously in the hope of high prices;

— a wish to bypass the existing distribution system and create a closer link between growers and roasters, who would get access to excellent coffees otherwise difficult to find.

Distribution Is Key

Auctions of this kind make it possible to trace rare, quality coffees directly to farmers by conducting a competition and to inform roasters directly of the results. In reality, however, the Brazilian auction could not have happened had the present distribution system not been solidly in place — and left in place for the transactions! Farmers and roasters are seldom equipped to handle intermediary export functions such as transportation, letters of credit, payments, documentation, shipping and so forth. For this reason, as part of the auction process, a respected exporter was nominated to handle all ten coffees — and to accept the potential risks and gains from the transactions. The idea that coffee can be sold by a small farmer directly to a small roaster was not in fact tested. Skipping the traditional export-import portion of the chain would not have been possible. So in the case of the auction, the coffee moved as it does for ordinary sales: Farmer –> Exporter –> Importer –> Roaster.

Size Matters

To make a profit from coffee, one cannot deal with small lots; a certain volume is necessary. This challenge becomes doubly difficult in a search for high-quality, gourmet coffee. In this coffee auction, the lot size of the coffees posed a problem from the beginning. Coffees are typically sold by the container, which is 250-300 bags. These lots were on average just below 100 bags. This meant that an importer would either have to piggyback his lot with other Brazilian coffees or pay the shipping on less than a container. Several importers decided not to participate for this very reason. Internet auctions of coffee are for exemplary quality only at the moment, and such quality sometimes comes in very small packages. Future auctions will have to address this problem and find co-operative shipping solutions fair to companies of all sizes. The best coffee should not be overlooked simply because the logistics to get it to port are difficult.

Risks

In the coffee auction, all parties took financial risks, especially the farmers. Without putting pressure on them and calling them every day, enough coffee would not have come forth for an auction of this kind. The project asked farmers to take a chance, to hold back selling their coffees in the hope that they would fetch better prices. Shortly before the auction, they sold the coffee to the nominated exporter under a formula worked out to split the premium. The opening prices were agreed and fixed two weeks before the auction. This was not easy, as the benchmark prices on the world market were heading up at the time.

Rigorous Planning Behind the Dream

The three-year Gourmet Coffee Project, under whose auspices this event took place, was completed by mid-2000. Five very different coffee-producing countries participated: Brazil, Burundi, Ethiopia, Papua New Guinea and Uganda. The project tested a range of activities from production methods to marketing tools. The objective was to try new methods of adding value to green coffee, enabling coffee producers to generate premiums. The internet auction of Brazilian coffees was one of the many activities of the project, and the lessons learned became available to all countries that are members of the International Coffee Organisation (ICO). The project was also presented to governments worldwide in an ITC presentation during its annual Joint Advisory Group Meeting. The main sponsor of the project was the Common Fund for Commodities. ITC was the executing agency.

Prior to the auction, the organisers (Table 6.1) worked out a long list (a very long list, in fact) of all the things that could go wrong. In addition to traditional issues such as disputes over the quality of the coffee, conditions for delivery and so forth, new areas had to be considered. Were bidding procedures clear enough? What would be done if a computer broke down or if the on-line connections got interrupted? How could one secure full discretion for the bidders? Would closing with last bids be at night in the United States, Europe or Japan? Many more questions of this type emerged as well.

Table 6.1. **Organisers behind the First Internet Coffee Auction**

Name	Functions
Brazilian Specialty Coffee Association	Liaison to farmers and the exporter; organisation of the competition for selection of coffees.
Co-operative Regional de Cageicultores em Guaxupe Ltda. – Cooxupe	Exporter of all ten coffees
The Gourmet Coffee Project	Funding and advice.
The Specialty Coffee Association of America	Promotion via its web site; technical organisation of the auction; contractual arrangements between all parties.

What Did the Bidders See?

Using a password, bidders around the world opened a screen with the information shown in Table 6.2.

Table 6.2. **Information Provided On-Screen**

Name	Description
Item:	A code for each of the ten coffees for sale.
Bags:	Number of 60-kg bags for sale.
Bid:	The highest bid per pound (lb.) expressed in dollars at any time. The opening prices were different and had been agreed upon between the individual farmers and the exporter.
Value:	The system automatically calculated the total sales price at any point, i.e. bags x bid (e.g. 49 bags at current bid of $1.55 cost $10 046.28).
High Bidder:	The secret code of the bidder having made the highest bid at any point. The bidders had been guaranteed full discretion during and after the auction, but all bidders who purchased one or several coffees made it publicly known afterwards.
Description:	Names of farms. By a "click" on the name, the bidder could obtain information on the farm and the coffee (of which he had received a sample already).
Time:	The auction opened with only one coffee (BGP 110) open for bidding. Every five minutes, a new coffee was added until the screen was full. The auction closed 48 hours later — also at five-minute intervals.
Status:	This column stayed Open for 48 hours. Thereafter it changed to Closed and the closing price to be paid by the "winner" could be seen in columns 3 and 4.

This screen shot, printed out during the auction (see Table 6.3), captures the bidding process at one point, 17 December, at 17.30 Central European Time. The screen shows that the auction had four minutes, 18 seconds left for bidding on Item BGP 105; and 24 minutes, 18 seconds left on the last Item, BGP 101. It was morning on the West Coast of the United States and the middle of the night in Japan.

Table 6.3. **List of Available Auctions**

Item	Bags	Bid	Value (US$)	High Bidder	Description	Time	Status
BGP110	102	$1.85	24 960.29	C18E2A	Carvalho Dias	-	Closed
BGP109	44	$1.65	9 603.16	968A94	Bittencourt	-	Closed
BGP108	134	$1.46	25 878.28	C18E2A	Nagona	-	Closed
BGP107	150	$1.50	29 761.87	9C27BF	Ferreira	-	Closed
BGP106	99	$1.38	18 071.41	D28CA3	Diamante	-	Closed
BGP105	49	$1.48	9 592.58	20F0F4	Fernandes	0:00:04:18	Open
BGP104	49	$1.32	8 555.54	C3E703	Watanabe	0:00:09:18	Open
BGP103	49	$1.55	10 046.28	20F0F4	Francischini	0:00:14:18	Open
BGP102	141	$1.80	33 571.39	F18EB1	Nannetti	0:00:19:18	Open
BGP101	50	$1.70	11 243.37	466DCC	Ottoni	0:00:24:18	Open

Is the Coffee Auction a Viable Model?

The internet coffee auction was an experiment, made possible only on the basis of great efforts and contributions by many parties in the form of risk-taking, man-hours and flat-out sponsorship. People made these contributions with the obvious hope that auctions of this kind could become viable in their own right in the long run. The turnover at the specific auction was around $200 000 for 900 bags only — a mere drop in the coffee ocean — but this was deliberate. If things had not worked out, the cost of remedy and compensation would not have reached an alarming magnitude. The auction attracted great attention in coffee circles, and the Brazilian parties began preparing new internet auctions of their coffees from 2000. The volume was to increase, the bidding procedures would be adapted, etc. It was assumed that a third auction in 2001 could be self-sustaining for all parties involved. Indeed, in late 2001, the Brazilians arranged — for the third time — a similar internet coffee auction but for larger quantities. All three Brazilian auctions held thus far have been successful regarding both technology and prices obtained for the coffees. In mid-2001, Guatemala organised an internet coffee auction of the same kind — also with very encouraging results. Others who might consider organising an internet coffee auction now have the valuable knowledge that it can indeed be done[1].

Nevertheless, the following cautions should be borne in mind:

— much tailor-made preparatory work is essential;

— parties will face risks bigger than those in the known day-to-day business, at least at the start;

— the first auction probably will not be economically viable on its own and may require external financial support;

— the coffees to be offered must be unique (in quality or as speciality or organic coffees) to create attention and justify a premium; and

— lot sizes probably need to be large enough to justify separate shipment.

Note

1. Further information on the internet coffee auctions can be obtained from www.intracen.org or scholer@intracen.org.

Part Three

Country Experiences and Local Experiments

Chapter 7

The Micro-Foundations of E-Commerce: Informational-Focused Development in Andhra Pradesh, India

Kyle Eischen

They are called computers, simply because computation is the only significant job that has so far been given to them. The name has somewhat obscured the fact that they are capable of much greater generality...To describe its potentialities, the computer needs a new name. Perhaps as good a name as any is "information machine".

Louis Ridenour, 1952.

Science, as well as technology, will in the near and farther future increasingly turn from problems of intensity, substance, and energy, to problems of structure, organisation, information, and control.

John von Neumann, 1949

"Software translates languages on Web"
Lotus Ireland, a subsidiary of International Business Machines Corp., said Wednesday it had developed a new software product allowing people speaking different languages to communicate across the Web. Lotus Translation Services for Sametime translates Web chat and communications as typed in real time, and will go on sale in September. The software employs Java technologies.

San Jose Mercury "TechTicker", 22 June 2000

As goes software...so goes business and, perhaps, even society itself.

Survey: Software, *The Economist*, 12 April 2001

The Micro-Foundations of E-Commerce

E-commerce has tremendous but unrealised potential to restructure the global environment. Yet understanding if and how this potential will be realised, particularly for developing economies, requires moving beyond e-commerce to consider the patterns that underlie information technologies (IT) generally. These general patterns, what makes IT a unique and transformative factor within the global environment, exist separately from the actual development of e-commerce as a viable and extensive economic and social reality. Mapping the central structures of IT that in turn structure the nature of e-commerce is crucial exactly because it frames analysis around the institutionalisation of new structures of inclusion, power and profit that operate separately from the development of specific economic sectors or technologies.

An essential method for beginning to define these broader patterns is to signal the fundamental difference between software and hardware.[1] This seems simplistic, but software is what underlies e-commerce, makes it dynamic and structures the nature of economic relationships within it. Software also embodies the informational as opposed to technological aspects of new information technologies. Informational development, whether focused on specific sectors (B2C, B2B, ICs, OSs) or outcomes (e-commerce, e-government, telemedicine), involves more than building hardware infrastructure. It requires that relationships and social patterns evolve around and become embedded in that infrastructure. From the protocols that offer interoperability between computers, access to on-line databases, processing of transactions and real-time communication to the "dancing paper clip" in Windows, software is a central tool through which interactions with and between networks are structured. In this way, e-commerce or other digital sectors, usually through software, are fundamentally information-framed and socially structured processes.

More importantly, informational production, products and industries (like software) reflect unique patterns that contrast with previous models of industrialisation[2]. On a micro-foundational level, IT production follows patterns that reflect an informational development process. This contrasts directly with industrial and manufacturing patterns, even within other high-technology hardware sectors. It suggests that informational industries entail different social, governmental and economic policies and institutions in their establishment, fortification and expansion. Patterns from previous industrial development efforts, particularly those focused on large-scale state investment in fixed and defined resources, will conflict with these new patterns, limiting the success of development efforts. State investment and policy remain central, but must be aligned with the development of an overall informational structure. Focusing on the technological or infrastructure aspects of IT, while comfortable within the framework of industrial policy and institutions, will not result in successful new economic and social development.

Bill Gates has argued that neither technology nor capitalism will alleviate the problems of the world's poor, but executives and policy makers from developing nations have advocated exactly such an approach. Understanding the general trends within IT helps evaluate such claims, to arrive at conclusions that reflect the complexity and truth in both arguments. The forecast of IT's transformation of India within five years by the CEO of Wipro, one of India's leading software firms, is probably accurate. It does not necessarily follow that such a transformation will entail the alleviation of the poverty Gates is concerned with, or that such a transformation will entail specific technologies or organisational patterns like e-commerce as currently conceived[3]. Recent statistics from India highlight such patterns (NASSCOM, 2001). In India as of December 2000:

— there were only 1.8 million internet subscribers (and more than 5.5 million users);

— 68 towns and cities accounted for 92 per cent of internet users;

— the capital cities (New Delhi and other state capitals) accounted for 79 per cent of internet connections across the country;

— there was a PC base of 5 million PCs. Of these, 3.7 million machines could be effectively used for the Internet;

— 91 per cent of India's corporate web sites were located overseas;

— the 1999-2000 total volume of e-commerce transactions in India was approximately Rs. 450 crore (or roughly \$96 000 000 as of December 2000 exchange rates), largely involving financial or B2B transactions;

— by 2005, forecasts predict that only 1.5 per cent of total e-commerce transactions will come from B2C;

— by 2005, there will be a \$9 billion business opportunity for Indian IT companies serving the global e-solutions services market.

The statistics highlight that e-commerce as a generalised phenomenon for the majority of people in India is unlikely anytime in the near future. However, e-commerce will transform business in India, creating large new markets and fundamentally altering the relationship between India and the global economy. How these new relationships are structured and supported — organisationally, technically and politically — will be the central way in which the majority of people in India are affected (positively or negatively, through inclusion or exclusion) by e-commerce and new information technologies.

As Dertouzos (2001) points out, digital technologies, as currently designed and implemented, will not instigate revolutionary change until they are structured to meet the needs of the 2 billion illiterate individuals in the world. This, again, does not mean that these 2 billion individuals will not have their economies and societies impacted upon by informational practices, products and industries. The very conceptualisation and implementation of digital technologies as text and computer based (assuming literacy, romanised character sets and a series of basic infrastructural supports) is already exclusionary for a vast majority of the world's population, including large portions of Indian society (particularly women). It does mean that the structure of that impact will be determined not by specific industries or products, but rather by the institutionalisation of patterns that structure the production, manipulation and dissemination of information as embedded in e-commerce and other applied technology formats. As highlighted by the statistics above, these are the exact patterns that are increasingly central issues for India in terms of e-commerce, IT and development in the coming decade.

Such questions and contradictions become more open to analysis when the micro-foundations of informational development, the mechanisms that translate information into products and power, are considered. Such explanations are important exactly because their absence limits an analysis of global processes generally, and the discussion of specific policies and development strategies in particular. Moving beyond any specific technological or sectoral focus to understand IT as an informational-driven practice (Brown and Duguid, 2000) requires detailing the processes, products and industry patterns that structure its development. This involves clarifying not only the technological aspects but also the informational patterns within new technologies that structure how information is created, distributed and managed.

A look at Andhra Pradesh, India provides an initial understanding of each of these issues, helping clarify the space for action and the possibility of overall economic and social growth within an "informational" development strategy. Although focused on building a local software sector, the policies pursued by Andhra Pradesh outline the overall social and economic impacts that informational strategies entail. Andhra Pradesh demonstrates that sustainable and widespread IT-focused economic development, even if targeted on one specific industry or sector, requires a reconceptualisation of resources, capacities and potential outcomes in line with the general patterns structuring informational development.

Opening the "Black Box" of Informational Processes, Products and Industry

The higher-level aspects of the information society are well established and theorised for both macro analysis of how "information societies" establish a new conception of social and economic reality and more detailed meso-level considerations of how this reality is structured geographically and organisationally. In the conceptual case, there is an extensive literature that seeks to understand the shift signalled by a move from a physical to an informational-based environment. Such analysis focuses on the nature of a "digital society" (Negroponte, 1995; Webster, 1995), the role of knowledge as the central resource (Drucker, 1993) and the spatial and symbolic impacts of such developments (Cairncross, 1997; Lash and Urry, 1994). This literature is complemented by analysis of the institutional and geographic structures that transmit and transform information on regional levels (Saxenian, 1994, 1999) and globally (Gordon, 1994; Borrus, 1993) through new organisational forms and mechanisms (Castells, 1996; Amin, 1994).

While analytically rich, this broader theorising fails to link to changes in concrete behaviour and practice. Defining the practices that underpin these general considerations is essential to understanding what precisely is unique about an informational-driven environment, in concrete terms with defined and predictable outcomes. As Rosenberg (1982, p. vii) states, "(T)his is because the specific characteristics of certain technologies have ramifications for economic phenomena that cannot be understood without a close examination of these characteristics". It is exactly these characteristics that are missing in much of the analysis of "information economies and societies".

Moving inside the "black box" of IT, it is possible to consider the "micro foundations of economic dynamics" (Dosi, 1984, p. 1) that link technical change with the macroeconomic and social forces that define a globalised information-driven environment. Focusing on micro-level practices — and their embeddedness in norms, organisations and practices that translate information into power and profit — opens a path to a more rigorous and systematic understanding of how global trends and micro-processes are interconnected, how IT is simultaneously technical and social, and how "information societies" compare with previous industrial transformations.

Outlining Informational Production: Finding the Information in Information Technologies

The Impact of Informational Patterns upon Norms, Organisations and Institutions

How social practices and knowledge are codified into information technologies becomes a central issue for understanding social and economic policies within an informational environment. IT generally is not only a physical architecture that facilitates global flows (Castells, 1996; Held *et al.*, 1999), but also structures how such flows occur. Assumptions about social processes are inherently built into the algorithms that comprise information technologies. As IT increases in importance in society, such assumptions increasingly impact upon how social relations are structured. This in turn suggests that IT increasingly shapes the strategic and organisational choices of governments, firms and civil society, whether consciously or not (Lessig, 1999; Mitchell, 1998).

IT is increasingly the central method for producing, storing, transforming and distributing knowledge. The structure of this process frames how social knowledge becomes embodied in actual products. In other words, informational practices increasingly define how information is produced and translated into power and profit on the "shop floor" (or in the cubicle). Informational production comprises a very tacit, unquantifiable process, which makes the regulation of both the inputs and outputs of that process extremely challenging. In many ways, it has an artistic and "free-speech" quality that challenges industrial forms of regulation and policy. In turn, informational industries reflect the basic patterns of informational production and

133

products. The organisational patterns of firms and the global structuring of production reflect patterns structured around the creation, manipulation and dissemination of information. The vertically integrated, product-centred firm — linked first to global networks of immigration and then to distinct regional centres of development globally — make organisational and strategic sense when viewed through the demands of information practices.

Informational production processes and organisational logics help elaborate on many key patterns visible in a global, information-driven society. At the most simple level, analysing informational practices explains how processes are both global (a global market for IT products and labour) and extremely regional (a need for local knowledge and interaction) simultaneously, and how such relationships are structured through global networks and flows. Understanding informational production processes helps link micro-level (shop floor) processes to broader organisational and institutional trends in the global environment.

More importantly, this analysis helps elaborate on the informational aspects of IT specifically and the "information economy" generally. The extensive literature that considers Fordism and Taylorism indicative of essential social relationships, production processes and organisational structures in the 20th century (Doray, 1988; Giordano, 1992; Waring, 1991) establishes a pattern for linking "shop-floor" and larger macroeconomic and social trends. Debates on the transformation of this structure, linked specifically to "Japanese-style" production systems (Jurgens et al., 1993; Sheldrake, 1996; Womack et al., 1991), indicate how such micro-level changes in the organisation of production occur and impact upon broader industry and social patterns. The predominance of IT in the economy, combined with its unique production process, suggests that informational patterns play a similar role within an information-driven environment.

Similar arguments have already been made for "high-technology" industries, particularly the semiconductor industry. In arguing for an analysis of IT as a "new mode of industrialisation", Henderson (1989, p. 4) considers that "(S)emiconductors are not only the heart of microelectronics and information industries generally, but semiconductor companies themselves constitute a production and organisational form that is a paradigm example for the global option in practice". Angel (1994) continues this line of reasoning by stating that semiconductor firms are optimised for innovation, which in turn shapes the organisational and geographic structure of the industry. This "structuring for innovation" is embedded in the linking of flexibility and innovation on the factory floor, shaping formal and informal learning and information exchange.

While correct in focusing on the impact of IT, a focus on semiconductors or other manufacturing-based high-tech industries fails adequately to frame analysis around an "informational mode of development" (Castells, 1989) that operates within a different supporting environment with distinct economic and social consequences. Simply, building a semiconductor industry has much more in common with an industrial model of development than with the promotion of software, biotechnology, multimedia, networks or other informational industries. The difficulty regions have experienced in moving from semiconductor to informational industries like biotechnology and software, in contrast with the move from electronics manufacturing to semiconductors, highlights this difference[4].

Overall, an informational mode of development signals that regions develop environments in support of informational practices and firms, as well as develop policy to address the social implications of such an environment. Detailing the general production, product and industry patterns that shape IT industries overall as "informational" opens up the possibility of understanding the possibilities and challenges of IT-focused development.

Informational Production: A Working Model

New information-based production patterns indicate how information is produced in the economy, supported by organisational forms that frame both this production and new social structures (and tensions). Innovation and competition will be centred on products and not processes, where access to unique sources of knowledge and human resources combined with market dominance are central to long-term competitive advantage. These patterns will play out on both the global and regional levels as firms seek global labour and product markets, but remain regionally focused, based on the need for agglomerating production and gaining access to unique domain knowledge.

The widespread nature of these patterns, and their similarity to "networked society" conceptions is not coincidence. An informational production model suggests that such an environment will be global with strong regional agglomerations formed by a need for skilled workers and domain knowledge. It will contain globally distributed mechanisms for congealing social knowledge as both a resource and an end product. It will include flexible and dynamic processes linked to the very tacit nature of its production process. Importantly, it will consist of new organisations and institutions to support such innovative, informational environments.

Focusing on processes, products and industries details the informational aspects that structure and interact with the overall global environment. A working model of "informational production" is comprised of several elements[5]:

Process

— It embodies a process organised around the definition, generation, manipulation and transmission of information into socially and economically applicable forms.

— Because it is socially structured and often determined, the production of such congealed knowledge will often take the form of craft-like (or creative or research-like) production systems where tacit (as opposed to explicit) knowledge is essential, peer or market review processes dominate and production processes are non-rationalised.

— Skilled human resources from multiple knowledge domains will be the central resource, with a weakly defined division of labour.

— Such production structures imply that extensive, as contrasted with intensive, production will take precedence. This constraint will apply no matter which organisational model, proprietary or open-source for example, is used to access sufficient skill and resources to develop and test new information-based products.

— Increasingly, value added will be greater in the design or mapping of the algorithmic aspects of a process, i.e. in the ability to define and model it, than in its actual implementation, manufacture or replication.

Product

— Informational products will have both functional and expressive qualities that will increasingly blur and extend existing legal codes and norms based on industrial models of intellectual property.

— Central debates will focus on balancing privacy, intellectual property, public and private goods and speech concerns around IT products.

— The social knowledge and assumptions embedded in IT products will result in the institutionalisation of norms prior to the application of the technologies in society.

— Business models, reflecting the difficulty of controlling distribution and replication of intellectual property, will move to establish products as *de facto* market standards and then control the pace of innovation with such standards.

— Given the limits of process rationalisation, products will be the central source of competition.

— Competition will centre on whether the translation and codification of existing processes into digital or algorithmic forms constitutes innovation or mere replication of existing knowledge.

— Products will inherently contain flaws derived from their non-rational production, the complexity of processes being mapped and the assumptions built into their design.

— The nature of competition will tend to produce dominant products and standards that structure the pace and direction of multiple industries.

Industry

— Flexible, networked organisational forms able to manage flows of information efficiently and rapidly (both its creation and applications), guide "information" or "knowledge" workers and implement new tools for manipulation and dissemination of information will take precedence.

— Organisations will locate in regional environments that both produce knowledge and stimulate its transformation into congealed, marketable forms.

— Regions globally networked through flows of individuals will tend to predominate, individuals being the key social institution for transmitting tacit knowledge as well as providing the highest value added within the global environment.

— Regional centres of information development (either independent or within a global firm) will be responsible for the full development cycle of individual products.

— Labour markets will increasingly be globally defined, although product markets will be fragmented.

— The social nature of domain knowledge, i.e. the place and context-specific understanding of processes, ensure that regions and culture will play a significant role in the development of IT.

— Firms will tend to be vertically integrated and dominant in specific knowledge domains.

— Monopolies will tend to occur, both through the establishment of standards and the drive of firms to control the innovation and product cycle.

Analysis of globalisation and the information society (Castells, 1996; Gordon, 1994; Held *et al.*, 1999; Amin, 1994; Drucker, 1993; Shapiro and Varian, 1999) has already established macro patterns similar to this working model for the nature of innovation and knowledge, patterns of global flows, network organisational forms and new social structures. Outlining informational patterns, however, serves as a clarification of why information is valuable and how it is structured and valorised in the global economy on a micro-level. It also opens up a method for linking these broader theories with individual case studies that lead to a clearer definition of the strategies and outcomes at play for new development efforts within the global economy, like that of Andhra Pradesh detailed below.

Building an "Information Economy": The Case of Andhra Pradesh, India[6]

On the southeastern coast of India, the state of Andhra Pradesh is undertaking a dramatic experiment in building what can justifiably be called an information society[7]. Over the last six years the state government has propelled Andhra Pradesh from virtual anonymity to status as a central location for software investment and development within the global economy. By 1999 Andhra Pradesh had 15 000 software professionals in 192 firms, with the number of companies growing by 70 per cent a year[8]. A central aspect of the regional initiative has been the social transformations linked to fostering an overall "informational" environment in support of the IT strategy. Yet, for most of the 1990s, no one would have foreseen the possibilities of development in Andhra Pradesh in general, let alone development centred on one of the most dynamic and leading industries of the coming century.

The central questions surrounding the development strategy focus on the ability of the region to promote IT development within exactly this economic and social environment. The resources and capacities that the regional strategy built on and created signal how the overall informational patterns above impacted upon policy and development efforts. Andhra Pradesh also directly addresses the question of IT generally, and software particularly, as an overall engine of regional growth. Most important, the nature of the strategy and the corresponding policies — regarding which industries, investments and programmes have or have not been targeted — frames informational strategies within a context that outlines the specific opportunities and challenges of IT for developing economies globally.

Initiating and Sustaining Informational Strategies

The general features of "information regions" or "technopoles" that support knowledge or information-focused development initiatives have been well-established (Castells and Hall, 1994; De Vol, 1999, 2000; Mytelka, 1999). In general, IT development strategies strive for three simultaneous goals: re-industrialisation as linked to a constant transforming of comparative advantage, regional development to ensure equitable and broad growth and the building of synergy to create new economic opportunities and vitality (Castells and Hall, 1994). In practice these goals evolve within the categories of public policy, comparative location benchmarking and social infrastructure development. The central catalyst in each is the state. "State and local governments, public policies, and the interaction between private and public sectors are crucial for the genesis, expansion and fortification phases of high-tech development" (De Vol, 2000, p. 3).

Distilling these general factors into a simple matrix helps simplify the complex milieu of factors that support informational regions and highlights the features, if any, that can be carried over from pre-existing development strategies. Very broadly, governments should focus on five factors central to the establishment and growth of an IT region:

— research centres;

— investments to jump-start development;

— human-capital development;

— capital and institutions for the commercialisation of research; and

— a governing and institutional culture and social environment that promote development.

Hidden within each of these factors is a double quantitative and qualitative characteristic crucial to evaluating the viability of the "genesis, expansion and fortification" of IT initiatives. The quantitative aspect involves fairly direct infrastructure and institutional initiatives that can be measured by standard financial and statistical measures. In Andhra Pradesh, these quantitative aspects are exactly those supplied by the national legacies that were crucial to the genesis of the regional strategy (Eischen, 2000*b*). The qualitative aspect involves the nature and quality of the institutions, cultures and relationships elaborated around the development initiative that ensure its expansion and fortification. Successful IT strategies involve the state as a catalyst of both economic and social transformation at different stages of the initiative. This implies that information-focused initiatives involve the region-state exactly because of the qualitative factors (social infrastructure, institutional culture, public-private partnerships) surrounding the institutionalisation and growth of the regional IT strategy.

As for most development initiatives, the initial kernel (or genesis) of an IT regional strategy may be quantitatively measured, but long-term success lies in the qualitative aspects of research, investment, human capital, commercial networks and governance structures. IT regions are inherently social projects for building new social norms and institutions to ensure long-term comparative advantage. Understanding and evaluating the Andhra Pradesh initiative involves analysing how regional efforts have framed both these quantitative and qualitative aspects within the overall patterns of informational development outlined above.

Information industries such as software require supporting social institutions and organisations to link local resources with the global economy. These institutional linkages are a mechanism through which IT industries access unique local social knowledge on which global competition centres. The specific features of IT processes, particularly the need for locally specific domain knowledge, represent one of the essential mechanisms through which local information is valorised in global economic and social circuits (Geertz, 1983). Information technologies such as software thus are incredibly flexible and dynamic processes, not only comprising how information moves in the global environment but also embedding local knowledge in the technologies themselves. Information industries build on pre-existing institutions, cultural patterns and social norms to access unique domain knowledge, while simultaneously creating new structures that slowly intertwine and transform these existing social relationships.

Fully understanding the implications of these broader patterns requires detailing the opportunities and challenges presented by the shift to information-focused processes, products, norms and institutions. The choice of software as a central focus of government policy and economic growth is not just a simple choice of policy or industry, but involves a restructuring of social and economic relationships in line with the qualitative aspects of the factors that support informational industries generally.

Such an understanding is clear when considering the three facets of the regional initiative: the replication of national resources on the regional level, the building of unique regional capacities and the fostering and capturing of private initiatives. The key thread running through each of these, given the essential quantitative and qualitative aspects of IT regions, is that they form an organic whole essential to developing the long-term viability of the information-focused strategy in Andhra Pradesh. This long-term viability goes beyond the mere fostering of "information industries or infrastructure" and entails the reformulation of social and political relations around an innovative IT environment — explicitly building the institutional framework that supports an informational region operating in a global economy. In this way, Andhra Pradesh is an ideal case in which to consider the social and economic framework within which new social relations are structured as regions pursue new informational models of development.

Extending, Incorporating and Building National Legacies into New Institutions

Given the challenges posed by the inherited national legacies and informational production structures, the specific policy initiatives of Andhra Pradesh (Table 7.1) outline the simultaneous building of an innovative environment and addressing the potential limitations of software as a driver of regional development. The uniqueness of the Andhra Pradesh initiative rests on the local resources, capacities and institutions that have spurred regional development relative to other regions nationally[9] and globally[10]. This regional advantage is supported by a real understanding of the innovative environment, i.e. the qualitative aspects of IT regions, that informational regions require. This overall understanding has allowed regional policymakers to incorporate national legacies, build innovative regional programmes and tap into global networks to both initiate and sustain the regional initiative.

Table 7.1. **Overview of Andhra Pradesh Regional IT Strategy**

Objectives	Initiatives
Capture National Resources	➤ Software Technology Parks, Hyderabad ➤ HI-TEC City Development ➤ Indian Institute of Internet Technology ➤ Indian School of Business ➤ Institute of DNA Finger Printing ➤ Government Bureaucrats and Administrators
Set Up Unique Programs and Institutions	➤ AP Biotechnology Park ➤ Andhra Pradesh Technology Promotion and Development Centre ➤ Apparel Export Park ➤ Regional-State Venture Capital ➤ Regional "SMART" Initiatives
Foster Private Initiatives and Networks	➤ The "Talking Heads" ➤ Satyam Corporation ➤ ICICI Knowledge Park ➤ ALEAP Industrial Estate

Overall, the Andhra Pradesh regional strategy focuses on the development of a "hi-tech habitat" that develops the infrastructure, partnerships, regulation, financing and social norms that will create an innovative region over the next two decades (Government of Andhra Pradesh, 2000). Key investments seek to build the infrastructure that will be the architecture within which software and informational development generally can take place. New partnerships with national, regional, private and international institutions for both expertise and financing support such infrastructure investments. The partnerships and initiatives have been directly supported by regulation within the control space delineated under the Indian constitution (Eischen, 2000*b*). These partnerships have also involved capturing national institutes to operate within regional objectives, either incorporating them into regional development coalitions or directly framing their policies to match regional initiative aims. The hope is that in combination these initiatives will create a synergy that will foster an innovative environment in which talented individuals will stay in the region and overseas Andhras will return and establish new ventures.

The overall direction of the regional strategy is important, but the new structures created in support of the initiative clearly highlight the social transformations entailed by the strategy. The combination of national legacies, regional innovations and private initiatives details the building of an information region in practice from the ground up. Overall, Andhra Pradesh provides detailed evidence of the sustainability and reach of the software-focused strategy as it moves from genesis to expansion.

Replicating and Capturing National Institutions and Resources: Filling in the Gaps

Much of the effort in Andhra Pradesh over the last six years has focused on replicating key national institutions or capturing existing national capacities for regional goals. While national legacies did provide key resources to initiate development in Andhra Pradesh, there were gaps in this inheritance compared with other regions nationally (Eischen, 2000*b*). Much effort has focused on replicating national institutions and capacities that facilitated IT industries in other regions in India. The national institutions and resources that did exist in the region have essentially been captured and transformed into *de facto* if not *de jure* regional resources. Key developments along both these lines have been:

Software Technology Parks, Hyderabad

The STP in Andhra Pradesh has become an integral part of the regional initiative, promoting software investment in Andhra Pradesh in direct competition with other regional STP centres in India. It is a key actor in the HI-TEC City project and has become a lead partner with the state in expanding STP services (telecommunications, single-window clearance) to new urban regions throughout Andhra Pradesh hoping to capture investments and small local software start-ups funded through new state-sponsored venture capital.

HI-TEC (Hyderabad Information Technology and Engineering Consultancy) City

The HI-TEC City is the premier targeted regional investment focused on constructing a software cluster. The $850 million software park, explicitly modelled on initiatives such as the Electronics City in Bangalore, has been central to attracting new investors, including Microsoft, Metamore and Oracle. Additionally, companies such as Motorola, Wipro and Baan Infosys have undertaken new or expanded investments in Hyderabad and are building campuses near the HI-TEC City. Structured as a land-for-equity swap (the regional government provided 158 acres of land in return for an 11 per cent equity stake), the venture is a public-private partnership between the Andhra Pradesh Investment Corporation (APIC) and L&T Engineering. Overall planning has focused on using urban land policy to link geographically new investments in software campuses, leading universities and research centres, new housing initiatives and telecommunication and transportation infrastructure, around which the software industry will expand region-wide.

Indian Institute of Internet Technology (IIIT)

The IIIT is an investment paired with the HI-TEC City. The aim is to build from the ground up an institution equivalent to the six existing Indian Institutes of Technology and Science found in other regions throughout India. The IIIT has drawn investments from many of the same firms investing in the HI-TEC City. Specific investments include: the Microsoft School of Software Technology, the Oracle School of Advanced Software Technology, the Metamore School of Excellence in Software Methodologies and the IBM School of Enterprise Wide Computing.

Indian School of Business (ISB)

The Indian School of Business is being constructed next door to the IIIT as a local variant of the five Indian Institutes of Management. The school is the idea of Rajat Gupta, a managing director of McKinsey & Co. The $80 million school was moved to Andhra Pradesh after strong regional advocacy by Andhra government officials and in reaction to resistance in Mumbai to the absence of student enrolment guarantees for scheduled castes. The school is being formed in partnership with the Wharton School of Business at the University of Pennsylvania and the Kellogg Graduate School of Management at Northwestern.

The Institute of DNA Finger Printing

This is a new nationally funded research institute specialising in basic R&D in DNA fingerprinting, molecular diagnostics and bio-informatics. It serves as the bio-informatics national node for the European Molecular Biology network (EMBnet), as well as the national centre for bio-informatics services including the biomolecular sequence, macromolecular structure and genome databases. It also contains a new graduate school in all fields of the life sciences. The institute fits perfectly with the regional focus on developing information-based industries backed by institutions to generate new research and skilled human resources.

Management Skills to Run Government Programmes

One of the truly extraordinary aspects of the development initiative in Andhra Pradesh has been its formulation, implementation and management by career national bureaucrats and locally based national research institutes. Capturing these national skills and resources and directing them to local needs has been one of the key factors in establishing the management and technical skills to develop and implement the regional initiatives.

Building Regional Institutions and Capacity

Adaptation of existing resources and building local models to fill in gaps in the national inheritance have combined with unique regional initiatives. Long-term success of the software strategy depends on building regional innovative capacity around information-focused production. Regional policies suggest that applying such skills to economic and social issues is a crucial aspect of developing innovative capacity. One of the central features of the regional initiatives is global benchmarking. Regional planners have freely borrowed or adapted programmes from successful initiatives in India, Southeast Asia, Europe and the United States. They have also created unique programmes to serve as models for other regional initiatives. Key programmes include:

AP Biotechnology Park

Like the HI-TEC City, the park is designed as a focus for commercialisation of biotechnology research and manufacturing as well a basis for the application of biotechnology to agricultural needs within the state. The park is set up explicitly to generate "synergy with other technology-based companies and public research organisations, creating opportunities for networking, collaborations and technology exchange".

Andhra Pradesh Technology Promotion and Development Centre

This government project provides a central location to help local industries and entrepreneurs reach and compete in global markets through technology innovation and the meeting of international standards. It is modelled directly on the Steinbeis Foundation for Economic Promotion in Baden Wurttemberg, Germany, designed to help SMEs in technology acquisition and global sales. The Centre operates as the central node in a network of dozens of regional and national research institutes and firms.

Apparel Export Park

The park is focused on the expansion of textile exports from the region. It is directly linked to the National Institute of Fashion Technology and the Apparel Training and Design Centre, built next to the HI-TEC City, that offer new technologies, design and human resources to the Apparel Park.

Regional-State Venture Capital

The government has created local VC funding totalling Rs. 15 Crore (approximately $4 million at current exchange rates)[11] that will be privately managed. This has been supplemented by regulations that will allow banks to invest in VC funds and tax pass-through benefits to avoid double taxation, irrespective of the form of venture capital.

Regional "SMART" Initiatives

The regional government philosophy is framed around the concept that "IT is SMART", meaning that IT is a political necessity to make government Simple, Moral, Accountable, Responsive and Transparent. The aim is to spread the benefits of the IT initiative to the population as a whole through governance, services and quality of life improvements. This combination of national skills, local domain knowledge and global best-practices, focused on applying IT to real social problems, is one of the central factors separating Andhra Pradesh from other regional IT efforts. Through the SMART initiatives, the government has reconceptualised information-focused development beyond economic goals towards a vision of IT as an integral part of governance and society. Key programmes include:

— *Chief Minister's Information System* (www.andhrapradesh.com) — an on-line database providing information on electricity, water, health and finance among other things, to gauge the daily progress of various infrastructure projects and government services on a state-wide basis.

— *APSWAN Fiber Network* — the backbone of an information and video conferencing network used for daily conferences between the central government and the 25 regional districts in the state, focusing on local issues and problems. The state is also experimenting with video-conferenced criminal trials in order to maximise scarce judicial resources.

— The *Computer-Aided Administration Department* (CARD) programme has streamlined the granting of land titles and paying land taxes on a state-wide basis. These various processes, inherited from the British and still performed by hand in many parts of India, had previously taken months to complete but now are finished while citizens wait.

— The *Twin Cities Integrated Services* (TWINS) programme seeks to build IT centres throughout the state, providing 18 services to the public. Birth and death certificates, drivers' licences and welfare cards are produced while citizens wait at the initial pilot centre in Hyderabad. The system also allows for the payment of basic utility bills.

— *Rural Internet Community Centres*, set up under an agreement with WorldTel, provide internet access in rural areas in the region that provides real-time and accurate prices to farmers, eliminating traditional brokers.

— *Secretariat Knowledge and Information Management System* (SKIMS) — a centralised database system that seeks to manage efficiently and integrate the information and knowledge of each government bureaucracy in order to improve efficiency and transparency.

— *Janmabhoomi Programme* — a rural initiative designed to combine financial and materials support with local community management and labour to develop educational, transportation and basic services infrastructure.

Private Initiatives and Networks: Capturing Synergy

In addition to these government programmes, private initiatives have supplemented regional initiatives and in some cases provided models for them. They are:

The "Talking Heads"

This is a local network of CEOs established by returning Indian executives to model the process of dialogue and networking that occurs in other regional IT centres like Silicon Valley, Austin and Seattle. They serve as an unofficial advisory board for regional policies and an entry point into global corporate, financial and human networks.

Satyam Corporation

Satyam, as one of the leading software firms in India, has provided an indigenous regional model of global-level software development. The company has built an entire infrastructure, in essence a corporate city (with employee housing, golf course, direct satellite uplinks and helicopter pad) that is a model of IT-based business within the region and the country. This is combined with a business culture that is distinctly local and global simultaneously. Satyam was the second Indian software firm listed on the NASDAQ, but retains its global headquarters an hour and a half outside the capital city of Hyderabad. It aims to be a global company, yet has been an active and even leading force in the development of a regional software industry. When the region was seeking Microsoft's investment in the HI-TEC City, Bill Gates was taken directly to the Satyam campus as a direct example of regional software development potential.

ICICI Knowledge Park

This is a private R&D park and network developed by the International Credit and Investment Corporation of India, the only universal Indian bank, and designed to facilitate research and technology exchange between universities, research institutes and the private sector. It has links with all the major national institutes in Andhra Pradesh, all of the IITs and IIS, the International Centre for Genetic Engineering & Biotechnology, Delhi and the National Institute of Immunology, Delhi.

ALEAP Industrial Estate

This is the country's first industrial estate exclusively for women entrepreneurs, developed by the Association of Lady Entrepreneurs of Andhra Pradesh (ALEAP) as a non-profit venture with support from the national government. It has served as a model for APIIC, the state agency charged with developing other industrial parks in the region.

Policy Implications: Understanding the Dichotomies and Possibilities of Informational Development

The story of Andhra Pradesh opens a window through which to consider how informational development strategies are initiated and sustained and how they impact upon regional structures over the long term. Underlying these aspects are potential dichotomies essential to evaluating the ability of information strategies to generate widespread economic and social development. For initiating a regional IT strategy, the dichotomy revolves around the central role of national legacies both in providing resources and in the inherent limits and challenges included in such legacies. The Andhra Pradesh experience clearly highlights this tension. National legacies played a key role in establishing the human, research, legal and infrastructure resources that the region drew on to establish a credible and viable software cluster. Yet they also limited the choices, given the failure of national industrial policy, and left dramatic social inequalities and challenges for the region to address.

For the choice of developing a software cluster, the dichotomy is that software, because of its unique informational production and organisational patterns, both fails to address social inequalities directly and is the region's best hope for overall economic development in the coming decades. The structure of a software cluster builds on or even exaggerates the social inequalities inherited from the national development model. Yet software, in its increasing dominance as a central global industry, its information-based production process, its ability to absorb and valorise local knowledge and its relatively unique economics, also offers an excellent chance for long-term regional growth relative to other industries.

Developing sustainable regional initiatives that can recognise and address these dichotomies requires understanding software (or informational industries more broadly) as not a product or an industry, but a process that epitomises knowledge valorisation within a global, networked, innovation-driven environment. The implication for regional development thus revolves around: *i)* creating regional innovation systems that support the constant evolution of products, services and firms (Malecki and Oinas, 1999); and *ii)* understanding the process by which such regional innovation systems network multiple local and global economic and social circuits. It is possible to work through these dichotomies by considering how Andhra Pradesh has managed exactly these issues.

Developing Regional IT Initiatives: National Legacies and Regional Innovation

Andhra Pradesh has not only established a software industry in a state that is 70 per cent rural, 40 per cent illiterate and was bankrupt in 1995, but it also has clearly pointed out key factors for other regions seeking to promote information-focused development. One of the central ironies of the Andhra Pradesh initiative is that policies and institutions that were weaknesses under national or industrial conceptions of development — chiefly skewed educational systems, lack of basic infrastructure, skewed legislative initiatives and regional factionalism — have become strengths under the regional software-focused development model. These are mirrored by positive national legacies including military research institutions, targeted telecommunications infrastructure, world-class universities and engineering and scientific human resources that provided the essential factors initiating the strategy (Eischen, 2000*b*).

The importance of Andhra Pradesh, however, is that policies undertaken over the last six years clearly indicate that national legacies alone are not sufficient to generate long-term development or address the shortcomings of failed national strategies. Regional initiatives are crucial to building and sustaining regional development, especially when focused on building regional innovation capacity that will support the expansion of an informational strategy. Andhra Pradesh has targeted specific investments in infrastructure, telecommunications and education that institutionalise and expand on many of the most crucial national legacies. The investments that Andhra Pradesh has pursued, as exemplified by the Microsoft investment, have focused on capturing not only leading firms but leading products that form central technologies of the future, such as Windows NT, Motorola's Digital Signal Processing designs or Oracle's Enterprise Resource Planning software. Furthermore, the strategy has focused not only on attracting investment, but also on linking business investment to additional investments in education and research. The creation of the IIIT and ISB are essential programmes that ensure the long-term commitment of firms to the region as well as the capacity to develop the innovative and human-resource bases that will insure the state's place in the global economy. These investments are complex alliances between the state, firms, local and international universities and non-resident Indians, all guiding these institutions to become spaces for global best practice and innovation.

Software as an Engine of Regional Growth: Addressing the Limits and Possibilities

The software-focused strategy creates a strong possibility that by building upon and adapting the positive aspects of the national legacies existing social inequalities will not be addressed. Even more significant, inequalities could become institutionalised within software-based development as resources and policies focus on expanding those legacies (e.g. investments in higher education and not literacy) essential to an innovating

147

region. Under these conditions, there is serious potential for a permanent digital divide (because access to technology, education and income are highly correlated), not between nations or regions but between social classes, cities or even neighbourhoods, as inequalities in education, quality of life, basic services and infrastructure are reinforced.

The overall social transformations linked to industrialisation generally — the rise of a middle class, urbanisation, consumerism, increased gender equity, expanded literacy and social movements — that have accompanied high-technology hardware industrialisation (Lubeck and Eischen, 2000; Rasiah and Best, 2000) have yet to be established as the default pattern for IT-focused strategies. In contrast with previous hardware-centred strategies, no clear trend or method has demonstrated the capacities and policies states should develop to manage these challenges (US Department of Commerce, 2000; Lessig, 1999). The formation of new IT clusters globally has replicated the labour and firm agglomeration patterns that have characterised the industry's development in places such as Silicon Valley (Benner, 2000). The most established regional centres of software development — chiefly in Ireland, Israel and Karnataka — have come to replicate the social and economic tensions present in Silicon Valley[12], starting from a significantly lower level of development and with much weaker mechanisms for social equity.

Strong and socially consensual policies are needed to embed development in the broader society rather than merely set up a parallel social and economic reality. If such policies do not exist, the risk is that social and economic development will remain relatively stagnant, while new institutions and targeted investments link small sections of the society to the global economy. In Andhra Pradesh, it is unlikely that export-focused and FDI-driven software can generate sufficient growth to address all of the state's challenges. Some 15 000 software professionals and $70 million in exports are not sufficient to address the challenges of inequality in a population of 80 million with 17 million living below the state poverty line. The ability of governments to generate policies that distribute and maximise the gains from information-focused strategies while maintaining the organisational and social structures that provide those gains, is one of the greatest challenges to regional IT initiatives.

The Hidden Possibilities in Information-Based Development Strategies

There are possibilities inherent in and unique to informational industries such as software that can address this possible institutionalisation of inequality. As outlined above, the opportunity around software, and industries following IT production patterns generally, is that local knowledge is needed and valorised within the production process itself. Regions should recognise that they are really developing a mastery of information-based production processes, not specific IT industries. In other words, focusing on synergy and developing the basic structures that promote an "ecology of innovation" in Andhra Pradesh will produce economic and social development far outside the software sector.

Software is and will remain a central factor within IT globally, much as it underlies the development of e-commerce. As outlined above, however, the blending of software with other industries and domain knowledge is what produces the real dynamism within information technologies. This, combined with the need for local domain knowledge, opens up the real possibilities for regional development strategies to overcome the potential limits of an IT strategy. Existing industries and research centres, from media and film to agriculture and education, can become an integral part of a successful strategy, expanding the impact of the development process and ensuring its sustainability over time. All of these factors combined will embed local knowledge into broader national and global processes, while giving some possibility that the most negative social and economic divisions are ameliorated.

The essential point for policy, one that Andhra Pradesh epitomises, is that within informational development strategies the space for building the innovative capacities of the region and addressing social inequality can and should be linked. Building an innovative environment means creating synergy between various sectors of the economy and society that can generate both the resources and ideas that produce new innovation. Adapting software and IT to local needs provides exactly such a synergistic environment in which local knowledge is valorised on a global level and global skills are applied to local needs. This is the unique opportunity provided by an information-focused strategy. Defining and clarifying the nature of IT processes like software help explain why information is valuable and how it is structured and valorised in the global economy on a micro-level. This process of commercialisation (or transformation into authority) of information creates strong similarities in production processes across software, biogenetics, film, music, academia, media, design, architecture and finance. The Andhra Pradesh software strategy, properly conceived as an informational strategy, provides a basis from which to provide widespread regional growth.

Lessons for Regional IT Development: Legacies, Adaptation and New Informational Industries

In evaluating the possibilities for sustained development, all of the basic factors outlined in the matrix are essential. Clearly a region's national inheritance, both positive and negative, shapes the initial genesis of an informational strategy. The long-term viability of the initiative depends on the local adaptation of these resources to address both the challenges of the legacies and the impact of the IT strategy itself. Addressing both of these challenges means linking different information-focused industries, skills and markets to revitalise existing industries and develop new growth opportunities. Institutionalising such synergy should be the goal of the overall development strategy. Such institutionalisation and the capturing of sectoral convergence involve social as well as economic transformations. In this way, viable IT strategies create "information societies", not information economies.

Andhra Pradesh highlights how various e-governance, education, infrastructure and investment policies overlap to build new markets, address social inequality and build a new social contract around an information-focused strategy. Its specific policy initiatives demonstrate that regional planners do understand the dichotomies and opportunities considered above. They have both built on and adapted national legacies to ensure that the initiative reproduces and expands the initial educational, research, infrastructure and management capacities that underlined the genesis of the strategy. The initiative has consciously sought to develop synergy between various types of information-based industries (specifically biotechnology and finance) or embed information technologies in traditional industrial sectors (apparel and agriculture). In the process, it has dynamically reinforced the overall innovative capacity of the region and widened its impact.

In many ways the initiative has sought directly to build an "information region" incorporating the general patterns that structure information processes and organisations into all social, economic and political facets of the region. In this way, it has built institutional bridges between global trends and local needs. A central example lies in the e-governance initiatives. These projects, by using local skills and knowledge, will gradually expand the market for local IT products and services as the government and society expand their capacities and demand for IT. A small example is the running of the entire computer system for the IIIT on Linux, managed by local university graduates. This both promotes Andhra Pradesh as a regional centre of software skill and offers the ability to apply such skills to local institutions and needs. Another example is the aim to develop a globally competitive apparel industry reinforced by the use of local IT skills, professional design, unique national and regional cultures and IT infrastructure. Global information technologies and architectures can also potentially feed directly into the thriving regional Telugu film industry that serves 80 million people locally as well as the global Telugu diaspora.

In each of these cases, the successful regional software strategy links regional government, culture and industry with global trends that reinforce and feed off regional initiatives. This potential is inherent in informational production processes generally (Table 7.2). In Andhra Pradesh, the failure to harness this potential would weaken the long-term viability of the regional software initiative, while adapting this potential to regional needs is crucial to establishing both a globally competitive software industry and software as a catalyst for broader regional growth. Overall, the development strategy in Andhra Pradesh is an ideal example of understanding an information economy and adapting its potential to regional political and social issues. While the long-term outcome of the initiative is not assured, Andhra Pradesh details the essential role of regional governments in building social, economic and institutional synergy around information-focused regional development. It is exactly such qualitative aspects that will most likely be the central determinant of successful regional initiatives over the coming decades.

Table 7.2. **Global Patterns Operating in Andhra Pradesh**

General Patterns	Specific Aspects	Specific Form in Andhra Pradesh
Informational Processes, Products and Industries	Tacit, innovation-driven and informational processes.	Development of software using skilled researchers, engineers and firms
	Products embedded and defined by social knowledge.	Use of AP exposure to foreign cultures.
	Global markets and regional, networked production for industries	Global software industry linked with local firms and institutions to access and market local labour
Institutional Mechanisms, Norms and Flows Structuring the Informational Environment	Immigration	Skilled global immigrant networks
	Investment	Ties to US venture capital
	Innovation networks	FDI by leading IT firms
	National and regional policy	National & regional development initiatives
	Private-public partnerships	Regional government-Satyam Partnership
	Entrepreneurial firms–global firm linkages	Global firm outsourcing linkages to local firms
Local Processes and Structures Interacting with the Informational Environment	Regional economic and social networks	Regional Andhra identity
	Unique local knowledge information	Weak existing industrial structure
	Regional governance institutions and capacity	IT used for better governance and regional development
	Unique social capital	Regional political party
	Unique cultural practices	Extensive immigrant networks in software firms globally
	Regional educational and scientific institutions	Over production of skilled SW labour and English-language university education

151

Implications of Informational Patterns: Mapping Interactions and Structures in a Networked Society

The four quotes that open this analysis offer entry points into a fuller understanding of information technologies and their impact on social and economic development. Ridenour describes the process of how computers can be and, as detailed above, have become "information machines". The key technological development of the last 30 years is exactly the creation of information technology as a general phenomenon with ever-greater distribution and connectivity. The key aspect is not, as is the usual focus, technology, but rather information. The increasingly connected and digitalised world we inhabit is structured by the flow of information and by how that information, as socially determined, gets congealed into new forms of profit and power.

Von Neumann, speaking over 50 years ago of science and technology, helps to explain the basic patterns of economic and social development as issues of structure, organisation, information and control under these informational flows. An information economy restructures social relationships in order to maximise the generation, manipulation, dissemination and commercialisation of information. This results in new organisational and institutional imperatives that offer both opportunities and challenges. A distinct informational pattern of production models how knowledge and information are produced and valorised in the global environment.

The IBM press release describes this entire process, in essence what the information economy is, in three short sentences. An Irish subsidiary of IBM has developed a web-based, real-time translation program based on Java. The knowledge to create (or recreate) such a program resides in the programmers who created it, in Ireland, even though they work for a global firm. The product is entirely digitally based and functions only on the internet, where it is instantly available globally. It enables real-time communication regardless of location or language. What these languages are, how well they are translated and how they structure communication is a function of the domain knowledge and assumptions of the programmers as structured in the program code. The ability to regulate the product is inherent in the coding of the program and the priorities of IBM, not in any government or social process.

The last quote serves to emphasise the social and informational nature of information technologies. Kranzberg (1985) states that "technology is neither good, nor bad nor neutral," meaning that society determines its application and impact. Yet informational technologies like the software produced by IBM already define frameworks for social action through their architectures and development processes. Informational products like software or gene patents are the vehicles through which knowledge and information are given form in a digital world, and as such they explicitly embody social knowledge. This means that prior to its application by society, IT is already structuring the forms that social interactions can take. Combined with Metcalfe's Law[13], this implies that once certain digital patterns of interaction become dominant — such as the protocols that shape internet communication or define how computers structure information — the social interpretation or regulation of these technologies is already limited. Furthermore, informational production, by its structure, tends to produce monopolies of both standards and firms, thus creating not only framed patterns of interaction but also extreme power inequalities with the network structures.

Analysis has tended not to recognise the central role of domain knowledge and its transformation on the micro-level within information technology. The informational aspect of IT signals not only communication but also the embodying of social practices and interactions in technology itself. These basic aspects, the micro-foundations and patterns of informational processes, pose the crucial questions surrounding issues of IT and development. E-commerce as a derivative of IT will impact upon economies and societies even if the effects are only secondary rather than through primary participation. Understanding the nature of this impact, and how societies and governments can negotiate such interactions, is a central policy question. Even as (or if) e-commerce becomes widely established, the domain-specific nature of informational processes and products ensures that it will reflect a myriad of local patterns, capacities and cultures that will be impossible to predict. How these local patterns are tied into broader networks, however — and more importantly how general informational development patterns may impact upon local communities — can be understood and planned for through a careful consideration of the micro-foundations of information societies.

Notes

1. Hardware, like software, is structured around algorithmic codes that determine the basic circuitry of an IC. In this way, hardware and software both follow the basic structures of binary, algorithmic logic. The real choice is between whether such patterns are "hardwired", with linked tradeoffs between flexibility, reliability, adaptability and cost. Software increasingly exceeds hardware in each of these areas (Armour, 2000).

2. A fuller analysis of the contrast between hardware and software and the implications for development can be found Eischen (2000a).

3. "Wrong Solution", by Kumar Venkat, *San Jose Mercury News*, 8 April 2001.

4. See the *Global Networks, Innovation and Development: The Informational Region as a Development Strategy* conference web site, http://www2.ucsc.edu/cgirs/conferences/globalnet/index.html, for an overview of these issues drawn from specific regional case studies.

5. See Eischen (2001) for a more detailed analysis of the development of the information model and patterns.

6. This section is derived in part from fieldwork conducted in 1999/2000.

7. Andhra Pradesh's average household income is $600 a year (four times the national value); 63 per cent of the households have electrical connections and 21 per cent of the inhabitants earn less than $49 per year (the Andhra Pradesh poverty line).

8. Interview: Joint Director Kumar, Software Technology Parks, Hyderabad.

9. See Bajpai and Radjou (1999) and Bajpai & Dokeniya (1999) for a comparative analysis of Tamil Nadu's IT strategy, and Parthasarathy (1999) on Bangalore.

10. See Lubeck & Eischen (2000) on Mexico, O'Riain (1999) on Ireland and Rasiah & Best (2000) on Malaysia for comparison.

11. While not large compared with VC funds in the United States (which can be as large as a billion dollars), 15 Crore is large by Indian standards. The federal government VC fund designated for all of India has only 100 Crore in funding. To match the same relative per capita commitment as the regional fund, the national fund would have to be 12.5 times as large.

12. While outside of the analysis here, the social and economic patterns surrounding IT industries such as software are clearly visible in other IT regions and industries, including Los Angeles (film), San Francisco (biotechnology and e-commerce), Austin (computers and ICs), New York (finance), Bombay (film) and Hong Kong (finance, e-commerce, film).

13. Metcalfe's Law states that the "value" or "power" of a network increases in proportion to roughly the square (for large numbers) of the number of nodes on the network, or more precisely N^2-N.

Bibliography

AMIN, A. (ed.) (1994), *Post-Fordism: A Reader*, Blackwell, Cambridge, MA.

ANGEL, D.P. (1994), *Restructuring for Innovation: the Remaking of the U.S. Semiconductor Industry*, Guilford, New York, NY.

ARMOUR, P.G. (2000), "The Case for a New Business Model", *Communications of the ACM*, Vol. 43, No. 8.

BAJPAI, N. and A. DOKENIYA (1999), "Information Technology-Led Growth Policies: A Case Study of Tamil Nadu", Development Discussion Paper 729, Harvard Institute for International Development.

BAJPAI N. and N. RADJOU (1999), "Raising the Global Competitiveness of Tamil Nadu's Information Technology Industry", Development Discussion Paper 728, Harvard Institute for International Development.

BENNER, C. (2000), "Navigating Flexibilities: Labor Markets and Intermediaries in Silicon Valley", doctoral dissertation, unpublished, Department of Urban Studies and Regional Planning, University of California, Berkeley, CA.

BORRUS, M. (1993), *The Regional Architecture of Global Electronics: Trajectories, Linkages and Access to Technology*, Berkeley Roundtable on the International Economy, University of California, Berkeley, CA.

BROWN, J.S. and P. DUGUID (2000), *Social Life of Information*, Harvard Business School Press, Boston, MA.

CAIRNCROSS, F. (1997), *The Death of Distance: How the Communications Revolution will Change Our Lives*, Harvard Business School Press, Boston, MA.

CASTELLS, M. (1996), *The Information Age: The Rise of the Network Society*, Blackwell, Cambridge, MA.

CASTELLS, M. (1989), *The Informational City: Information Technology, Economic Restructuring, and the Urban-regional Process*, Blackwell, Oxford, UK.

CASTELLS, M. and P. HALL (1994), *Technopoles of the World: The Making of 21st Century Industrial Complexes*, Routledge, New York, NY.

DERTOUZOS, M.L. (2001), *The Unfinished Revolution: Human-Centered Computers and What They Can Do for Us*, HarperCollins, New York, NY.

DE VOL, R.C. (2000), *Blueprint for a High-Tech Cluster: The Case of the Microsystems Industry in the Southwest*, Milken Institute, www.milken-inst.org.

DE VOL, R.C. (1999), *America's High-Tech Economy: Growth, Development, and Risks for Metropolitan Areas*, Milken Institute, www.milken-inst.org.

DORAY, B. (1988), *From Taylorism to Fordism: a Rational Madness*, Free Association Books, London.

DOSI, G. (1984), *Technical Change and Industrial Transformation*, St. Martin's Press, New York, NY.

DRUCKER, P.F. (1993), *Post-Capitalist Society*, HarperBusiness, New York, NY.

EISCHEN, K. (2001), "Mapping the Micro-Foundations of the Informational Society: Linking Software Processes, Products and Industries to Global Trends", Center for Global, International and Regional Studies, University of California, Santa Cruz, CA.

EISCHEN, K. (2000*a*), "Information Technology: History, Practice and Implications for Development", CGRIS Working Paper 200-4, Center for Global, International and Regional Studies, University of California, Santa Cruz, CA.

EISCHEN, K. (2000*b*), "National Legacies, Software Technology Clusters and Institutional Innovation: The Dichotomy of Regional Development in Andhra Pradesh, India", paper presented at the Association of Collegiate Schools of Planning Annual Conference, 2-5 November 2000, Atlanta, GA.

GEERTZ, C. (1983), *Local Knowledge: Further Essays in Interpretive Anthropology*, Basic Books, New York, NY.

GIORDANO, L. (1992), *Beyond Taylorism: Computerization and the New Industrial Relations*, St. Martin's Press, New York, NY.

GORDON, R. (1994), "State, Milieu, Network: Systems of Innovation in Silicon Valley", Working Paper 94-4, Center for the Study of Global Transformations, University of California, Santa Cruz, CA.

GOVERNMENT OF ANDHRA PRADESH (2000), *AP First: Information Technology Policy*.

HELD, D., A. MCGREW, D. GOLDBLATT and J. PERRATON (1999), *Global Transformations: Politics, Economics and Culture*, Stanford University Press, Stanford, CA.

HENDERSON, J.W. (1989), *The Globalisation of High-Technology Production: Society, Space, and Semiconductors in the Restructuring of the Modern World*, Routledge, New York, NY.

JURGENS, U., T. MALSCH and K. DOHSE (1993), *Breaking from Taylorism: Changing Forms of Work in the Automobile Industry*, Cambridge University Press, London.

KRANZBERG, M. (1985), "The Information Age: Evolution or Revolution?", *in* B.R. GUILE (ed.), *Information Technologies and Social Transformation*, National Academy Press, Washington, D.C.

LASH, S. and J. URRY (1994), *Economies of Signs and Space*, Sage, Thousand Oaks, CA.

LESSIG, L. (1999), *Code: and Other Laws of Cyberspace*, Basic Books, New York, NY.

Lᴜʙᴇᴄᴋ, P. and K. Eɪsᴄʜᴇɴ (2000), "Silicon Islands and Silicon 'Valles': Informational Networks and Regional Development in an Era of Globalization", *in* N. Kʟᴀʜɴ, P. Cᴀsᴛɪʟʟᴏ, A. Aʟᴠᴀʀᴇᴢ and F. Mᴀɴᴄʜóɴ (eds.), *Las Nuevas Fronteras del Siglo XXI/New Frontiers of the 21ˢᵗ Century*, La Jornada Ediciones, México, D.F.

Mᴀʟᴇᴄᴋɪ, E. and P. Oɪɴᴀs (eds.) (1999), *Making Connections: Technological Learning and Regional Economic Change*, Ashgate, Brookfield, VT.

Mɪᴛᴄʜᴇʟʟ, W.J. (1998), *City of Bits: Space, Place and the Infobahn*, MIT Press, Cambridge, MA.

Mʏᴛᴇʟᴋᴀ, L.K. (1999), *Competition, Innovation and Competitiveness in Developing Countries*, Development Centre Studies, OECD, Paris.

NASSCOM (2001), *Internet & E-commerce — The Indian Scenario*, New Dehli, National Association of Software & Service Companies, August, www.nasscom.org/it_industry/int_ecomm_home.asp

Nᴇɢʀᴏᴘᴏɴᴛᴇ, N. (1995), *Being Digital*, Alfred A. Knopf, New York, NY.

O'Rɪᴀɪɴ, S. (1999), "The Flexible Developmental State: Globalization, Information Technology and the 'Celtic Tiger'", conference on Global Networks, Innovation and Regional Development: The Informational Region as Development Strategy, 11-13 November, University of California, Santa Cruz, CA.

Pᴀʀᴛʜᴀsᴀʀᴀᴛʜʏ, B. (1999), "Institutional Embeddedness and Regional Industrialization: The State and the Indian Computer Software Industry", conference on Global Networks, Innovation and Regional Development: The Informational Region as Development Strategy, 11-13 November, University of California, Santa Cruz, CA.

Rᴀsɪᴀʜ, R. and M. Bᴇsᴛ (2000), "Industrial Transition in the Malaysian Electronics Industry", unpublished working paper, United Nations Industrial Development Organization, United Nations Development Programme.

Rʜᴏᴅᴇs, R. (ed.) (1999), *Visions of Technology: A Century of Vital Debate About Machines, Systems and the Human World*, Simon & Schuster, New York, NY.

Rᴏsᴇɴʙᴇʀɢ, N. (1982), *Inside the Black Box: Technology and Economics*, Cambridge University Press, New York, NY.

San Jose Mercury News (various), www.sjmercury.com.

Sᴀxᴇɴɪᴀɴ, A.L. (1999), *Silicon Valley's New Immigrant Entrepreneurs*, Public Policy Institute of California, San Francisco, CA.

Sᴀxᴇɴɪᴀɴ, A.L. (1994), *Regional Advantage: Culture and Competition in Silicon Valley and Route 128*, Harvard University Press, Cambridge, MA.

Sʜᴀᴘɪʀᴏ, C. and H.R. Vᴀʀɪᴀɴ (1999), *Information Rules: A Strategic Guide to the Network Economy*, Harvard Business School Press, Boston, MA.

Sʜᴇʟᴅʀᴀᴋᴇ, J. (1996), *Management Theory: from Taylorism to Japanization*, International Thomson Business Press, Boston, MA.

US Dᴇᴘᴀʀᴛᴍᴇɴᴛ ᴏꜰ Cᴏᴍᴍᴇʀᴄᴇ (2000), *Digital Economy 2000*, Economics and Statistics Administration, Washington, D.C.

WARING, S.P. (1991), *Taylorism Transformed: Scientific Management Theory since* 1945, University of North Carolina Press, Chapel Hill, NC.

WEBSTER, F. (1995), *Theories of the Information Society*, Routledge, New York, NY.

WOMACK, J.P., D.T. JONES and D. ROOS (1991), *The Machine that Changed the World*, Harper Perennial, New York, NY.

Chapter 8

Cellular Phones in Rural Bangladesh: A Study of the Village Pay Phone of Grameen Bank

Salahuddin M. Aminuzzaman*

Introduction

Bangladesh suffers one of the lowest telephone penetration rates in the world, even the lowest in the South Asian region. It has only three fixed and mobile phones per 1 000 people, compared with five in Nepal, 15 in India, 20 in Sri Lanka and 25 in Pakistan[1]. Most of the rural population is poor and cannot afford subscription to fixed telecommunication lines. About 95 per cent of Bangladesh's villages thus lack any access to a phone. Moreover, the start-up cost of a fixed-line telephone in Bangladesh is the highest in South Asia[2] and involves a long waiting period of 5-10 years[3].

In March 1997, Grameen Telecom (GT)[4], a sister company of Grameen Bank (GB), launched its cellular operations in rural Bangladesh. Twenty-eight GB borrowers became pioneering operators of telephone services in their villages. By early 2001 the number reached 1 500. GT plans to provide GSM cellular phone service to 100 million rural inhabitants over the next four years in Bangladesh's 68 000 villages. The expansion programme will be carried out by GB micro-credit network. GT also aims to organise the Village Pay Phone (VPP) service further as an income-generating project for village operators.

This chapter describes the VPP system and presents the results of a unique study to assess its efficacy in reducing the information poverty of villages that have obtained access to mobile phones. More specifically, the study sought to analyse the ways in which the VPP is operated, how the service is used and by whom and its impact on the economic and social empowerment of individuals and communities[5].

---

* This study was supported by a research grant of NORAD and Telenor, Norway. In addition to the author, the research team was composed of Prof. Harald Baldersheim, Department of Political Science, University of Oslo, and Dr. Ishtiaq Jamil, Associate Professor, Department of Administration and Organisation Theory, University of Bergen, Norway.

The Grameen Telecom System

To address the problem of poor telecommunications in rural areas, GT seeks to introduce modern technology (cellular phones) that overcomes the lack of appropriate public telephone services and the prohibitively high cost of traditional telecommunications infrastructure. It uses GB loans to enable operators to underwrite the initial investment of acquiring a handset for hiring out to local callers (the phone and accessories cost an estimated $420). A GB client, most frequently a woman, borrows about $300, then starts marketing the service to the village people. From the ensuing profit, she earns a living besides paying back the loan. In selecting VPP operators, GT follows certain criteria: at least two years as a GB member, a record of on-time loan repayments, knowledge of English digits, a centrally located house or place of business, one or two other sources of income and access to electricity (to charge the phone). If qualified, the woman is lent the necessary capital at 22 per cent interest with a three-year grace period. A VPP is normally installed at the operator's residence, although during the day it is placed in a tea stall or shop along a main village road or close to the bazaar. The VPP operator charges the market retail rate while GT charges her half that rate. The VPP owner initially uses a banner or poster to draw the attention of potential users. In due course her house may become popular and be known locally as *Phone Bari* (house with phone). During our field visits we noticed that in a given village almost everybody irrespective of age could indicate the *Phone Bari* or the VPP holder by name.

Objectives of the Study

The study on which this paper is based aimed at assessing the efficacy of the VPP in reducing the information poverty of villages that have obtained access to mobile phones. It analysed how the VPPs are operated, how the service is used and by whom, and its impact in terms of the economic and social empowerment of individuals and communities[6].

The formulation of specific research questions was guided by the notion of information poverty (Nafstad and Iversen, 1996). For present purposes, the term designates a situation in which an inadequate telecommunications infrastructure — in terms of quantity and price — limits the range of choices available to individuals by making it too costly to seek out information about alternative courses of action. The structure of hypotheses was guided by the theories of asymmetrical information and cultural perspectives on collective action. Asymmetrical information is characteristic of situations in which the quality of the object of the exchange is fully known to only one of the parties. The inherent uncertainty that it generates may reduce the volume of transactions that would otherwise take place. Sometimes the use of special information is downright prohibited (insider trading). A number of social mechanisms exist to rectify the problem and thus encourage transactions, e.g. the sale of goods and services with guarantees attached, or the introduction of licensing or quality programmes. A reduction of the asymmetry of information distribution should improve the functioning of markets (Olsen, 1989). Asymmetrical information may also become the basis of power relations. Such relations can be observed in an extreme form in Bangladesh, where an illiterate majority depends on transactions with a literate minority. Cellular phones may have the potential to even out the distribution of information and thus reduce such asymmetries.

Recent elaboration of the theory of collective action has emphasised the cultural foundations of collective action. Trust has been shown to be a prerequisite for collective action, i.e. for overcoming the free-rider problem (Putnam, 1993; Fukuyama, 1996). Interpersonal trust has cultural roots. Societies vary in the inclination of people to trust each other spontaneously. In low-trust societies collective action is difficult to organise beyond the extended family or the village. Such societies tend to be fragmented socially and highly state-centred. State authority provides a substitute for the social cement of the mutual trust of civil society. The introduction of cellular phones in a low-trust context should facilitate transactions that might otherwise not take place or take place at higher costs. A cellular phone may enable the parties to check out on the spot information given by the other and thus allay fears of being cheated.

Methodology and Analytical Model

The study was based on a sample survey of 350 VPP owners/operators and users. Samples were drawn on the basis of geographical locations and time since the introduction of VPP in the locality. In addition, a number of distant beneficiaries (persons who had received calls from VPPs) were interviewed. To supplement the survey some case studies were also carried out.

The basic research issue in the study concerns the identification of the processes that influence the success of VPP operations. What makes for the success or failure of a technology-driven development initiative such as the VPP? The approach adopted was a demand-and-supply model supplemented with contextual analysis. One would expect the intervention to succeed if it meets a pent-up demand, if the supply is technologically adequate and if the costs fall within the customer's willingness or capacity to pay. Insofar as both demand and supply may be influenced by contextual factors, however, such factors can also impinge upon the success of the VPP. They may be related to the economic, social and cultural environment of the communities into which the VPPs are introduced. Some economic activities may generate more demand for phones than others: businessmen, for example, may *ceteris paribus* need to make more calls than peasants. Communities with many migrant workers living abroad may also grasp the opportunity for better communications more eagerly than those with few such individuals. Some VPP holders may be more active in promoting the service than others so that the supply side is different. The technology may work better in some places than others for geographical reasons. Cultural factors may also come into the equation. For example, more conservative communities may take longer to get used to or accept new gadgets; they may also object to women as operators. Both situations may hamper demand. Changing the supply side by letting men take over the day-to-day operations may stimulate demand in such settings. The basic model is sketched in Figure 8.1. Some key details of the model are listed below the figure.

Figure 8.1. **An Analytical Model of the VPP Intervention**

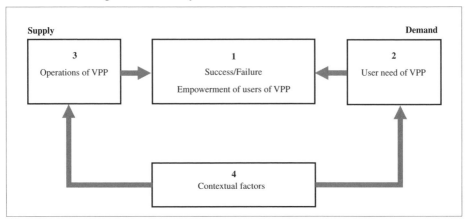

— Success and failure are measured in terms of users' empowerment as indicated in interviews.

— User need is an indirect measure built by classifying users into professional categories (e.g. housewives, businessmen, peasants, etc.), as well as age and education groups, that show different communication needs.

— VPP operations are not systematically analysed in relation to user empowerment because observations during the study revealed them to be fairly standardised. Some indications of technological and other problems in VPP operations are reported, however, as are holders' perceptions of the impacts of the VPP.

— The contextual categories are used mainly to distinguish between the Chittagong and Dhaka zones. Chittagong is well known for its distinct regional culture. It is both economically entrepreneurial and socially conservative. Thanks to its port and a strong merchant tradition, as well as the unusually high proportion of migrant workers, it is open to the world. At the same time, long-time traditions are held in high esteem, as reflected for example in the preference accorded to marriages within the region. Chittagong's entrepreneurial character may be expected to generate more communication needs and therefore higher intensity in the use of the VPP. Its social conservatism, on the other hand, may constitute an obstacle to accepting the VPP and its special features of operation, chiefly female holders/operators.

Main Findings

Profile of the VPP Stakeholders

Generally, the users are younger than the owners. Around 75 per cent of owners are between 35 and 55 years old, with the largest group in the 35-45 age bracket. Among the users, the largest age group is 24-35 years old, with 19 per cent less than 25. Few users are above 55, so the use of the telephone is definitely something for the younger generation. Most of the owners (91.8 per cent) are female while the majority of the users (88 per cent) are male. All but one of the owners are married. Reflecting the high marriage rate in rural Bangladesh, it is very rare for mature women to remain unmarried. Fewer users (67.7 per cent) are married because they are also younger

Literacy among both owners and users is higher than average for rural Bangladesh. Only 4 per cent of users and 12 per cent of owners are illiterate, as against an 80 per cent general illiteracy rate for adults. More than 80 per cent of users have education beyond the primary level, while among the owners 47 per cent have such schooling. Both groups represent something of an educated elite in rural Bangladesh. The difference in educational levels between users and owners reflects the contrast in school attendance among boys and girls, the owners being mostly female and the users mostly male.

Most of the owners (77.6 per cent) are primarily housewives engaged in household activities. Only a few have other activities such as entrepreneurship (12 per cent), trading (4 per cent), services (4.7 per cent) and agricultural work (2.4 per cent). On the other hand, as many as 41.1 per cent of the VPP users are traders and 22.8 per cent are small entrepreneurs. Some users also do household activities (11.4 per cent) and some are service providers (13.3 per cent). Only a tiny proportion of users works in agriculture (3.2 per cent).

Call Patterns

The average number of calls made in a month is 16, with a range from one to well over 50. The most usual call frequency is in the range of 11 to 25 calls every month, signifying a good number of users of the VPP service that make calls almost every day or every second day. This pattern clearly demonstrates that the VPP has identified a need and effective demand arising out of that need. An analysis of the call frequency of various occupational groups indicates as expected a conspicuous contrast between them (Figure 8.2). Traders, service providers, entrepreneurs and students most frequently use the VPP, while those in agricultural occupations and housewives do so more intermittently. Calls therefore are probably driven mostly by professional and economic motives. Social motives, however, top the list of reasons for calling. Calls to family members and relatives dominate among them. Business calls come second, while official (government-related) and political errands are quite rare. The last may reflect the limited role that the government plays in the life of the villages.

Figure 8.2. **Distribution of Average Monthly Call Frequency by Occupation**

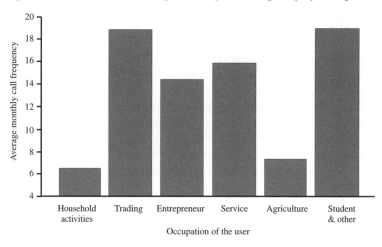

Business-Related Impacts

The study sought to identify the impacts of the VPP on individual and community life. "Impact" refers to the difference that access to the VPP has meant to the individuals in the study areas. Assessments of impacts are based on the self-reported advantages of VPP access that the interviewees indicated. Users reported a number of business-related advantages (Table 8.1). Access to the VPP has meant above all the creation of more opportunities and choices, but it has also provided help in managing uncertainty. Moreover, existing business relations have been strengthened.

Table 8.1. **Business-Related Advantages of VPP**

VPP has helped in	Percentage of Users
Providing more choices for decision making	78.50
Taking uncertain decisions	68.40
Strengthening relationships with business partners	59.50
Motivating the user to take new initiatives	53.80
Creating new economic and income-generating opportunities	40.50

Note: The percentages are based on cases, not on responses. Because of multiple responses, the total exceeded 100 per cent.

166

The advantages that the users feel the VPP has given them in business transactions relate above all to the reduced access time to get information (Table 8.2). Many also mention an enhanced feeling of security by being able to convey messages rapidly. Reduced communication expenses are also important.

Table 8.2. **Advantages of VPP to Users as to Collection of Information**

Advantages	Percentage of Users
Reduced access time to information	44.1
VPP has become an information centre, can easily be shared	17.9
Reduced feeling of physical distance to the information centre	29.6
Reduced communication expenses	27.9
Negates physical presence	26.4
More security through transmitting the message instantly	39.7

Note: Percentages are based on cases, not on responses. Because of multiple responses in each case, the total exceeded 100 per cent.

Social and Family Relationships

In rural areas people remain isolated from their family members and friends who do not live in nearby places. Also, because Bangladesh is a manpower exporting country, as many as 3 million Bangladeshi, mostly semi-skilled and unskilled labourers, live abroad, many of them in the Middle East and Far East. A good number of non-resident Bangladeshi also work both legally and illegally in various European and North American countries. These expatriate Bangladeshi and their relatives stay in touch mostly through letters. As most people in rural areas are not literate, they depend on others to write and read letters for them. Hence, they cannot maintain privacy and are prevented from instant sharing of joys and sorrows. VPP has the potential to provide emotional relief for people by allowing them to contact their loved ones in situations of privacy. VPP can also potentially help in situations requiring medical advice and assistance. Furthermore, rural women are more isolated than men in Bangladesh because of the traditional *purdah* system (seclusion of women from men). After marriage, many women cannot visit their families because of the prevailing, male-dominated cultural practices. They are expected to concentrate on their household duties, and they themselves cannot take the decision to visit their parents because their husbands and in-laws exercise authority over them in such matters (Firdhouse and Zamen, 1994). In such situations, the VPP represents an opportunity for a woman to maintain contacts with parents, brothers and sisters.

VPP has been extensively used for making social calls. VPP owners have reported that social calls[7] dominate both incoming calls (64.22 per cent on average) and outgoing calls (61.44 per cent)). In many cases these social calls also have business purposes. When a migrant labourer calls to his family, in most cases the call includes a message related to monetary transactions, i.e. sending or receipt of money, purchase of livestock or land, construction of a house, etc. In response to how VPP affected family relationships, user opinions were distributed along three dimensions. The calls:

— helped in easier sharing of private emotions (36.9 per cent) by providing more privacy than other modes of communication;

— strengthened family relationships by reviving broken or forgotten relationships (34.4 per cent); and

— reduced suspicions, which again led to better relationships (30.3 per cent).

Changes in Conceptions of Time and Space

Most users (96.2 per cent) reported having saved time through VPP. Savings seem to have been substantial for most purposes for which the telephone was used. Most users (96.2 per cent) also stated that VPP has enabled them to save on transportation costs. For the majority of the users (71.7 per cent) transportation cost savings have been up to Tk. 500 a month.

Nearly half of the users (48.7 per cent) considered that VPP helped them to prepare better for the natural disasters that so often can happen in Bangladesh, but only 39.2 per cent have used VPP for seeking medical assistance (as against 71.8 per cent of the owners). The low rate of medical-oriented use could reflect the nature of health service-seeking behaviour of the rural population. People in the rural areas generally visit traditional healers (spiritual healers, homeopathic doctors, village quacks, etc.) rather than health service delivery points. Moreover, those points cannot, as a rule, be reached via the phone.

As VPP has affected users' and owners' time and costs, it has also had an impact on their transportation needs. Most of the users (91.1 per cent) and owners (95.3 per cent) confirmed that VPP has affected travel patterns. For the users, the VPP's impact on transportation costs is significantly correlated with VPP impact on travel ($r = 0.60$, sig. 0.01 level). Fewer trips mean less travel cost. Among the users, 38.2 per cent stated that their frequency of travelling for business purposes was reduced and 22.9 per cent said that they were not required to travel at all after access to VPP. Overall, 15.6 per cent of the respondents mentioned that their frequency of travel for official purposes had been reduced.

Economic Empowerment

Empowerment is the reduction of dependency relations. The figures emphasise the role of communication and information in producing alternatives and choice and thus breaking cycles of dependency. The VPP is a channel for communication and dissemination of information about alternatives. A by-product is the opportunity for maintaining or widening social networks, which again may produce more information. In rural Bangladesh, people have very little scope for choice in work or social relations but remain confined to the village and its limited income-earning opportunities. The scope for women is even narrower than that for men. Owners as well as users thus experienced a variety of changes after their access to the VPP — changes more pronounced for owners than for users, which may be natural because the VPP is a direct income opportunity for the owners. Being mostly women, owners may also have started from more restricted life situations than the users did. Both groups experienced increased income, widening networks and more business. More detailed information on this is presented below.

Economic empowerment refers not only to increases in income but also to having control over resources and resource management, decision-making power and involvement in and control over economic transactions. Obviously, VPP as a business venture provides an opportunity for financial gain for the owners. Most of the owners (94.10 per cent) found VPP profitable as an investment. VPP has brought significant changes in the range of average monthly incomes of the owners (Table 8.3). In most cases, owners' incomes increased with the length of time of VPP ownership. Those operating the VPP for 1-6 months had an increase in average income of Tk. 2 204.55, those in operation for 6-12 months had a Tk. 3 453.49 gain and owners in the VPP business for 12-18 months enjoyed an average income Tk. 3 125 higher. There was also a substantial increase for the 24-30 months group. Apparently the VPP has been a success for the owners as an income opportunity.

Table 8.3. **Distribution of Owners' Average Monthly Incomes before and after Owning VPP**

Average Monthly Income (Tk.)	Percentage of Owners	
	Before VPP	After VPP
1 500 and below	19.7	7.4
1 500–3 000	33.3	12.3
3 000–6 000	23.5	33.3
6 000–9 000	8.6	22.2
9 000 and above	14.8	24.6

Social Empowerment

VPP has had a remarkable effect in widening the networks of the beneficiaries. Most of the users (95.6 per cent) spoke in favour of VPP as helping to widen their contact/clientele groups. Almost two-thirds (63.2 per cent) stated that VPP helped to a great extent. The VPP's impact on the expansion of users' social circles is significantly correlated with their increase in incomes ($r = 0.31$, sig. 0.05 level). Obviously, gains in social capital relate to financial gain. A similar pattern appeared among the owners.

Box 8.2. Another User's Voice

Use of VPP has led to a significant widening of my business network. Now I can communicate with many people through someone else's reference and can easily establish business relationships. Before VPP, it was not always possible to establish contact with people because in many cases it was not cost effective for me.

In rural Bangladesh, owning a phone is a symbol of social prestige and power, not because it relates to income-earning power but because owning a VPP in itself bears the mark of social prestige and honour. As mentioned earlier, the house of the VPP owner is commonly named as *Phone Bari* (house with phone). In some cases the VPP owner is also lightly called *Phone Bibi* (lady with phone). Most of the owners (92.9 per cent) held the opinion that owning a VPP did bring them social prestige. A significant proportion (39.2 per cent) said that because of VPP they have become "reference personalities" in their villages.

Change in Bureaucracy-Citizen Relationships

People may have to contact public offices and officials for many different purposes, including dispute reporting, information gathering, official reporting, complaining, *tadbir*[8], political influencing, etc. In Bangladesh, getting a job done or collecting any information can be time-consuming, particularly in public offices. People may have to go to public offices or contact public officials repeatedly even for small errands. It is more difficult for poor people without good connections. The introduction of VPP has made it easier to reach the bureaucracy. Through the VPP users can communicate more easily with the *Thana* (the local police station), government officials and political leaders, especially members of parliament. They do call them for varied reasons. Comparatively more calls are made to government officials and political leaders than to the *Thana*. Dispute reporting dominates among the calls made to the *Thana* (57.1 per cent). Information collection and official reporting/interaction predominated among those made to GOB officials (28.9 per cent and 26.7 per cent respectively). *Tadbir* and information collection were the main objectives of calls made to political leaders (34 per cent and 36.2 per cent respectively).

Women's Empowerment

VPPs have created an income-generation opportunity for rural women and provided scope for interacting with a wider cross-section of people. Before they had VPP, women's access to phones was difficult. To assess if VPP could, aside from financial gain, also facilitate the economic empowerment of women, the study probed not only VPP owners' feelings about their empowerment, but also the users' perceptions of it. When asked about the VPP's role in empowering women, most owners (81 per cent) stated that VPP had added to their social prestige. That they are known as VPP owners has indeed changed their social image. To them, ownership itself is a matter of social dignity although in most cases they are not responsible for the day-to-day operation of the VPP.

From the point of view of women's economic empowerment, it is also vital to take into account who is responsible for the actual operations of the VPP. Because of the very nature of Grameen Bank policy, most of the VPP owners are female (91.8 per cent). Yet the female owners operated only 4 per cent of the VPPs themselves. Male family members of the female owners operated 96 per cent of the VPPs. Such exclusion from the VPP practicalities may lead to women's exclusion from decision making involved in VPP operations and from the use of income from VPP businesses. When owners are not involved in VPP transactions, they are probably also less exposed to social interactions. Moreover, as mentioned above, only 22 per cent of VPP users are female. It seems, therefore, that in rural Bangladesh, in both the use and operation of the VPP, the traditional seclusion of women from the wider society has been maintained. Apparently, tradition and culture influence both the demand and supply side of the VPP. Nevertheless, for a significant minority of women, the VPP has entailed some change. Two-thirds of the users said that VPP had an impact on women's empowerment, but most of them also felt that introduction of VPP had not caused any change in men-women relationships. Only 25.9 per cent thought they had noticed any change in this respect.

Impact on the Distant Beneficiary and User

It has been assumed that, besides affecting owners and users, the introduction of the VPP also affects people who are the regular contact persons of the VPP users. The study termed them "distant beneficiaries" or "distant users" of VPP phones. Distant beneficiaries include traders, service owners, students, local political leaders and housewives. All of them said that they had indeed benefited from the introduction of the VPP. The most commonly stated benefits were reduced communication time (100 per cent) and saved communication cost (88 per cent). Significant percentages also felt that the VPP had extended their communication networks (36 per cent) and widened their business networks (66 per cent). Before the introduction of VPP, communicating with the present users was a cumbersome process. The distant beneficiaries had to go to them physically or send representatives. Sending letters took a long time. Most of the distant beneficiaries (80 per cent) often sent representatives. With VPP, 28 per cent of the distant beneficiaries received between one and five calls from the users per week and 44 per cent made one to five calls to the users per week.

What are the Most Important Impacts of the VPP?

The VPP has entailed a series of changes in social and economic relations. So far in this study a quite rich and varied picture has emerged. A series of impacts has been identified, most of them in the expected direction. It is more difficult, however, to assess the relative magnitude and significance of the various changes and impacts from the detailed analysis. This section tries to arrive at a more comprehensive understanding of the impacts of the VPP and the forces that help shape them.

To obtain a summary picture, all the variables seeking to identify such impacts were re-coded into dichotomous variables. They were then subjected to factor analysis. The factor solution yielded seven different factors, which were used as guidelines for the construction of indices of impact. These indices can also be interpreted as dimensions of empowerment associated with the VPP. The indices were standardised to a scale of 0-100. Figure 8.3 shows the results of the analysis. Note that it is based on data about users only.

Figure 8.3. **Impact of Cellular Phones as Assessed by the Users**

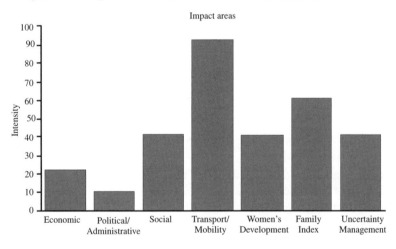

The strongest impacts of the VPP appeared for transport and mobility and family relations. The VPP enhances the geographic reach of the users while at the same time reducing the need to travel to obtain information. These, of course, are quite obvious effects once the VPP becomes operational in an area, but the ability to make the VPP operational could not be taken for granted and data therefore were collected on the seemingly "obvious" aspects of the telephone's benefits. Significant effects also emerged with regard to the social life and status of users, women's empowerment and uncertainty management in general. Surprisingly, the VPP has had less impact on the economic activity of the users. Recall, however, that the direct economic benefits were more pronounced for owners than for users, for whom the economic benefits were primarily indirect.

Overall, then, the VPP allows a more efficient use of time and enhancement of social and family relations by making it possible to stay in touch more frequently and more directly. This is no small advantage in a family-oriented society such as Bangladesh. Easier access to information through the VPP also reduces uncertainties and anxieties in daily life and helps quicker and better decisions in the various occupations of the users. This must be regarded as a step towards a more efficiently functioning society. It has also meant an increase in the volume of social and economic transactions, as predicted by the theory of information asymmetry as well as that of social capital.

Explaining Variations

The preceding sections have noted variations in the uses and impacts of the VPP. They have suggested a number of supply-side, demand-side and contextual factors that may account for such variations. Their impacts are analysed in Table 8.4. Reading the table vertically, the columns show how the factors (independent variables) affect the level of users' empowerment in particular impact areas, for example family relations. The higher the beta coefficients, the stronger the impact. Reading horizontally, a row shows the impact that a given factor has across different impact areas.

For the overall impact (general index) summarised for all areas, the driving forces are the ages and occupations of users. Younger users and those occupied as traders have particularly felt the advantages of the VPP. Both of these effects seem intuitively reasonable. Younger people are prone to make use of new gadgets more quickly than their elders. Villagers working as traders will likely have a greater need to get in touch with customers and suppliers easily and may hence welcome phones even more than those in other walks of life.

The factors identified here do not so well explain the transport and mobility impacts, perhaps because the impacts are of a rather general nature and therefore felt equally by most users. Family-oriented impacts are felt less by the entrepreneurs than by those in other occupations, and they are more manifest in the Chittagong zone than in the Dhaka zone. This may reflect the larger number of migrant workers from Chittagong, using the phone to be in touch with their families. It may also be a manifestation of the strong regional identity of the region and therefore the strong pull of regional roots.

Table 8.4. Factors Affecting Impacts of VPP on Users: Regression Analysis.

Factors (Independent Variables)	General Impact Index	Transport and Mobility	Family	Social	Women	Uncertainty Management	Economic	Political & Administrative
				Impact Areas (Dependent Variables)				
Age of user	-.258**							
Education of user					-.339***			E***
No. of family members of user								
Monthly family income of user (in Taka)								
Distance from the nearest Thana town (in km)								
Occupation: Household	.284**				-.481***			
Occupation: Trading			-.299**				.342***	
Occupation: Entrepreneur		-.250**	-.310**					
Occupation: Service				-.344**				
Occupation: Agriculture								
Occupation: Student								
Zones: Chittagong=1 Dhaka=2			-.272**		-.233**			
Call frequency (monthly)						.284**	.277**	
Period used VPP (months)					.329***			
Adjusted R^2	.214	.052	.135	.012	.275	.070	.186	.120

Note: Levels of Significance: * = .05 level, ** = .01 level, *** = .001 level.

174

Women's empowerment is driven by education, occupation, zone and practice as a VPP user. Surprisingly, the VPP is seen as bringing women's empowerment more by those with low education than those with higher education. Those working outside household activities see women as more affected than those who are primarily occupied in the home. Again, Chittagong dwellers are more prone than the Dhaka dwellers to see women's empowerment coming from the VPP. Such a perception has a lot to do with how long the user has had access to the VPP. The impact of (low) education may indicate that the VPP will likely make more of a difference to people with low education than to those with higher educational achievements, who also have access to information through other channels. The negative perceptions of householders (mostly housewives) on the VPP's impact on female empowerment may suggest that individuals confined to the house have more difficulty in seeing the wider benefits of the phones. Yet they may perhaps also tend to generalise from their own confined existence to women's empowerment in general. Furthermore, women's empowerment tends to be emphasised more the longer the user has had access to a VPP, which can be given a quite straightforward interpretation.

Enhancement of economic opportunities is related to call frequency and occupation. Traders, primarily, feel they have become more economically empowered by the VPP. These are demand-driven relationships. Empowerment in relation to political and administrative bodies relates to education levels in the expected way. Those who use the phone more to get in touch with Thana, administration and political leaders have more education than those who don't.

Reading the table horizontally, it is apparent that no single factor or group of factors explains variations in impact equally across the board, in all impact areas. Occupation is an important factor in the call patterns — some occupations (especially traders) have more need of the phone than others. In some areas age and education turned out to be important but not ubiquitously so. Such presumably demand-driving factors as family income and distance from nearest centre play very little role. The same is true of family size. All in all, the explanatory power of these regressions may not be too impressive (as indicated by the row of adjusted R^2s), but it did help to explain variations in some cases. It worked best for female empowerment and economic enhancement.

Conclusions

Any large-scale mobile phone programme like Grameen Telecom's Village Phones will bring changes to the village economy and village life in general. The VPP has expanded considerably the transaction boundaries of the local village market, reducing the isolation and fragmentation of the village economy. GB's style of managing communications can help significantly to expand access to this vital information input for all segments of the population, reduce inequality and thus enhance the broad-based, pro-poor orientation of rural development strategies. There are significant non-economic benefits, such as rapid and effective communications between family members, stronger kinship bonding, etc.

Access to mobile phones has had a noticeable effect on development and entrepreneurial activity in rural Bangladesh. Effective demand exists and appears to be growing. The mobile phone has also brought some attitudinal change in social acceptance of women as lead agents in creating conditions appropriate for the spread of information technology. The experience of Grameen Telecom in Bangladesh indicates that mobile phones can deliver telecommunications to impoverished rural areas efficiently and profitably. It has also demonstrated that in a technology-shy society like Bangladesh, a high technology can indeed find use, provided it is channelled through a well designed institutional framework that does not disturb social norms and values.

Notes

1. Grameen Phone (1999), *Annual Report.*

2. Grameen Phone (1999), *Annual Report*, p. 44.

3. Grameen Phone (1999), *Annual Report*, p. 44.

4. Grameen Telecom is a not-for-profit company registered under the laws of Bangladesh for attaining certain social objectives. In its efforts to extend the village phone service in rural areas, it has the advantage of being assisted by its peer, Grameen Bank, an internationally recognised bank for the poor with an extensive rural network and understanding of the economic needs of the rural population. Grameen Telecom administers the village phone services to villagers and trains the operators as well as handling all service-related issues.

5. At a general level, Coates and Jarrat (1990) have suggested a series of typical social impacts of mobile phones: acceleration of transactions, thereby providing competitive advantages; expansion of scope of short-term transactions, e.g. the convention of on-the-spot meetings; production of more choice (a buyer may for example compare prices in one store with those of another with a call from the first location); provision of opportunities for immediate feedback, e.g. phone voting; stimulation of certain kinds of actions (both desirable and undesirable); increase in public and individual safety; alteration of concepts of time, space and distance; raising expectations.

6. See note 5.

7. Social calls refer to calls made or received by users for exchanging greetings between and among friends, relatives and family members, as well as for knowing their whereabouts.

8. That a client must employ extensive persuasion by using social and political links to get things done in a public office is an element typical of a bureaucratic culture.

Bibliography

COATES, J.F. and J. JARRAT (1990), "Future Use of Cellular Technology — Some Social Implications", *Telecommunications Policy*, Vol. 14, No. 1.

FIRDOUSE A. and N. ZAMAN (eds) (1994), *Infinite Variety,* UPL, Dhaka.

FUKUYAMA, F. (1996). *Trust. The Social Virtues and the Creation of Prosperity*, The Free Press, New York, NY.

NAFSTAD, H. and A.W. IVERSEN (1996), "The Role of Information Technology in African Development", *Telektronikk*, Vol. 1, No. 1.

OLSEN, T.E. (1989), "Effektiv ressursallokering under asymmetrisk informasjon" (Effective Resource Allocation Under Information Asymmetry), LOS-senteret, Bergen.

PUTNAM, R. (1993), *Making Democracy Work. Civic Traditions in Modern Italy*, Princeton University Press, Princeton, NJ.

Chapter 9

Local Content Creation and E-Commerce: A South African Perspective

Carey-Ann Jackson and Johan Eksteen

Introduction

During the recent corrections in the technology sector across the world's stock markets, it became clear that the "click-and-mortar" model is a more robust business model in the e-commerce arena. This model sees e-commerce as an extension and enabler of existing, non-virtual businesses. Lessons learned from these events can apply directly to the area of local content creation and e-commerce, and it is this learning which informs the subject of this paper.

In discussing this subject, the paper recognises the need to address local content creation and e-commerce as a holistic value chain located in a global environment. The paper presents a view that such a value chain spans both virtual and physical dimensions and stretches across a wider range of activities than just consumption activities. Further, local content and e-commerce value chains have a number of different channels, infrastructures, drivers and enablers, which run along the length of the chain and differ considerably between one point and another.

In contrast with this approach, discussions of local content creation and e-commerce commonly refer only to considerations of consumption and the market, typically located at the latter parts of value chains. In promoting another option for developing-country participation in global e-commerce, there is a need to understand and support the whole value chain and in so doing account for differences of environment, channels, infrastructures, drivers, enablers, potential risks and threats. The paper refers to pilot research and development projects in South Africa and uses these projects to illustrate what environmental conditions and associated enablers come into play in the early and middle parts of the value chain.

The Argument

The approach to local content creation and e-commerce outlined in the paper emphasises the need to think about these issues as a holistic value chain. The argument begins with reference to the realities faced by all South African initiatives addressing local content creation and e-commerce: the environment is dominated by the presence of poverty and inequities in access to information and communications technologies (ICTs), and these realities provide the background for the paper's arguments about local content creation and e-commerce.

Poverty alleviation is one of the highest developmental priorities in South Africa. Almost half of all South Africans live in impoverished households (Statistics South Africa, 1997). Most poor South Africans live in rural areas (Table 9.1) and a significant proportion live in households headed by women. Widespread poverty impacts directly upon participation by South Africans in global markets and on the country's presence on the World Wide Web.

Table 9.1. **Poverty in South Africa**

Province	Households living in poverty (%)	Individuals living in poverty (%)	Non-urban population (%)
Eastern Cape	40.4	50.0	63.4
Free State	56.8	64.0	31.4
Gauteng	29.7	41.0	3.0
KwaZulu-Natal	36.1	47.1	56.9
Mpumalanga	33.8	45.1	60.9
North West	15.4	21.1	65.1
Northern Cape	38.2	48.0	29.9
Northern Province	61.9	69.3	89.0
Western Cape	14.1	17.9	11.1
South Africa	35.2	45.7	46.3

Source: Adapted from Statistics South Africa 1997 data.

It would be remiss in a paper concerned with e-commerce not to describe access to ICTs in South Africa. Common parlance recognises South Africa as a country with a digital divide, yet some domestic commentators have criticised the use of the phrase "digital divide" because it masks the social, economic, educational and commercial inequities that predate the existence of anything digital. The provision of technological infrastructure alone cannot eradicate these inequities and several strategies are needed to do so, some of which are:

— strengthening and diversifying the human resource and competence base;

— ensuring participation by small, medium and micro enterprises (SMMEs) in the economy;

— supporting job creation and black economic empowerment;

— providing impoverished households with access to finance;

— addressing the affordability of a range of basic services; and

— ensuring women's empowerment.

Table 9.2 shows current access to telephones (including cellular or mobile telephones). It exemplifies the disparities between two groups of South Africans (http://www3.sn.apc.org/africa/). While "Africa's information infrastructure is by far the least developed in the world" (UNECA, cited in Hall, 2001), South Africa is comparatively a continental "giant", responsible for almost 95 per cent of all African internet hosting. South Africa has over 100 000 hosting facilities, sophisticated IT infrastructure in the finance and retail sectors, an advanced cellular communications infrastructure and a growing community of internet subscribers — a profile similar to those in some European countries (Hall, 2001) (Table 9.3). Several private South African organisations have established web presence. Financial institutions, large clothing and food chain stalls, general service providers and Internet Service Providers (ISPs) provide on-line users with services such as electronic banking, booking and reservation facilities, auctions, secure purchasing of anything from fast-moving consumer goods (FMCGs) to motor vehicles, and job applications and recruitment, for example.

Table 9.2. **South African Access to Telephones**
(percentages)

	All	African	White
Universal service	34	20	89
Universal access (15 minute walk)	71	60	99
Universal access (30 minute walk)	83	78	100
Universal access (60 minute walk)	90	87	100

Source: Adapted from AISI data for South African access to telephones.

Table 9.3. **Internet Access, Use and Service Provision in South Africa**

Use, Access and Service Provision	Frequency
Dialup subscribers	650 000
Leased lines	5 000
Estimated total users	1 800 000
Major dialup ISP	Mweb World Online ABSA
Leased line & national network providers	Internet Solutions UUNet Africa SAIX

Source: Network Wizards' Internet Domain Survey.

South Africa is expected to play a role in development and expansion of internet connectivity across the Southern African Development Community (Table 9.4). Yet "within South Africa, there are huge contrasts between the urban, largely white and increasingly commercial users of information and communications technology, and rural, overwhelmingly African, communities who have only partial access to basic telecommunications" (Hall, 2001).

Table 9.4. **Host Statistics in Egypt and Sub-Saharan Africa**

Country	Number of Hosts
South Africa	122 025
Egypt	2 013
Namibia	640
Zimbabwe	599
Botswana	550
Mozambique	69
Swaziland	330
Angola	4

Source: Network Wizards' Internet Domain Survey

A word of caution is in order about describing access among individuals and households in poor and rural communities in static terms. Most data sets lack reference to demographic data on migration and mobility. Both are features of daily life, particularly among impoverished individuals, and in South Africa large portions of the population travel significant distances between their family households and working (or work-seeking) places. This is a legacy of apartheid urban and rural planning as well as a reflection of the social and economic changes underway in the society. Given the frequency of significant movement of large groups of people in the society, describing access (or the lack thereof) in statistical terms needs a clearer understanding of migration and mobility data because they may, inadvertently, mask the real inequities of access to infrastructure.

South Africa has implemented its ICT policies and regulations as attempts to address the poverty and inequity that exist within the society. Through the provision of an exclusivity period to the national telecommunications provider, the South African government defined social responsibility rollout targets associated with extending universal access. Similar social responsibility targets were included in the licences granted to telecommunications players such as the public broadcasters and GSM service providers.

A topical ICT debate underway in South Africa during the writing of this paper concerns the formulation of the White Paper on e-commerce[1]. It is not uncommon to hear argument that e-commerce in South Africa should be linked to poverty reduction and wealth redistribution. Some community activists, leaders of organised labour, policy makers and intellectuals want to ensure that e-commerce legislation is developed so that benefits accrue for all. During the White Paper development process, Stavrou *et al.* (2001) have promoted such an approach, inspired by the work of Amartya Sen, that connects a livelihoods concern with e-commerce. Stavrou *et al.* (2001) highlight the need to emphasise the assets and abilities of the poor and recognise that poor households face a diversity of risks, such as natural and environmental hazards, price fluctuations, policy changes, social relationship changes, conflicts and "unbanked" money or cash management strategies. Risk aversion is widely attributed as characteristic of poor households and the ways in which they manage their assets in relation to perceived and actual risk. Those risk management strategies can, depending largely upon the level of poverty of the household, result in a vicious cycle of poverty (Stavrou *et al.*, 2001). Their approach argues that access to information can support improved risk management strategies and impact upon the household's livelihood. Lack of information or incorrect information can add substantially to poor households' costs of living compared with households that do have better informational access. Other key points about the livelihoods approach, taken from Stavrou *et al.* (2001) are as follows:

— it recognises the possibility of exchange failure;

— it allows for separation of proximate resources for livelihood generation from intermediary resources;

— it recognises that unwired households are disadvantaged economically further by lack of connectivity;

— it emphasises diversification of income sources as crucial for sustainable livelihoods; and

— it acknowledges that engagement with diversified activities permits households to try different tactics for generating adequate and sustainable livelihoods.

This paper extends the livelihoods approach to e-commerce by arguing for thinking about local content creation and e-commerce as a holistic value chain. This permits impoverished households to participate as creators of knowledge and generators of value, not just as consumers, which is currently the case with the Stavrou *et al.* (2001) approach.

Local Content Creation in South Africa

Tackling local content and e-commerce presents a challenge for several reasons. First, significant international attention and debate have focused on regulatory issues surrounding content, particularly phenomena of child pornography, hate and violent speech, copyright, ISPs' liability and advertising. Those issues are not within the scope of this paper. Second, there is difference in opinion of what is meant by content. For clarification, this paper recognises content as everything accessible on an electronic platform (such as a web site) and presented in a range of ways using graphics, text or audio. There are many examples of local content (e.g. learning and teaching resources or current affairs) but this paper restricts its focus to content from historically marginalised, cultural and indigenous knowledge systems (IKS) unique to South Africa.

Across the South African telecommunications sectors, a range of departmental policies and regulations addresses local content creation, but all share commitment to nation building, unique identity promotion and protection, industrial growth and job creation (Table 9.5). One of the major players is the regulator, the Independent Communications Authority of South Africa (ICASA). It offers two main reasons for regulating local content in South Africa — first, the need to develop, protect and promote a national and provincial identity, culture and character; and second, the need to create vibrant, dynamic, creative and economically productive local industries. The regulator specifies that content needs to "reflect and engage with the life experiences, cultures, languages, aspirations and artistic expressions that are distinctly South African". Local content quotas are set to create incentives for music, television and broadcasting industries, develop talent, invest in high quality technology, improve the quality and variety of South African music and television programming, and redress historical imbalances in the cultural and broadcast industries.

Table 9.5. **Governmental and Regulatory Bodies Involved in Local Content Creation**

Entity	Domains
ICASA	TV and radio broadcasting Language representivity Quotas for local content
DACST	Cultural Industry Growth Strategy Film, culture and television industries National Film and Video Foundation Cultural Heritage Resource Management
DoC	Broadcasting and telecommunications E-Commerce Green Paper (2000) Support development of local content in broadcasting sector

The Department of Arts, Culture, Science and Technology (DACST), another player, has been concerned with local content in several areas and several ways. The Cultural Industries Growth Strategy and the National Film and Video Foundation are DACST initiatives that focus on local industry growth and stimulating export of South African film, video and other content as well as promotion of South African talent and production resources. A third player is the Department of Communications (DoC), which is concerned with local content creation within its e-commerce and broadcasting policy processes. The DoC's White Paper on Broadcasting Policy (1998) includes regulations on appropriate scheduling of local content, enhanced production quality for exportation and the establishment of the South African Broadcast Production Agency to support local content development.

Local content creation across other technological platforms such as the internet has not received much attention. The only reference to e-content exists in the 1999 amendment to the Film and Publications Act (Act 34 of 1999) and there is no South African case law on internet content regulation. Some have criticised the apparent lack of clarity regarding local content and e-commerce and have debated at length which agencies have jurisdiction to regulate content on the internet. In its discussion paper on local content creation, ICASA recognises that convergence has an impact on local content and states that "new communications and information technologies, as well as the growing convergence between media, entertainment and telecommunications, pose both a threat to indigenous cultures and an opportunity to extend the creation and distribution of cultural products and services. The trend internationally is towards the worldwide homogenisation or standardisation of culture resulting from the increasing dominance of US cultural content... (L)ocal content regulation will be severely tested by the emergence of new distribution platforms..." (http://www.iba.org.za/local_content.doc)

E-Commerce in South Africa

At the time of writing this paper, the South African government is engaged in compiling a White Paper on e-commerce. Some issues included in the green paper are development of and access to ICTs, taxation, security and privacy, convergence, protection of intellectual property, content development and regulation, electronic payment systems and standards and interoperability. A lot of energy has been directed at writing into forthcoming legislation what the role of government should be. Different views obviously exist. Some demand a light touch from government, others want self-regulation by industry and yet others expect clear policy and regulatory directives on job creation, alleviation of poverty, black economic empowerment and redressing inequities. The South African approach to e-commerce shares some similarities with international approaches and debates, but there are some differences that impact on the local content creation and e-commerce value chain.

Intellectual Property and Indigenous Knowledge Systems

An environmental difference as well as an enabler relates to Intellectual Property (IP) and IKS. While the World Intellectual Property Organisation (WIPO) mediates and arbitrates IP infringements, South African IP faces additional risks from ICTs because of:

— the legacy of institutionalised destruction of IKS;

— the dominance of Western paradigms in creation and management of IP and associated value chains;

185

— the absence of adequate legislation relating to the protection of indigenous South African IP; and

— a poor or limited presence in South Africa of adequate capacity, instruments and mechanisms to monitor and protect IP rights.

There remains a concern that amendments to South African IP law (the South African Intellectual Property Law, Act 38 of 1997) do not address adequately all of the main challenges presented by e-commerce to local content. South Africa participated in the WIPO IKS discussions and various institutions such as research organisations now involved in e-commerce development and cultural preservation signalled that IKS in South Africa had been actively destroyed by apartheid. Some difficulties continue to exist with respect to IKS and patent protection. For example, foodways, which include recipes for producing hemp-based health products that were developed collectively and dynamically over several generations, are not currently protected by patent law because that knowledge is considered to be in the public domain.

Technologies and Applications in E-Commerce

In the current South African policy process, e-commerce is defined as "the use of electronic networks to exchange information, products, services and payments for commercial and communication purposes between individuals (consumers) and businesses, between businesses themselves, between individuals themselves, within government or between the public and government and, last, between business and government" (Department of Communications, 2001). This is a broad definition and implies a wider range of interactions and players than solely commercial ones.

The technologies involved in facilitating these interactions need to be flagged because of concerns with affordability and access for impoverished South Africans. The internet is a major network over which e-commerce interactions occur, but mobile networks may be more affordable or accessible in the local context. Therefore, adopting a technology-neutral perspective is necessary. This is especially pertinent in South Africa where, for example, m-commerce using cellular phones is potentially more affordable and accessible than e-commerce via personal computers, plain old telephone systems (POTS) or digital lines.

One way to think about the different dimensions at play across the local content creation and e-commerce value chain is to refer visually to the application of technology in context (ATC) model (Eksteen, 2000; Jackson and Eksteen, 2000) (Figure 9.1). The ATC model has three dimensions, which allow innovation, risk or investment to be plotted with respect to each dimension. Most developed country e-commerce focuses on activities in the application-technology plane and on issues such as the hunt for the next "killer app" or automation of processes. In South Africa, an attempt is made to focus on the other two planes, namely the context-technology plane and the context-application plane. Some of the issues that would be considered in the context-technology plane include combating technological illiteracy or building public understanding of science and technology.

Figure 9.1. **The Application of the Technology in Context Model**

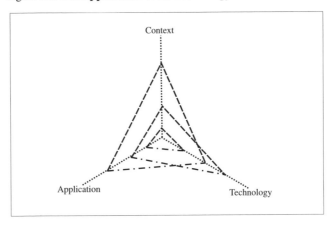

Notes:
The technology axis examines issues such as the technologies involved, the degree of modification or customisation required and so on. For example: Does the technology exist and is it affordable?
The application axis examines issues such as the underlying business models involved, the supporting process technologies required and the market opportunities. For example: Will the application form the core of a small enterprise?
The context axis examines issues such as the needs of the potential users and the cultural, ethical and social implications of the technologies or application. For example: Will the technology and application violate a person's right to privacy?

The ATC model is useful for describing visually the different channels, infrastructures, drivers and enablers that run along the length of the value chain of local content creation and e-commerce. As the next section of the paper highlights, approaching these value chains holistically requires attention to context, application and technology dimensions, and a wide range of issues within the context-technology and context-application planes.

Local Content Creation and E-Commerce Pilot Research and Development Projects

South Africa has several research projects and initiatives addressing local content creation and e-commerce. The selection of projects for mention here is based on their objectives and the need to illustrate the ATC dimensions of the value chain. Before describing the pilot projects, one should recognise that important learning regarding value chains is derived from the open-source movement, and was used in an attempt to enhance the local content creation and e-commerce value chains underlying the various projects described in this paper. These lessons were particularly valuable when local content was sourced from IKS. Although the paper does not explore IKS and open source in detail, it uses the open-source example of the Linux operating system to illustrate how the success of the open-source model enhanced understanding of the value chains related to local content creation. IKS and open source have at least three characteristics in common:

— distributed "ownership" by communities and developers;

— distributed contributions to the whole; and

— creation driven by need, not profit.

Linux is a PC-based operating system produced through a distributed software development effort. The effort involved more than 3 000 developers and countless other contributors located in about 90 countries. It is difficult to provide an accurate figure for the number of programmers who contributed to the Linux operating system and associated utility programs: published estimates range from several hundred to more than 40 000 (Shankland, 1998; Raymond, 1999). In its first few years of development (1991-95), over 15 000 people submitted code or comments to the three main Linux-related newsgroups and mailing lists. This trend continues today at an ever-increasing pace.

The simplified value chain (Figure 9.2) begins with the development and creation of the Linux code. The drivers and value in this activity are typically personal (i.e. non-financial, like peer recognition) or the result of a specific need for functionality. This happens in a distributed fashion, and, typically, the Linux community, and not the individual developer, owns the results. The consumption of the Linux operating system ranges from the developer community itself to commercial institutions. The Linux community often takes care of distribution and packaging and uses open systems such as File Transfer Protocol (FTP) or the World Wide Web.

Figure 9.2. **Simplified Value Chain of Linux Creation, Distribution and Consumption**

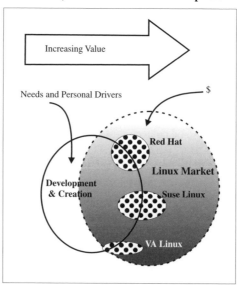

Further, several commercially orientated opportunities that were identified and then exploited were recognised as located on the border between the developer community and the broader market. Examples of this include the packaging, enhancement, distribution and branding of Linux by companies such as VA Linux, Red Hat and Suse. Although the content included in the "commercial" channels created by these groups is open source and hence free, it creates value through services and packaging, enhancement, distribution and branding. This value is then translated into financial terms.

It is possible to regard these efforts as examples of different channels within the open-source value chain. The following lessons are relevant:

— Local content creation (like IKS) does not need to happen only to satisfy a market need. As with Linux, the creation drivers are often not financial or market orientated.

— Various channels, by adding value, serve to translate local content creation activities into value measurable in financial terms.

— Not all the channels in the value chain need to be commercially oriented.

— The consumption and creation communities overlap in many instances. With Linux, the creation community was and still is part of the consumption community.

Exploitation and creation depend on each other. In the Linux case, the balance between creation and exploitation favours the former. Without sustainable creation activities, exploitation will fail, even though the creation activities are independent of the exploitation efforts. This illustrates how different drivers exist at different parts of the value chain. For ensuring the sustainability of local content value chains it means that a similar focus is needed to ensure that sustainable and appropriate creation is available.

Community-Inclusive Value Chains

The Poverty Alleviation through Processing Technologies and Job Creation Initiative is a multi-million Rand state-funded initiative intended to support rural people in realising their strengths and potentials through implementation of projects that result in small and micro enterprises, job creation and poverty relief. The importance of this initiative, for this paper, is that IKS content and development of products within an agrarian context can form the basis of a sustainable source of income for impoverished communities and allow for participation of the poorest of the poor in South Africa's e-commerce development. The initiative focuses specifically on value addition to available local resources, mainly from the agricultural sector but including IKS. Several projects support the emergence of sustainable value chains for resources such as hemp, wild silk, leather and indigenous foods. Community participation is essential in the initiative and community ownership is consolidated in, among other things, establishment of legal and governance entities such as community trusts and community-owned businesses. This approach, an alternative to supporting individual entrepreneurs, maximises job creation across the communities.

An activity within this initiative was the design of an architecture for a virtual trade house which, in itself may not be difficult, but was challenged by the fact that poverty alleviation and job creation are the overarching objectives of the initiative. The participatory nature of the initiative was crucial, hence design of a virtual trade house, for example, had to be consultative and dialogic with the community stakeholders. Processes and functionality of the virtual trade have to be understood by all community players — an ongoing challenge because of the low levels of public understanding of science, technology and e-commerce business models.

In its design, the trade house is not conceptualised as a single entity or as merely an information technology system. Rather, it is an overall architecture that integrates systems (e.g. an e-commerce system), activities (e.g. retailing), governance structures (the board of trustees), legal entities (such as community trusts) and role players (e.g. creators). Generic and quite typical functionalities are designed into the virtual trade house, such as distribution, payment, optimisation, centralisation, auditing and customer account management. A number of unexpected challenges are identified in the design of the architecture (Table 9.6).

With poverty alleviation and job creation as fundamental objectives, the virtual aspects of a trade house are not developed using only mainstream e-commerce and web-enabled commercial marketing approaches. Approaches based on assumptions and principles of corporate capital accumulation run counter to the principles of this initiative. Caution has to be applied when commissioning technological implementation because "off the shelf" products and "mainstream process technologies" may reinforce accelerated corporatisation.

The livelihoods approach to poverty alleviation underlines that participation is essential and stresses the need to pay attention to issues such as "acceptance literacy", legitimacy and buy-in of both the specific projects and the overall initiative. The sustainability of the value chain is put at risk unless there is attention to ongoing training and awareness, as well as to governance and communication, which ensure that breaks or blockages in the value chain do not result and that the communities involved are not alienated.

Table 9.6. **Problems Met in Designing a Trade House Architecture**

Branding	There is a need to decide on branding across several entities ranging from, for example "[brand name] hemp" or "[community name] product" or "[community trust name] products" or "Collective virtual trade house [name]". The brand management process is complicated and decisions still need to be made about the level at which branding is required. The decision, however, has an impact on what income from royalty payments, for example, can be generated by participating communities.
Quality control	Quality control impacts more on certain products than on others, particularly those that use IK. For example, hemp products used for health care may need to be quality controlled for toxicity, and an "external" quality control process and associated disclaimers need to be visible on products. The South African Bureau of Standards (SABS) approval or a "fair trade" approval may add to the value of the product and perceptions of brand purity. This process, however, presents a risk that IK involving traditional healing processes is transformed, which runs counter to preserving that knowledge.
Financing	Refers to consequences associated with success, namely that as a legal entity the trade house may have enhanced access to external financing options or may itself evolve into a financial service provider. This raises the possibility of development of the "next generation" community bank, providing financing to impoverished households or SMMEs. Hence, it transforms the trade house into a legitimate micro-lending entity, which could be a route for further development.
Depersonalisation	This is a risk associated with success because as the community collective becomes more successful, it may reach a transition point from which its personalised and community-flavoured services and products are lost as it transforms into a quasi or real corporate, even without any changes in its legal composition or governance.
Knock outs	A risk that some products or product ranges such as hemp clothing and hemp-based health care products become so successful that they knock out the smaller and less popular products such as wild silk linens. This would run counter to the principle that the overall collectively owned trade house enhances value for all.

A second project is the Culture Preservation Project, also a state-funded multi-million Rand entity. Among the several publications available that outline the project's objectives and its innovations in methodologies and technologies, Jackson and Eksteen (2000) discuss IKS and the impact that globalisation and ICTs have on its management. IKS is understood dialectically as a) a recognition that indigenous people are inventors and custodians of technology and knowledge, and b) having multiple manifestations, many of which are directly interlinked in communal cultural practices, traditions and symbols.

Because IKS is a rich source of local e-content, the impact of digitisation on that e-content needs understanding. Commonly used technologies include digitisation technologies, 3D modelling tools, encryption algorithms, digital libraries and so on. From a purely technological perspective, once digitisation and technological communication functionality are in place, little or no technological modification is required to set up a B2C e-commerce service. The actual impacts of ICTs on IKS are not always positive. Current ICTs are applied largely to support global commercial transactions and as a result, knowledge — indigenous or otherwise — is a commodity, potentially controlled and sold without attention to cultural preservation.

In IKS, a simple technological intervention such as digitally watermarking a digitised cultural artefact can have unintended cultural consequences. A digital watermark is a pattern of binary digits inserted into the artefact that provides information about copyright. It is not visible and must be robust enough to continue to exist if the digital artefact is changed in some way. Digital watermarking cannot guarantee the authenticity of a cultural artefact in cultural terms (i.e. that the e-content is an authentic representation of a culture). It provides a trace of origin of ownership. It contributes towards the commodification of IKS-based e-content and its management. The addition of a watermark can be perceived to provide authenticity. In those cases, the perception is very different from real authenticity. It is not inconceivable that perceptions can be manipulated or misrepresented, particularly if the e-content supports purely short-term commercial interests.

IKS e-content can be used for various purposes, such as education, cultural preservation, public awareness and virtual cultural tourism. The principles of its digital protection and preservation rest on enhanced restitution and human worth, and permit current and future communities to have continued and authentic access to the symbols, values and traditions which shape and define them as unique. The act of preserving digitally cultural artefacts is not a once-off activity. It is ongoing, requiring investment and commitment and it is at this point that concerns with "sustainability" often arise. One view suggests allocation of finite state funding based on the reasoning that the state must "manage" IKS on behalf of the people. The risk is that state funding can change or disappear, particularly when priorities, policies or social conditions change. A second view opts for "soft commercialisation", where not-for-profit income for particular services is rechannelled into purely preservation activities. Two additional views suggest doing nothing at all or pursuing "hard commercialisation" — wholesale commodification of knowledge based on the rules of the game defined by the global market place.

With respect to creating channels for use of local e-content in the global market place, some regard cultural tourism as a soft commercial application that balances tensions between preserving indigenous cultures and economic reconstruction and development. Cultural tourism, as defined by the World Trade Organisation, is a process whereby an individual is motivated to travel to a different country and culture for aesthetic, intellectual or spiritual development. Yet it also is a business transaction and a marketing exercise, facilitated by ICTs. The act of preservation of the indigenous culture for use as local e-content is a necessary condition, but there is a risk that investors may want higher financial returns on the investment made in preservation.

Virtual cultural tourism is a growing market, but digitised IKS for commercial e-consumption could present cultures in a trivialised or paternalistic way. In designing a compelling cultural virtual website, one challenge is to avoid such trivialisation. Retaining authenticity without making the experience compelling risks losing consumers who want more excitement. Tension rules between market need and preservation.

Sourcing IKS for e-content risks reinforcing the historical marginalisation of indigenous people and their knowledge. Digitisation of indigenous content demands sensitivity to the historical and human systems within which it exists. It also requires high technical skills. Given that the artefact is neither neutral nor ahistorical, digitisation cannot occur without understanding the cultural and curatorial aspects at play.

Local content regulation and management are complicated because digitisation creates a new artefact and not merely a reproduction of the original. As a result, different rules and information management processes (subject to different perceptions) come into play. A way of ensuring that the creators of knowledge accrue benefit, either financially or by acknowledgement, has been formulated and the establishment of a Universal Digital Original (UDO) master index suggested. The UDO concept involves a high-quality master digital copy or representation of an artefact, concept, event or natural phenomenon. The UDO would meet certain international standards for digitisation and be accompanied by an authenticity certificate. UDOs could be registered and managed, possibly by or on behalf of the state, and would list licence agreements as well as commercial and non-commercial rights as defined by use regulations. This would make it possible to address some of the issues of compensation or recognition for communities involved in IKS-based e-content supply, so that they are able to support preservation of IKS.

The view offered here has highlighted some technological, context and application considerations in the local content creation and e-commerce value chain, especially when one of the channels is cultural tourism. Some of the solutions developed may appear to observers from developed countries as too cumbersome or to have too much governmental involvement, but from a developing country perspective, as in South Africa, a wider range of considerations than only market demand has to be considered.

A Possible Future Instantiation of Value Chains

Impoverished households have assets and abilities but simultaneously face a diversity of risks affecting their options and opportunities for securing sustainable incomes (Stavrou *et al.*, 2001). Most, particularly rural ones, are headed by women, many of whom are grandmothers performing childcare work without remuneration and reliant on income from social-support grants (pensions, disability and child support grants) or *ad hoc* employment by some or all members of the household, including children.

The Storytellers' Network Initiative, the third project for discussion here, is conceptualised within this context. It seeks to source stories and knowledge embedded in the daily lives, activities and memories of impoverished community members, particularly (but not exclusively) older women, in order to provide opportunities for commercial and non-commercial use of that content. South Africa has a rich history of storytelling, poetry, music and creative expression. The initiative assumes that supplying local content for development into e-content is one way that impoverished households and communities can simultaneously participate in South Africa's e-commerce development and secure additional and sustainable income sources for themselves.

Trained community members source the local content in the community. Cultural authenticity is established through rigorous yet creative mechanisms. Digitisation of the content follows guidelines specified according to international approaches that seek to preserve cultural content with technical and cultural care. One of the channels available for creating income-generating opportunities uses the content to develop IKS-based early childhood development programmes. Early childhood development (ECD) is an educational and developmental imperative. South African psychological and educational literature recognises that the notions of childhood and development are not compatible with traditional, unquestioned assumptions that development is "coherent". The ECD channel seeks to source knowledge about child development as well as content and tools, such as stories, games, indigenous toys and play, across a range of cultural systems indigenous to South Africa. In combining educational, ethnographic and anthropological research and community participation in sourcing indigenous cultural childrearing practices, rich ECD learning content and programmes emerge. The community itself can benefit both from the sourcing function it plays and from income created for women who establish ECD centres in their communities. Future plans exist for supplying content to South Africa's publishing, broadcasting and tourism industries as well as providing exportable ECD content in an electronic format (e.g. on CD and DVD) from which royalty fees will be available to the community.

A second available channel sources content as the basis of printed and electronic material, such as postcards, poetry anthologies, story anthologies, historical descriptions and product-packaging descriptions of other products from the region. The arts and crafts channel co-packages this content with hand-made arts and crafts created in the region and allows households or groups of them to provide products for cultural stores, both physical and virtual. An option provides these as corporate gifts, which South African organisations can purchase and distribute to international and local clients. The Storytellers' Network Initiative also faces "acceptance literacy" problems among community participants and the risk of "knock outs", as well as issues about the impact of digitisation of indigenous content similar to those faced by the Culture Preservation Project.

As already noted, the use of cellular or mobile telephones is increasing in South Africa. The behavioural patterns of using that infrastructure are very interesting. South Africans, like their counterparts in many other countries, use SMS functionality on their cellular telephones in very significant proportions. Its rapid increase signals a trend that people want to and do use their cellular phones primarily to connect with other people. This suggests that content may not be as dominant in the future as it is currently. Focus will go instead on providing infrastructure, channels and services that connect people who are "consumers" directly with those who are creators. At present, content acts in an intermediary way between consumers and creators but it is likely that social networks rather than distribution and intermediary networks may become dominant. These value chains may thus become predominantly social ones, with a challenge to the Storytellers' Network Initiative to ensure that the value chain can evolve towards a social one. Different drivers, channels, infrastructure and enablers will come into play across the length of the value chain. As with the open-source example, several commercially orientated opportunities may appear either on the border between consumers and creators or in totally unexpected locations. This development will not be without risk. South Africa could take the lead in exploring future instantiations of local content and e-commerce value chains. Even if environmental factors such as poverty or inequitable access to ICTs prevail (but are much reduced, one may hope) future concepts of value chains could become shaped more by humanism and people-driven communication than currently.

Conclusion

This paper has attempted to present thinking about local content creation and e-commerce in terms of holistic value chains that span both virtual and physical dimensions and stretch across a wider range of activities than simple consumption. It suggests that a number of different channels, infrastructures, drivers and enablers run along the length of the chains and differ considerably between different points on them.

Several local content creation and e-commerce initiatives are underway in South Africa. The paper discusses three of them. Drawing on local content sourced from IKS and agrarian, rural and predominantly impoverished settings, it showed how the poorest of the poor can indeed participate as more than merely consumers. It referred to a possible future instantiation of value chains and the need for urgency — in developing countries — to accelerate research and pilots on alternative and innovative local content and e-commerce value chains, premised on principles not exclusively commercial.

Note

1.   Subsequent to the publication of this paper, the White Paper process has resulted in the formulation of the current Draft Electronic Communication and Transactions Bill (http://www.gov.za/gazette/bills/2002/23195.pdf).

Bibliography

AFRICAN INTERNET CONNECTIVITY, http://www3.sn.apc.org/africa/, last accessed 6 April 2001.

DEPARTMENT OF COMMUNICATIONS http://www.doc.pwv.gov.za last accessed 6 April 2001.

EKSTEEN, J (2000), *The Application of Technology in Context Model*, unpublished paper, CSIR, Pretoria.

HALL, M. (2001), *Africa Connected*, First Monday, http://www.firstmonday.dk/issues/issue3_11/hall/index.html, last accessed 19 April 2001.

INDEPENDENT COMMUNICATIONS AUTHORITY OF SOUTH AFRICA (2001), *Discussion Paper on the Review of Local Content Creation*, http://www.iba.org.za/local_content.doc, last accessed 6 April 2001.

JACKSON, C.-A. and J. EKSTEEN (2000), *Device-ive Artefacts*, paper presented at the South Africa — China Indigenous Knowledge Systems Summit, Beijing, China, October.

NETWORK WIZARDS (2000), cited in HALL (2001).

RAYMOND, E.S. (1999), *The Cathedral and the Bazaar: Musings on Linux and Open Source by an Accidental Revolutionary*, O'Reilly & Associates, Sebastopol, CA.

SHANKLAND, S. (1998), *Linux Shipments up 212 per cent*, available at CNET News.com http://news.cnet.com/category/0-1003-200-336510.html, last accessed 19 April 2001

STATISTICS SOUTH AFRICA (1997), http://www.statsa.gov.za, last accessed 6 April 2001

STAVROU, A, J. MAY and P. BENJAMIN (2001), "E-Commerce And Poverty Alleviation In South Africa: An input paper to the Government Green Paper on E-Commerce", University of Natal, Durban.

UNECA (2000), cited in HALL (2001).

LIST OF PARTICIPANTS
AND
CONFERENCE AGENDA

List of Participants

Salahuddin Aminuzzaman	Professor, University of Dhaka, Bangladesh
Pier Giorgio Ardeni	President, SDIC-University of Bologna, Italy
Annaflavia Bianchi	Fellow, Telecom Italia, Italy
Jorge Braga de Macedo	President, OECD Development Centre, France
Kyle Eischen	Director of Programs and Development, CGIRS-UCSC, United States of America
Johan Eksteen	Research Fellow, CERNA-École des Mines, France
Patrizia Fariselli	Consultant, Nomisma, Italy
Gary Gereffi	Professor, Duke University, United States of America
Andrea Goldstein	Senior Economist, OECD Development Centre, France
Paolo Guerrieri	Professor, University of Rome, Italy
David Hallam	Division Chief, Food and Agriculture Organisation, Rome
Brian Hammond	Division Chief, OECD Development Co-operation Directorate, France
John Humphrey	Fellow, Institute for Development Studies, United Kingdom
Carey-Ann Jackson	Consultant, South Africa
Gilles Leblanc	Research Fellow, CERNA-École des Mines, France
Aaditya Mattoo	Senior Economist, World Bank, United States of America
Sagren Moodley	Researcher, CSDS-University of Natal, South Africa
Lynn Mytelka	Director, UNU-INTECH, Netherlands
Catherine Nyaki Adeya	Research Fellow, UNU-INTECH, Netherlands
David O'Connor	Senior Economist, OECD Development Centre, France
Danilo Piaggesi	Division Chief, IADB, United States of America
Fabiola Riccardini	Economist, ISTAT, Italy
Morten Scholer	Senior Adviser, International Trade Centre, Switzerland
Susanne Teltscher	Economic Affairs Officer, UNCTAD, Switzerland
Paul Timmers	Head of Sector, DG INFSO, European Commission, Belgium
Mark Tomlinson	Research Fellow, University of Manchester, United Kingdom

4 May 2001

9:30 *WELCOME ADDRESS*
Pier Ugo Calzolari, Rector of the University of Bologna

10:00 *INTRODUCTION TO THE WORKSHOP*
Pier Giorgio Ardeni (Director, SDIC)
Jorge Braga de Macedo (President, OECD Development Centre)

Session 1: General Issues

10:15 *E-COMMERCE FOR DEVELOPMENT*
Patrizia Fariselli (SDIC)
David O'Connor (OECD Development Centre)
Discussant: Lynn Mytelka (UNU-INTECH, Maastricht)

12:00 *THE IMPACT OF THE INTERNET ON GLOBAL VALUE CHAINS*
Gary Gereffi (Duke University)
Discussant: Annaflavia Bianchi (Telecom Italia, Venice)

Session 2: Learning from Best Practices

14:30 *MEASURING E-COMMERCE IN DEVELOPING COUNTRIES*
Susanne Teltschler (UNCTAD, Geneva)
Discussant: Fabiola Riccardini (ISTAT, Rome)

15:15 *ACCESS TO TELEPHONY AND THE INTERNET: THE BANGLADESHI EXPERIENCE*
Salahuddin Aminuzzaman (University of Dhaka) & Ishtiaq Jamil
(University of Bergen)
Discussant: Mark Tomlinson (University of Manchester)

16:15 *INTERNATIONAL COOPERATION*
Danilo Piaggesi (Inter-American Development Bank, Washington)
Paul Timmers (European Commission, Brussels)
Discussant: Brian Hammond (OECD Development Co-operation
Directorate)

5 May 2001

9:00   *TRADE POLICIES FOR ELECTRONIC COMMERCE*
        Aaditya Mattoo (World Bank, Washington)
        Discussant: Paolo Guerrieri (University of Rome)

Session 3: Case Studies: Part I

9:45   MANUFACTURING
        GLOBAL SUPPLY CHAINS IN THE CAR INDUSTRY
        Andrea Goldstein (OECD Development Centre,)
        Sagren Moodley (University of Natal, Durban)
        Discussant: John Humphrey (IDS, University of Sussex, Brighton)

10:45   PRIMARY COMMODITIES
        THE IMPACT OF INTERNET TRADING IN THE COFFEE INDUSTRY
        Morten Scholer (International Trade Centre, Geneva)
        Discussant: David Hallam (Food and Agriculture Organisation,
        Rome)

Session 4: Case Studies: Part II

11:45   *E-COMMERCE AND THE ICT INDUSTRY: IMPACT ON LOCAL DEVELOPMENT IN INDIA*
        Kyle Eischen (CGIRS, UC Santa Cruz)
        Discussant: Gilles Le Blanc (STICERD-LSE & École des Mines,
        Paris)

12:30   *E-COMMERCE & LOCAL CONTENT CREATION IN SOUTH AFRICA*
        Carey-Ann Jackson (Consultant, South Africa)
        Discussant: Catherine Nyaki Adeya (UNU-INTECH, Maastricht)

13:30   Closing Address
        Fabio Roversi Monaco, (President, Fondazione CARISBO, Bologna)

OECD PUBLICATIONS, 2, rue André-Pascal, 75775 PARIS CEDEX 16
PRINTED IN FRANCE
(41 2002 09 1 P) ISBN 92-64-09954-9 – No. 52759 2002